Shoes

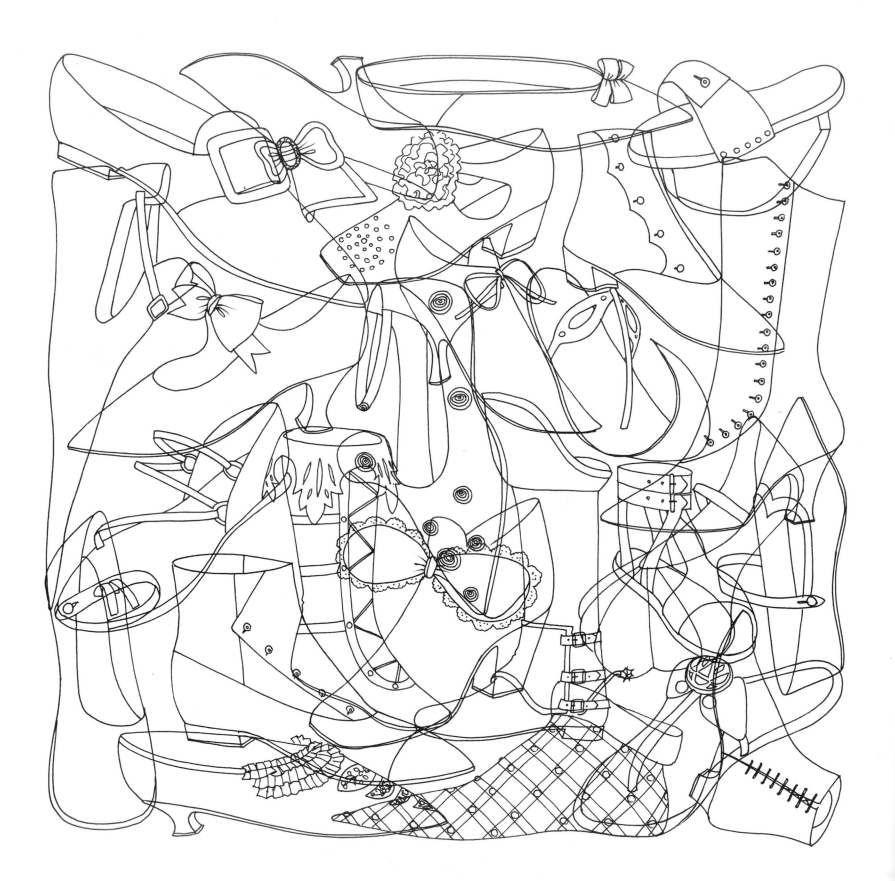

Shoes
The Complete Sourcebook

John Peacock

with over 2,000 illustrations, over 750 in colour

Thames & Hudson

To Zoë Thomas Webb

First published in the United Kingdom in 2005 by
Thames & Hudson Ltd
181A High Holborn
London WC1V 7QX

www.thamesandhudson.com

British Library Cataloguing-in-Publication Data
A catalogue record for this book is available from the
British Library

ISBN-13: 978-0-500-51212-8
ISBN-10: 0-500-51212-4

Printed and bound in China by Midas Printing

Contents

Introduction

Shoes: The Complete Sourcebook follows the history of footwear from ancient times to the present day. My main aim in this study is to illustrate the evolution of footwear, including shoes, sandals, slippers and boots, showing as many types and styles as possible, and concentrating on those that I consider to be the most representative of each period, and of greatest interest and usefulness to the designer, student and non-specialist to whom this book is directed.

The examples presented are, in the main, those worn by fashionable women and men, though on occasion I have chosen to illustrate interesting or unusual footwear, as well as military, sports or workmen's shoes and boots, where I feel them to be appropriate or informative.

The book is divided into six parts, of sixteen pages each. The end of each section is followed by eight pages of schematic drawings and detailed descriptions of each item illustrated.

The first section illustrates footwear in Antiquity, starting with Ancient Egypt and covering the period 2500–600 BC. Most people wore sandals outdoors as protection from hot sand and walkways. Royalty, priests and those of high rank or social standing wore simple sandals with soles made from natural fibres held onto the foot with narrow thongs: some had piked toes (toes with elongated upturned points) or were elaborately painted, sometimes decorated with gold. During the Mesopotamian period, 1000 BC–AD 200, people wore sandals very similar to those of the Egyptians, but also soft leather ankle boots with pointed toes. The Greeks were well known for their exquisite footwear during the 'Golden Age' of 480 to 400 BC. They produced shoes, sandals and boots of very high quality. From 800 to 200 BC Etruscan men and women favoured Greek styles, particularly the long boot, known as the endromis, made from rawhide with its fur lining and leather leg bindings. The design of Roman footwear between 753 BC and AD 323 was also influenced by that of the Greeks, though the latter had been conquered by Rome in 146 BC. While Greece remained the fountainhead of civilization to the end of Antiquity, during the Byzantine Empire of *c.* 400 BC to AD 1100, royalty, people of high birth and the indulgent wealthy wore shoes made from costly fabrics that were richly embroidered and bejewelled.

In the second section of the book Western styles are covered from AD 100 to 1699. In the early period in Northern Europe, commoners wore practical shoes and boots made from untanned animal skin, often with criss-crossed garters around the leg for extra protection. The influence of the Romans was much in evidence during their occupation of Northern territories until they withdrew their legions in the fifth century. Until the eleventh century footwear remained practical, with a prevailing Roman design influence. Eleventh-century fashion became dominated by Oriental designs brought back from the Christian crusades. Conspicuous in the twelfth century were shoes made from luxurious fabric, often decorated with embroidery and complete with extended pointed toes. By the thirteenth century the pointed toe had lengthened considerably, and in the fourteenth century, between 1300 and 1350, the extension had increased from two inches to twelve inches beyond the end of the foot. The fantastic 'snouted' toe was padded with moss, hay or wool and shaped with whalebone. Such shoes became known as poulaines in France and crackowes in England (so-named because Poland was where the fashion was supposed to have originated). Pikes, or beaks, went out of fashion towards the end of the fifteenth century, when round-toed slippers and mules became popular, whether in vermilion, scarlet or violet velvet, or in satin, often exquisitely embroidered and sewn with pearls. The wide 'bear's foot' blunt toe reached the height of its popularity in the mid-sixteenth century, when a sumptuary law was passed, imposing a width limit of six inches. Costly fabrics necessitated the wearing of protective cork-soled clogs or wooden pattens for outdoors. These developed into exaggerated platforms, up to thirteen inches high, supporting mules known as chopines. It was from the chopine and the patten that the modern heel developed. The cork wedge was the first form of heel, sandwiched between the leather sole and upper, the thickest part of the wedge set under the heel. It was during this period that the feminine heel known as the French or Louis XIV heel first appeared. In the years to follow, the medium-high heel of Venetian origin, made from wood and painted red, became widely recognized as the sign of a gentleman.

The third section covers the period 1700–1899. It was in the eighteenth century that the masculine shoe took on its modern form, the low broad heel making its appearance in the 1730s. By mid-century these shoes were being produced in the modern conservative colours of brown or black, and had buckles concealing latchet fastenings. Women of the eighteenth century favoured slippers made from fine morocco leather, silks, velvets, brocades and damasks, all very often embroidered. Clogs and pattens were still worn with thick leather soles or hinged wooden soles, and some were covered in fabric to match the shoes. In the nineteenth century the boot, mostly in black, was the most important accessory in the masculine wardrobe. Worn on all occasions, these boots, whether heavy or lightweight, long or short, plain or fancy, had medium-high, stacked leather heels. At the beginning of the century dainty, fragile, heelless pumps with long ribbon ties around the ankle were in vogue for the fashionable lady, or else Greek-style sandals or fine, pale-coloured, kidskin ankle boots. In 1858 in Abingdon, Massachusetts, Lyman R. Blake invented a shoe sewing machine capable of attaching the sole to the upper. The machine lightened shoe construction by making it possible to build shoes with thread rather than with nails and pegs.

The last three sections of this study I have confined to the twentieth century and the first few years of the twenty-first. The twentieth century hailed the birth of the shoe designer as opposed to the shoemaker. Names such as Pietro Yanturni, André Perugia, Salvatore Ferragamo and Roger Vivier were designing and making shoes for a grand and wealthy elite. American manufacturers mass-produced many of their designs using the revolutionary shoe sewing machines and in consequence fashionable styles were now available to everyone at lower prices. The range of designs and colours grew, as did the demand.

Styles in women's footwear appear and reappear throughout the century. Boots from the 1900s have been constantly reinvented – in the 1960s as knee-length and close-fitting, in the 1970s as thigh-length with six-inch platform soles, in the 1990s as above-knee-length in see-through plastic with 1950s-style elongated winklepicker toes and five-inch metal spike heels. Shoes with pointed toes and bar straps reappeared in the 1950s with stiletto heels, and the platform soles and blunt toes of the 1930s and '40s became exaggerated out of all proportion in the 1970s. In the late 1990s and at the beginning of the twenty-first century, shoe fashions were as inconsistent as ever. Vivienne Westwood's twelve-inch platform-soled shoes, with thick high heels to match, were made in brightly coloured lacquered snakeskin. At the same time, Jimmy Choo produced delicate, ultra-feminine shoes in pale pistachio-ice-cream-coloured suede decorated with beads and feathers. Manolo Blahnik, on the other hand, designed immaculate fine calfskin slingback shoes with elongated pointed toes and high stiletto heels.

Men's shoes, on the other hand, have altered little over the past century. The lace-up leather shoe of 1900, with its toecap and brogue detail, is indistinguishable from any classic style of today. Certain changes have, however, occurred. Step-in shoes, or slip-ons, appeared in the 1940s. In the 1950s teddy boys adopted crepe soles with combined heels, while others wore shoes with pointed toes that aped contemporary womenswear, or indeed the fashions of the fourteenth century. The 1960s brought in elastic-sided chelsea boots, favoured by the Beatles, with high, shaped, stacked heels and pointed toes reminiscent of those worn at the beginning of the 1900s. Since the 1970s lace-up white canvas sports shoes with ridged rubber soles – trainers, or sneakers – have become universally popular for both men and women.

At the end of this book are several pages which chart the development of shoes from Antiquity to the present and outline at a glance the principal changes that have taken place. Brief biographies and histories of some of the important designers also appear at the end of this book. Finally, a bibliography lists those works which have been especially useful in compiling this survey.

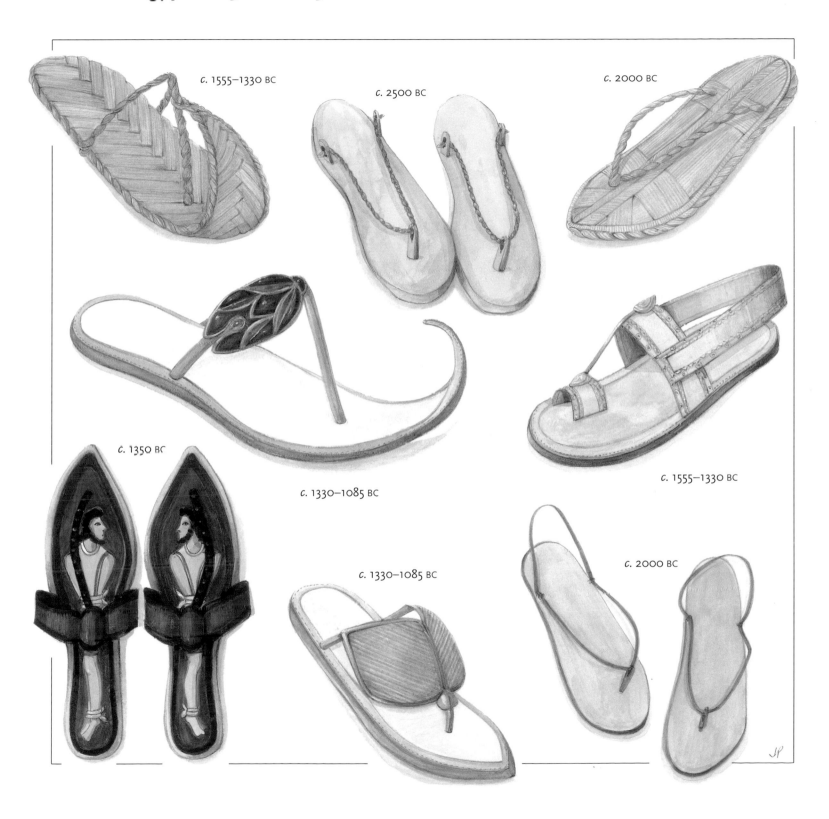

c. 1555–1330 BC

c. 2500 BC

c. 2000 BC

c. 1350 BC

c. 1330–1085 BC

c. 1555–1330 BC

c. 1330–1085 BC

c. 2000 BC

Ancient Egypt *c.* 1555–600 BC

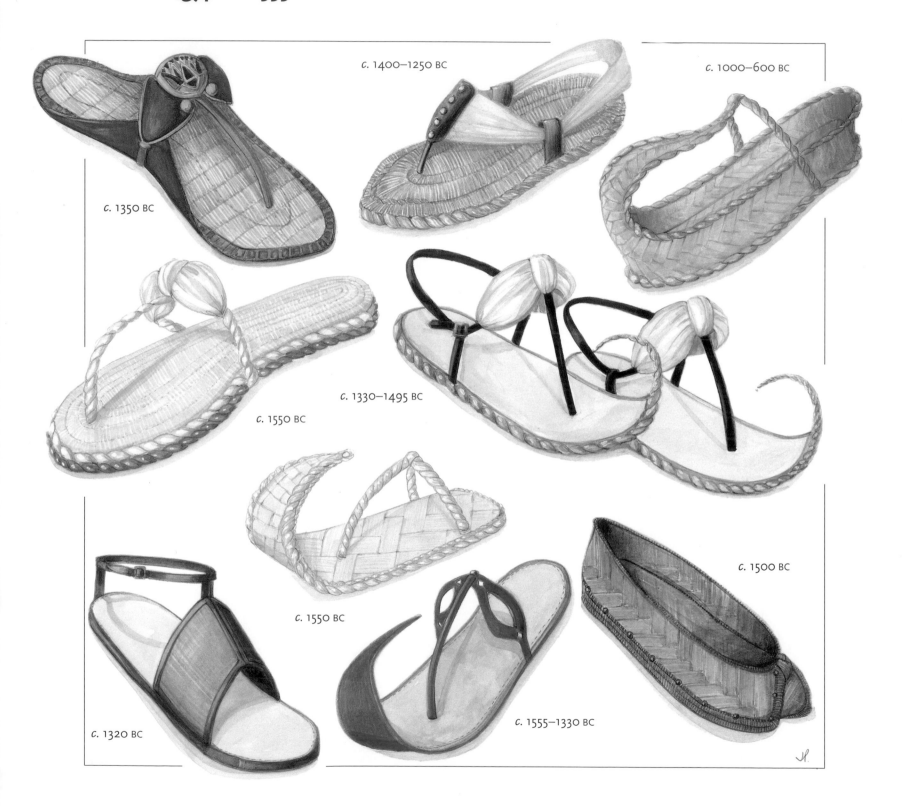

c. 1400–1250 BC

c. 1000–600 BC

c. 1350 BC

c. 1550 BC

c. 1330–1495 BC

c. 1550 BC

c. 1500 BC

c. 1320 BC

c. 1555–1330 BC

Mesopotamia *c.* 1000 BC–AD 200

Persian *c.* AD 100

Assyrian *c.* 1000 BC

Assyrian *c.* 900 BC

Babylonian *c.* 500 BC–AD 100

Babylonian *c.* 500 BC

Babylonian *c.* 900 BC–AD 100

Babylonian *c.* 900 BC

Persian *c.* AD 200

Mesopotamia *c*. 1000 BC–AD 200

Assyrian *c*. 1000 BC

Assyrian *c*. 200 BC

Babylonian *c*. 500 BC

Babylonian *c*. 500 BC

Persian *c*. AD 200

Babylonian *c*. AD 200

Assyrian *c*. AD 100

Persian *c*. AD 200

Ancient Greece 480–400 BC

c. 450 BC

c. 480–400 BC

c. 400 BC

c. 450 BC

c. 480–400 BC

c. 450–400 BC

c. 400 BC

c. 450 BC

c. 450 BC

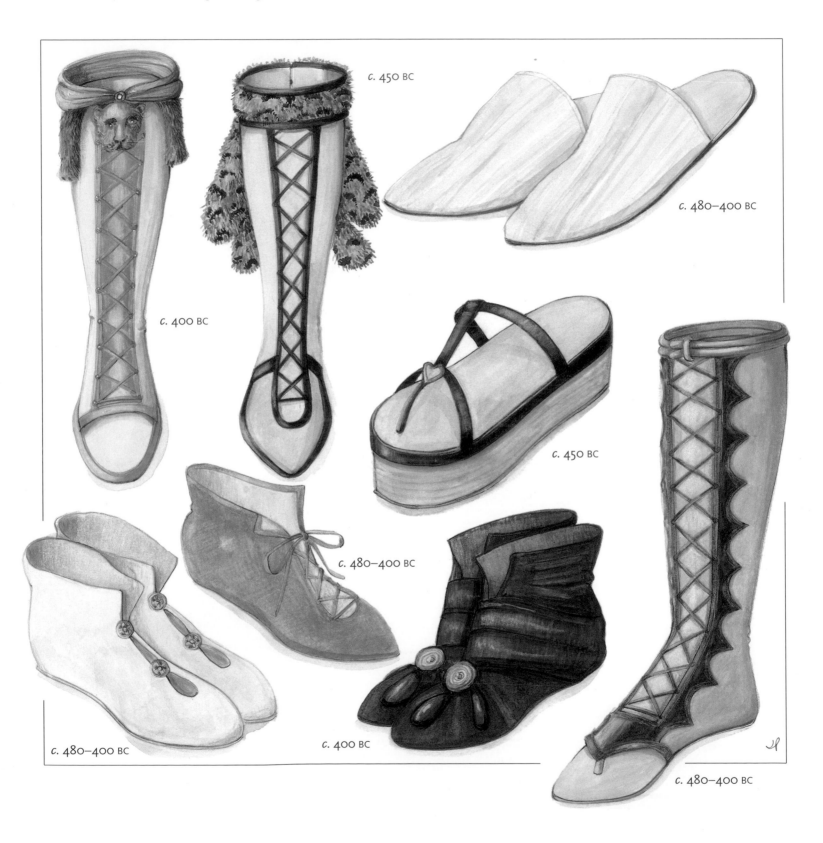

c. 450 BC

c. 480–400 BC

c. 400 BC

c. 450 BC

c. 480–400 BC

c. 480–400 BC

c. 400 BC

c. 480–400 BC

Ancient Greece 480–400 BC

c. 480 BC

c. 480 BC

c. 400 BC

c. 400 BC

c. 450 BC

c. 450 BC

c. 480–400 BC

c. 450 BC

c. 400 BC

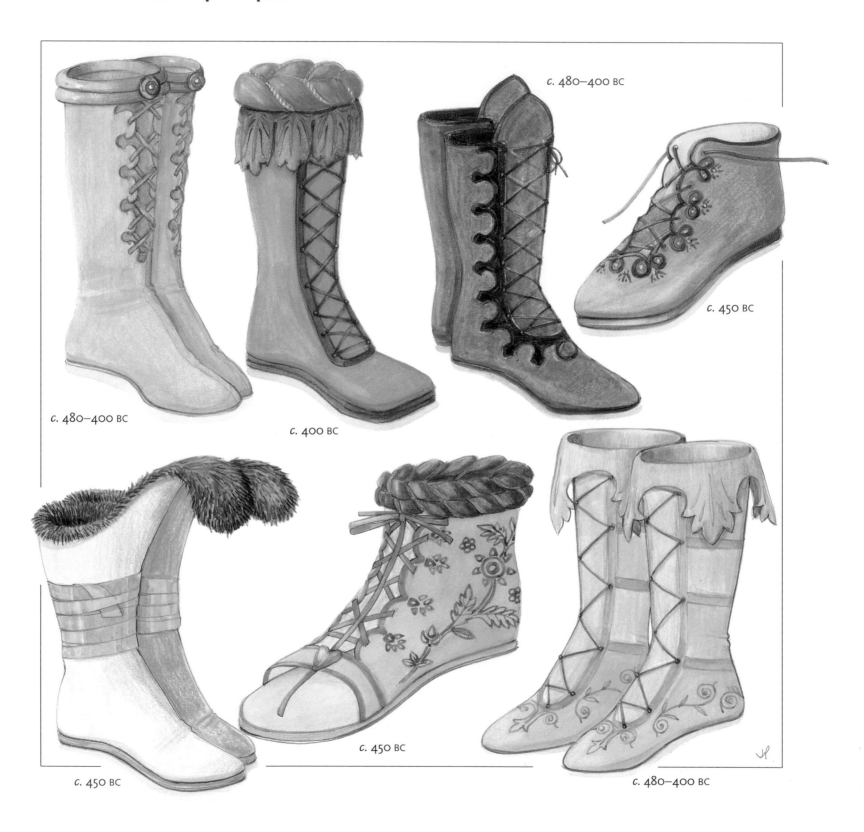

c. 480–400 BC

c. 480–400 BC

c. 400 BC

c. 450 BC

c. 450 BC

c. 450 BC

c. 480–400 BC

Ancient Greece 480–400 BC

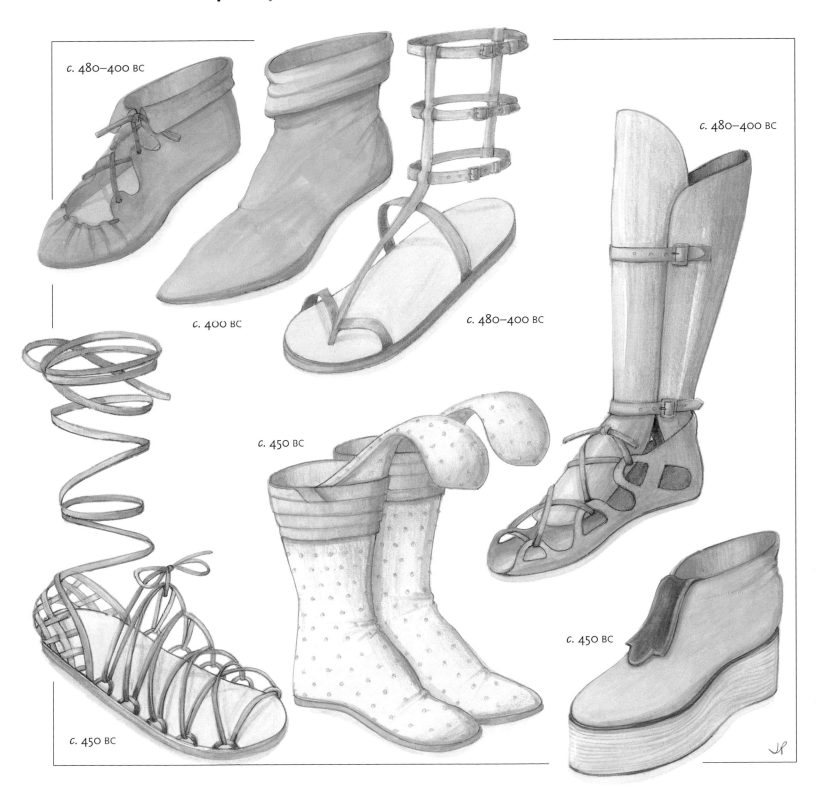

c. 480–400 BC

c. 400 BC

c. 480–400 BC

c. 480–400 BC

c. 450 BC

c. 450 BC

c. 450 BC

Soldier's sandal

Woman's boot

Woman's shoe

Woman's mule

Soldier's boot

Woman's shoe

Hunting boot

Woman's sandal

Hunting boot

Man's boot

Ancient Rome 31 BC—AD 323

c. AD 200–300

c. AD 100

c. AD 100–323

c. 31 BC–AD 100

c. AD 100–200

c. AD 200–300

c. AD 200

c. AD 100

c. 31 BC–AD 323

c. AD 300

c. AD 100

c. AD 200

c. AD 100–200

c. AD 100–300

c. AD 100–300

c. AD 100

c. AD 100

c. AD 300

c. AD 100

c. AD 100

c. 31 BC–AD 200

c. AD 200

c. 31 BC–AD 323

c. AD 100–300

c. AD 150

c. AD 150

c. 31 BC–AD 323

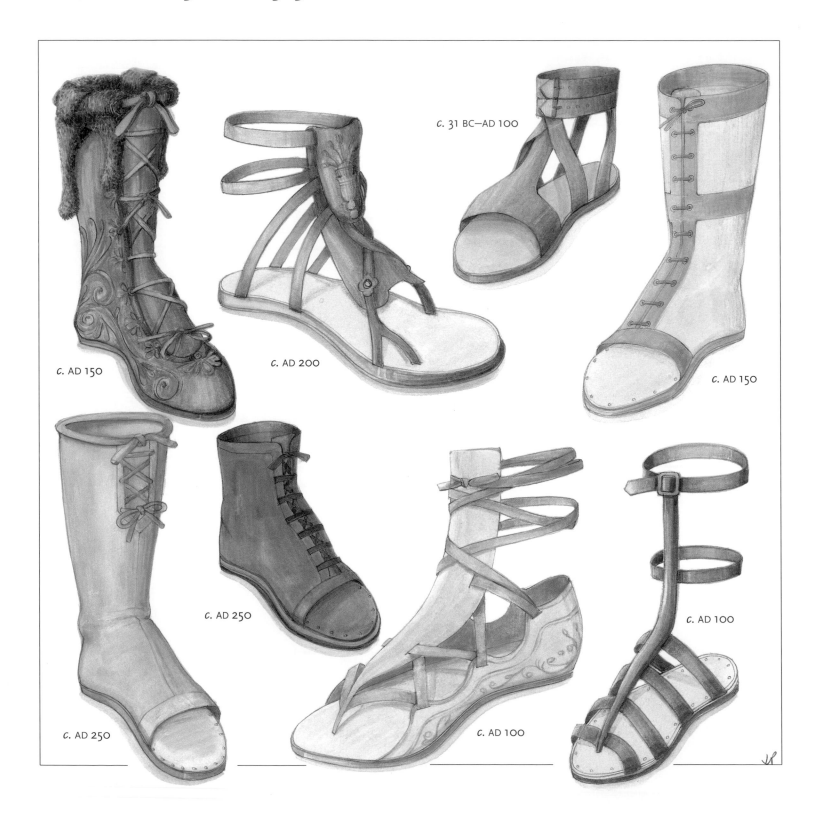

c. AD 150

c. AD 200

c. 31 BC—AD 100

c. AD 150

c. AD 250

c. AD 250

c. AD 100

c. AD 100

Byzantine AD 400–1100

c. AD 400–500

c. AD 400–500

c. AD 400–500

c. AD 400

c. AD 550

c. AD 550

c. AD 450

Byzantine AD 400–1100

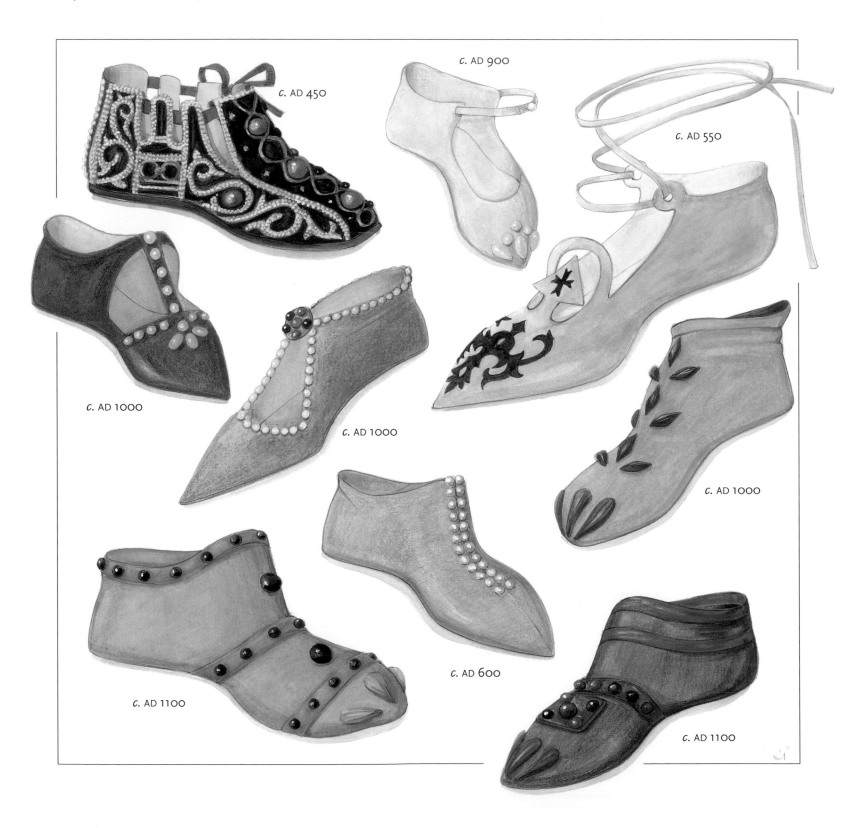

c. AD 900

c. AD 450

c. AD 550

c. AD 1000

c. AD 1000

c. AD 1000

c. AD 600

c. AD 1100

c. AD 1100

Ancient Egypt *c.* 2500–1085 BC

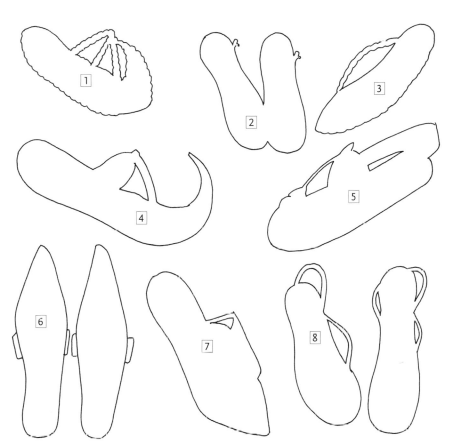

1 Sandal *c.* 1555–1330 BC. Woven vegetable fibre sole, shaped for left foot, piked toe attached to a twisted thong passing between big and second toe, matching strap over instep. 2 Workman's sandals *c.* 2500 BC. Wooden soles, shaped for left and right feet, vegetable fibre straps secured in wooden pegs. 3 Sandal *c.* 2000 BC. Woven vegetable fibre sole, shaped for left foot, pointed toe, single strap of twisted palm fibre passing between big and second toe, ending each side of heel. 4 Royal sandal *c.* 1330–1085 BC. Thick ox, cow or buffalo hide sole, sewn with waxed thread to upper of lamb or goatskin, fine white linen lining, piked toe, leather thong passing between big and second toe, matching strap over instep passing under wide shaped bar, painted decoration with raised gold-embossed detail. 5 Royal sandal *c.* 1555–1330 BC. Thick ox, cow or buffalo hide sole, sewn to fine leather upper with waxed thread, dyed kidskin lining, gold-embossed instep, heel and toe straps, gold linking bar between instep and toe strap. 6 Pair of sandals *c.* 1350 BC. Thick ox leather soles, stitched with waxed thread to fine dyed kidskin upper soles, pointed toes, linen lining painted with a figure depicting a bound captive or enemy, two-colour leather thong passing between big and second toe, attached to wide strap over instep. 7 Royal sandal *c.* 1330–1085 BC. Thick ox or cow hide sole, shaped for right foot, stitched with waxed thread to goatskin upper sole, white linen lining, pointed toe, wide wing-shaped gold-embossed leather strap over instep, leather thong between big and second toe. 8 Pair of outdoor sandals *c.* 2000 BC. Thick ox, cow or buffalo hide soles, shaped for left and right feet, stitched to finer upper soles with waxed thread, short leather peg between big and second toe, attached thong straps to side instep and behind heel.

Ancient Egypt *c.* 1555–600 BC

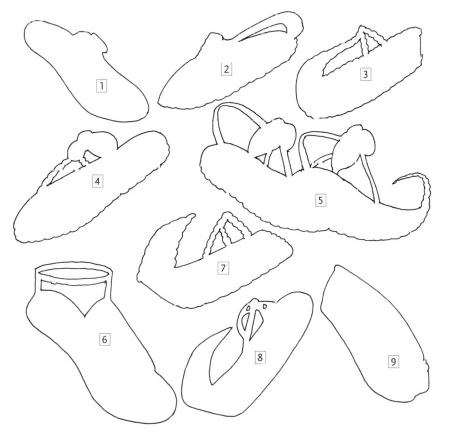

1 Royal sandal *c.* 1350 BC. Brightly coloured dyed fine kidskin sole with pointed toe and curved side panels, matching leaf-shaped instep strap surmounted with painted and gilded lotus flower plaque, woven and stitched palm fibre insole, shaped for left foot, dyed kidskin thong passing between big and second toe to under instep strap. 2 Outdoor sandal *c.* 1400–1250 BC. Woven vegetable fibre sole, shaped for left foot, pointed toe, short leather thong between big and second toe under leather bar decorated with gold studs, wide white linen strap around foot, secured by leather side straps. 3 Outdoor shoe *c.* 1000–600 BC. Open boat-shaped woven vegetable fibre shoe, high sides and back, long piked toe attached to instep strap. 4 Sandal *c.* 1550 BC. Bleached vegetable fibre double-thickness sole, lower sole dyed red, twisted thong between big and second toe, attached to matching thong bound with linen over instep. 5 Royal sandals *c.* 1330–1495 BC. Vegetable fibre soles, shaped for left and right feet, lined with bleached linen, long piked toes, dyed leather strap between big and second toe, matching buckled heel straps, side supports and linen-covered instep strap. 6 Soldier's sandal *c.* 1320 BC. Thick ox, cow or buffalo hide sole, shaped for right foot, stitched to finer leather upper sole with waxed thread, wide leather strap-over instep with buckled leather strap above, attached at back of heel, no toe hold. 7 Priest's sandal *c.* 1550 BC. Woven bleached vegetable fibre sole, high piked toe, squared-off at back of heel, twisted toehold between big and second toe, matching instep strap. 8 Royal sandal *c.* 1555–1330 BC. Dyed leather undersole, stitched to kidskin upper sole with waxed thread, long piked toe, shaped for right foot, thong between big and second toe under wide openwork instep strap. 9 Outdoor shoe *c.* 1500 BC. Woven vegetable fibre shoe, shallow piked toes and sole made in one piece, high sides and back, low-cut front.

Mesopotamia *c.* 1000 BC–AD 200

1 Persian queen's sandal *c.* AD 100. Platform sole and shallow wedge heel covered with gilded leather, linen lining, two gold rings either side of filled-in heel-back to hold contrasting-colour triple-thong instep strap, matching bindings and straps from above toehold. 2 Assyrian king's sandal *c.* 1000 BC. Thick dyed leather sole, fine kidskin lining, single flat leather strap secured on one side of sole, continued across instep to opposite side and threaded though gold rings attached to filled-in heel-back, matching double toehold. 3 Assyrian sandal *c.* 900 BC. Thick leather sole, linen lining, metal rings on either side of double-strap heel-back securing leather thongs criss-crossing over instep, double strap toehold. 4 Babylonian king's shoe *c.* 500 BC. Thick dyed leather platform sole, fine kidskin lining, filled-in heel-back to above ankle-level, lined with brightly coloured dyed kidskin, matching linings of embroidered and jewelled straps across open front. 5 Babylonian soldier's sandal *c.* 500 BC–AD 100. Thick ox hide sole, shaped for left foot, stitched to thinner leather upper sole, flat coloured leather toehold strap between big and second toe, attached to straps over instep, heart-shaped metal locking slide adjuster. 6 Babylonian sandal *c.* 900 BC–AD 100. Platform sole covered with gilded leather, matching toehold, filled-in heel-back and triple straps across instep, bead decoration and jewelled clasp. 7 Babylonian king's shoe *c.* 900 BC. Thin leather sole, pointed toe, linen lining, multicoloured dyed kidskin, cut and seamed to form stripes, bound edges. 8 Persian shoe *c.* AD 200. Thin leather sole, pointed toe, linen lining, dyed leather upper, central strap with matching instep straps and long ties around ankle.

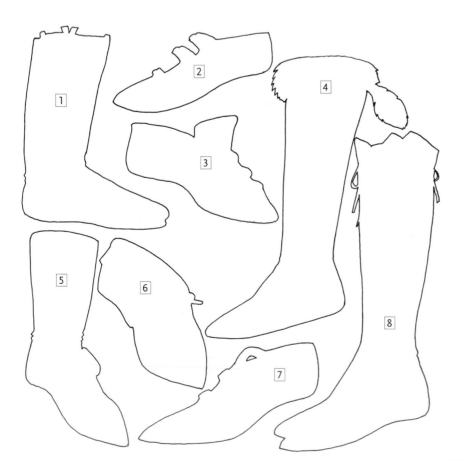

Mesopotamia *c.* 1000 BC–AD 200

1 Assyrian hunting boots *c.* 1000 BC. Calf-length pale-coloured leather, open front in-filled with wide full-length tongue, flat leather laces, ends tied around calf, thin heelless soles. 2 Assyrian king's shoe *c.* 200 BC. Heelless thin leather soles, lined with linen, pointed toe, low-cut upper, dyed kidskin embroidered with coloured silks and gold thread, set with precious and semi-precious stones, three matching instep straps, gold button fastenings. 3 Babylonian shoe *c.* 500 BC. Heelless thin leather sole, pointed toe, high sides and back, dyed kidskin lining, matching high tongue and slashes on each side of centre front opening, jewelled button trim. 4 Babylonian boot *c.* 500 BC. Knee-length pale-coloured leather, heelless thin leather sole, pointed toe, open front in-filled with full-length tongue, topstitched detail, laced from instep to under deep animal-fur cuff, complete with tail. 5 Persian nobleman's boot *c.* AD 200. Mid-calf-length fine leather, heelless thin leather sole, pointed toe, upper with central seam, large jewelled clasp above instep. 6 Babylonian shoe *c.* AD 200. Soft leather, heelless thin leather sole, pointed toe, fine leather lining, tied at front above instep with flat thong from under turned-down cuff running around high back and sides. 7 Assyrian queen's shoe *c.* AD 100. Pale-coloured goatskin embroidered with coloured silks and gold thread, thin leather sole, pointed toe, three instep straps, jewelled button fastenings. 8 Persian boots *c.* AD 200. Heelless thin leather soles, pointed toes, light-coloured goatskin, knee-length, fitted closely to legs with leather laces, shaped top edges, open sides, open fronts with full-length tongues.

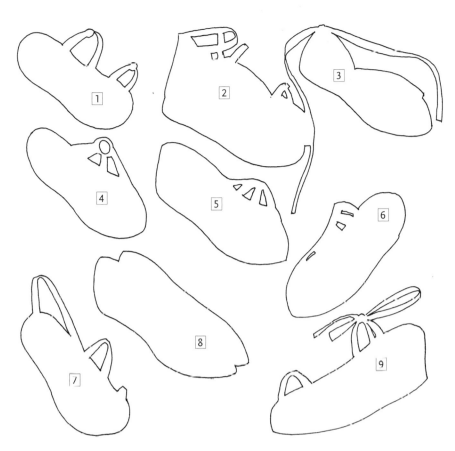

Ancient Greece 480–400 BC

1 Woman's sandal c. 400 BC. Thick leather sole, pale-coloured kidskin lining, flat leather instep strap, button trim, leather strap over toes. 2 Woman's sandal c. 450 BC. Thick sole made from layers of leather, front shaped to toes, kidskin lining, thong between big and second toe from under instep strap, filled-in heel-back, buckled straps around ankle. 3 Woman's shoe c. 480–400 BC. Thin leather sole, goatskin lining, open front, thong between big and second toe, metal slide adjuster, low-cut sides, long ribbon ankle ties attached to filled-in heel-back. 4 Woman's sandal c. 450 BC. Thick leather sole, pale-coloured kidskin lining, coloured leather straps attached at sides and threaded through metal ring on instep. 5 Woman's shoe c. 480–400 BC. Thick leather sole, pale-coloured kidskin lining, flat leather straps crossing over instep, matching filled-in heel-back, cloth-lined behind heel and on side fronts. 6 Woman's sandal c. 450–400 BC. Layered thick leather sole, pale-coloured kidskin lining, coloured cloth straps over toes and instep, decorative plaque on front. 7 Woman's sandal c. 450 BC. Thick sole covered in dyed goatskin, matching straps over instep, over toes and around heel. 8 Woman's shoes c. 400 BC. Thin soles, pointed toes, fine light-coloured kidskin uppers, embroidered and painted design. 9 Woman's sandal c. 450 BC. Cork and leather platform sole covered in dyed goatskin, matching shallow wedge heel, cloth lining, cloth ribbon straps over toes and around ankle, tying over instep.

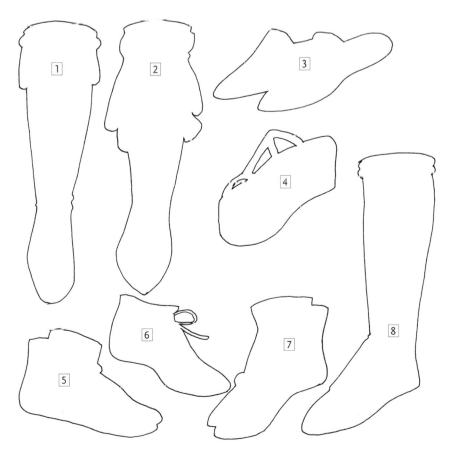

Ancient Greece 480–400 BC

1 Woman's boot c. 400 BC. Thick leather sole, kidskin lining, open front, criss-cross leather thong laces from above open toe to under small animal head, top edge trimmed with fine fabric, animal legs and fur. 2 Woman's boot c. 450 BC. Pale-coloured leather upper, pointed toe, thick sole dyed bright colour, matching bindings and trim, open front, criss-cross leather thong laces from low front to under leopard-fur-trimmed cuff, matching fur hanging on either side. 3 Woman's mules c. 480–400 BC. Thin red leather soles, fine fabric uppers, pointed toes, kidskin linings. 4 Woman's sandal c. 450 BC. Platform cork and leather sole, kidskin lining, dyed leather trimming, matching thong between big and second toe with heart-shaped slide adjuster, flat straps across instep and toes with joining strap. 5 Woman's boots c. 480–400 BC. Heelless thin leather soles, blunt toes, pale-coloured goatskin uppers, open fronts, two engraved metal button fastenings from low front to under ankle-level. 6 Woman's boot c. 480–400 BC. Heelless thin leather sole, pointed toe, brightly coloured goatskin ankle-length upper, open front, criss-crossed ribbon laces. 7 Woman's boots c. 400 BC. Heelless thin leather soles, pointed toes, brightly coloured dyed goatskin ankle-length uppers, decorative slashes above toes, matching wide binding around instep and heel, engraved gold plaque above instep. 8 Woman's boot c. 480–400 BC. Heelless thin leather sole, open toe, thong between big and second toe, open front, criss-cross gilded leather lacing from instep to knee-level, matching bindings and edges to scalloped contrast-colour leather inserts.

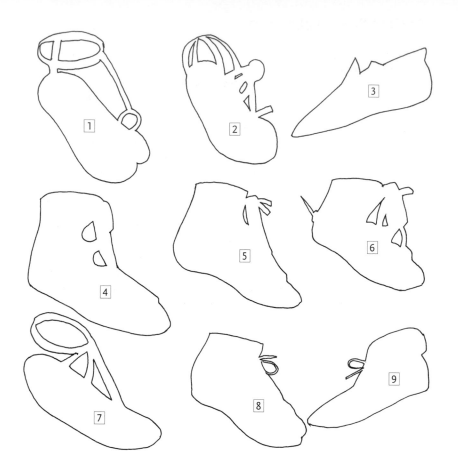

Ancient Greece 480–400 BC

1 Man's sandal c. 480 BC. Thick leather sole, front shaped to toes, kidskin lining, leather thong between big and second toe connected to metal ring on centre of instep, adjustable leather bar below buckled ankle strap, restraining band behind heel. 2 Man's sandal c. 480 BC. Thick leather sole, kidskin lining, flat leather straps between big and second toe, three instep straps with front clasp fastening and two heel straps interlaced on sides. 3 Man's shoe c. 400 BC. Heelless thin leather sole, pointed toe, dyed fine goatskin upper, high vamp split on centre front, high sides and back. 4 Man's sandal c. 400 BC. Layered thick leather sole, open toe, goatskin lining, ankle-length leather upper, cut-away open side panels, adjustable central securing strap over instep and under ankle-level turned-down cuff. 5 Soldier's sandal c. 450 BC. Layered thick leather sole studded with metal spikes, open toe, goatskin lining, ankle-length thick leather upper, narrow flat leather straps crossed and tied under central adjustable securing instep strap. 6 Soldier's sandal c. 450 BC. Thick leather sole, blunt toe, goatskin lining, ankle-length dyed leather upper, flat leather thongs laced through scalloped sides, fastening under central adjustable securing strap over instep, heel-back reinforced with thick leather, metal studs and a long spike. 7 Man's sandal c. 480–400 BC. Layered leather sole, blunt toe, cloth lining, adjustable strap between big and second toe connected to instep and ankle straps. 8 Man's shoe c. 450 BC. Layered thick leather sole, front shaped to toes, ankle-length thick leather upper, open front, flat leather criss-cross lacing between scalloped sides. 9 Man's shoe c. 400 BC. Heelless thin leather sole, pointed toe, ankle-length leather upper, open front, criss-cross leather laces from instep to under turned-down cuff.

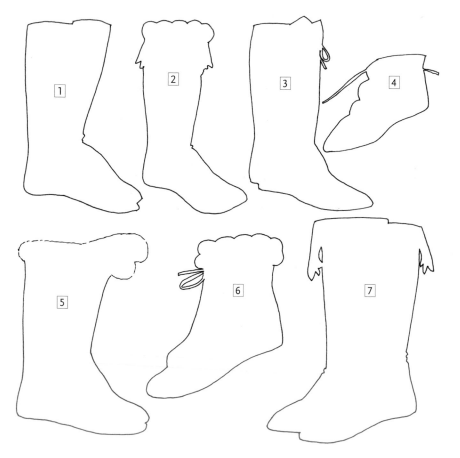

Ancient Greece 480–400 BC

1 Man's riding boots c. 480–400 BC. Heelless thin leather soles, pointed toes, light-coloured goatskin knee-length uppers, open front from padded top, with clasp fasteners, to ankle-level, fastened with criss-crossed leather laces between scalloped edges. 2 Man's hunting boot c. 400 BC. Layered thick leather sole, square toe, knee-length leather upper, open front fastening with criss-cross leather laces from low instep to under decorative padded fabric cuff and foliate leather pelmet. 3 Man's riding boots c. 480–400 BC. Heelless thin leather soles, pointed toes, brightly coloured dyed goatskin knee-length uppers, open fronts to low instep, criss-cross leather lacing over full-length leather tongue, contrast-colour inset edging and painted decoration. 4 Man's ankle boot c. 450 BC. Layered thick leather sole, pointed toe, dyed goatskin upper, open front with lacing between scalloped edges from low instep to ankle-level. 5 Man's hunting boots c. 450 BC. Layered thick leather soles, blunt toes, thick hide knee-length uppers, fur lining, matching high front cuffs, leather gartering around and above ankle-level. 6 Man's shoe c. 450 BC. Layered leather sole, blunt toe, kidskin lining, open toe with leather thong between big and second toe, heart-shaped metal adjuster, fine pale-coloured leather upper, embroidered floral design on side fronts, open front with scalloped edges bound in contrasting-colour leather, matching criss-cross lacing from above toes to under padded ankle-level decoration. 7 Man's riding boots c. 480–400 BC. Heelless red leather soles, pointed toes, pale-coloured goatskin knee-length uppers, embroidered decoration on fronts and sides, low-cut open fronts bound in contrasting-colour leather, matching inset bands around legs, fine leather thong lacing over full-length inset tongues from low instep to under contrasting-colour leather foliate-design pelmet.

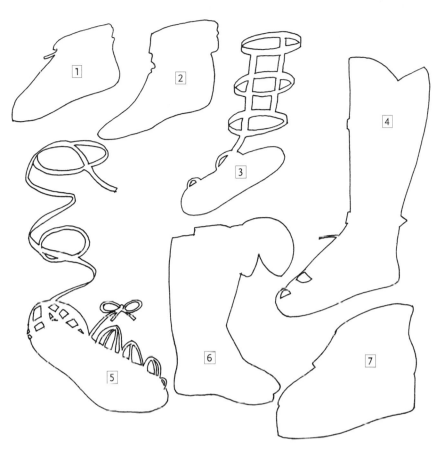

Ancient Greece 480–400 BC

1 Peasant's shoe c. 480–400 BC. Heelless leather sole, blunt toe, ankle-length hide upper, open front, criss-cross leather thong laces between scalloped edges from low-cut instep to under turned-down ankle-level cuff. 2 Actor's shoe c. 400 BC. Heelless thin leather sole, pointed toe, soft leather upper, ankle-level cuff. 3 Soldier's sandal c. 480–400 BC. Layered thick leather sole, blunt toe, kidskin lining, leather strap between big and second toe, joining toe, instep and buckled leg straps. 4 Soldier's footwear c. 480–400 BC. Leather heelless soles and shoe sides cut in one piece and moulded to foot shape, open front with scalloped edges, criss-cross leather laces from over open toes to ankle-level through large holes, thick hide knee-length two-piece leg-guard, high front extending to cover instep, below-knee-level back panel to under heel-back inside shoe, two straps and buckle fastenings. 5 Man's sandal c. 450 BC. Layered thick leather sole, kidskin lining, blunt toe, leather thongs criss-crossed over toes and instep, threaded through leather rings attached to edges of sole, open latticework heel-back. 6 Man's hunting boots c. 450 BC. Heelless thick leather soles, blunt toes, fitted mid-calf-length light-coloured calfskin uppers, perforated decoration, extended leaf-shaped front cuffs, leather strap binding below. 7 Actor's shoe c. 450 BC. Layered thick leather and cork platform sole, ankle-length pale-coloured soft leather upper, contrasting-colour leather tongue decoration over instep.

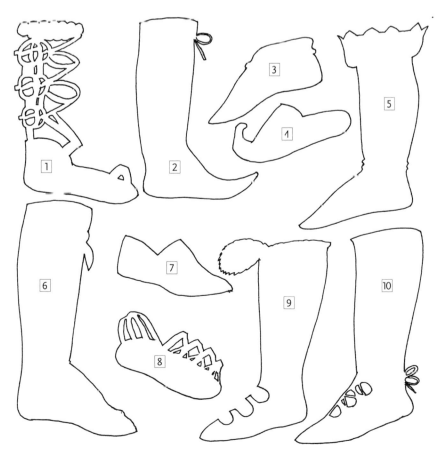

Etruscan c. 800–200 BC

1 Soldier's sandal. Thick leather sole, blunt toe, goatskin lining, wide leather straps over toes and instep, filled-in heel-back, leather laces criss-crossed over front of leg and through graded leather-covered rings on sides from instep to below twisted bands of leather at knee-level. 2 Woman's boot. Peaked toe revealing brightly coloured heelless thin leather sole, knee-length contrast-colour soft leather upper, embroidered decoration from back heel to over instep on each side, fine leather thong laces from instep to under wide pale-coloured leather cuff. 3 Woman's shoe. Heelless thin leather sole, pointed toe, pale-coloured soft leather upper, decorated around top edge with multicoloured semi-precious stones. 4 Woman's mule. Thick wooden sole, leather lining, thick leather upper with long peaked toe, instep decorated with two bands of coloured leather. 5 Soldier's boot. Heelless thin leather sole, knee-length calfskin upper, leather strap binding around upper leg under wide turned-down cuff, crenellated edge lined in contrasting colour. 6 Hunting boot. Heelless thin leather sole, knee-length dyed leather upper, slashed decoration above blunt toes, contrast-colour binding and embroidered decoration on edges of open front, fine leather thong laces, leather strap binding around knee. 7 Woman's shoe. Heelless thin leather sole, pointed toe, light-coloured calfskin upper, wide contrast-colour leather binding on top edge. 8 Woman's sandal. Thick leather sole, blunt toe, kidskin lining, four leather cross straps secured through thongs attached to sides of sole, two leather heel straps. 9 Hunting boot. Heelless hide sole, pointed toe, light-coloured fur-lined hide knee-length upper, matching fur tail cuff on front edge, three open slashes over instep, leather strap binding around calf. 10 Man's boot. Heelless leather sole, pointed toe, knee-length leather upper, scalloped-edged open lower front, laced with fine leather thongs over instep and around ankle, wrap-over boot-leg covering back only.

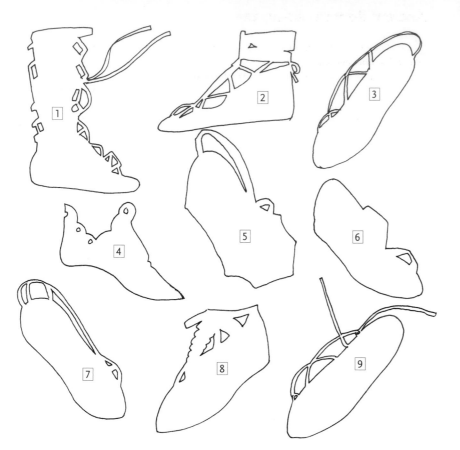

Ancient Rome 31 BC–AD 323

1 Woman's boot c. AD 200–300. Layered thick leather sole, kidskin lining, mid-calf-length upper comprised of interwoven flat leather straps, laced through open front with leather straps from above open toes to leather band at mid-calf-level. 2 Woman's shoe c. AD 100. Thin leather sole, kidskin lining, fine leather upper, high heel-back with embroidered detail to side, tongue strap over open front laced with leather thong from between big and second toe through rings set on scalloped sides to instep, tied behind heel, leather strap bindings around ankle. 3 Woman's sandal c. AD 100–323. Thin leather sole, kidskin lining, fine leather thong straps from between big and second toe from edge of sole, criss-crossed over instep and around heel through two leather guides. 4 Woman's shoe c. 31 BC–AD 100. Heelless thin leather sole, pointed toe, ankle-length fabric upper, open scalloped sides with punched hole decoration. 5 Woman's sandal c. AD 100–200. Deep sole of layered leather and cork, shaped at front and sides, inner sole lined with kidskin, leather strap between big and second toe, metal heart-shaped adjuster, leather strap around heel from side fronts. 6 Woman's shoe c. AD 200–300. Raised woven vegetable fibre sole, matching straps between big and second toe, three straps over instep and filled-in heel-back. 7 Woman's sandal c. AD 200. Thick leather sole, cloth lining, leather straps crossed over toes, matching side and heel straps. 8 Woman's shoe c. AD 100. Thick leather sole, open toe, shallow sides, straps over instep, sides and ankle, gilded leather leaf-shaped tongue, filled-in heel-back. 9 Woman's sandal c. 31 BC–AD 323. Thick unlined hide sole edged with four rings guiding leather thong straps crossed over toes and instep, and tied behind heel.

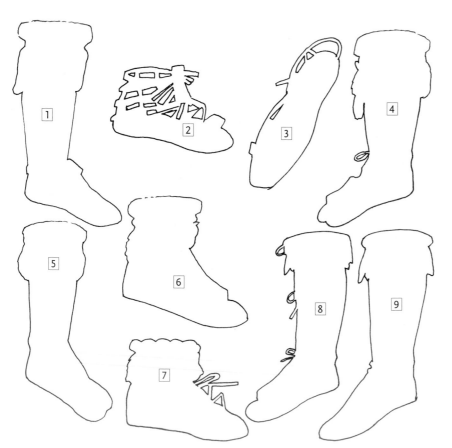

Ancient Rome 31 BC–AD 323

1 Man's riding boot c. AD 100. Heelless thin leather sole, blunt toe, knee-length soft leather upper embroidered with gold threads, open front bound with contrast-colour leather, matching tied strap around ankle, inset band at toe-level, criss-cross laces and securing strap around fur-trimmed top, complete with animal head and legs. 2 Man's sandal c. AD 300. Layered thick leather sole, fine leather lining, wide strap over toes, ankle-length upper comprised of interwoven flat leather straps, open front fastened with leather laces, decorative tongue strap of tooled leather. 3 Man's sandal c. AD 200. Thick leather sole, square toe, fine leather lining, shallow sides, strap over toes, matching instep, side and tied ankle straps, large heart-shaped metal strap adjuster. 4 Man's hunting boot c. AD 100–200. Layered thick leather sole, front shaped to toes, leather lining, knee-length pale-coloured soft leather upper, contrast-colour leather on open toe, matching laces over open instep and securing strap around knee-level fur cuff, complete with animal head and legs. 5 Man's riding boot c. AD 100. Thin leather sole, front shaped to toes, knee-length pale-coloured soft leather upper, open toe with contrast-colour shaped binding between big and second toe, heart-shaped metal adjuster, matching tied ankle strap, binding of open front and thick criss-cross laces from mid-calf-level to under fur cuff, painted decoration on upper side leg. 6 Emperor's boot c. AD 100–300. Layered thick leather sole, blunt toe, kidskin lining, ankle-length dyed goatskin upper, all-over gold thread embroidered design, gilded leather bindings to open front, open toe, leather thong between big and second toe, gold adjuster, fine laces to under fur-trimmed top edge, complete with animal head and legs. 7 Senator's boot c. AD 100. Dyed thick leather sole, embroidered soft leather upper, open front with criss-crossed laces over instep, twisted fabric cuff above carved ivory animal head, fur paws. 8 Man's hunting boot c. AD 100–300. Unlined heelless thick leather sole, knee-length leather upper, open toe bound in contrast colour, matching thong laces on instep, at mid-calf-level and above crenellated cuff. 9 Man's hunting boot c. AD 300. Thick leather sole, knee-length fitted leather upper, contrast-colour leather crenellated cuff and padded roll edge.

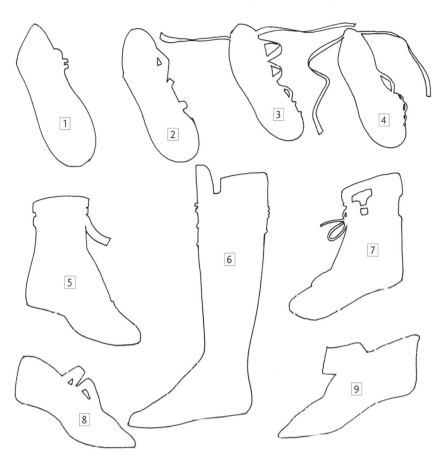

Ancient Rome 31 BC–AD 323

1 Man's sandal c. AD 100. Unlined thick leather sole, blunt toe, open front, narrow adjustable strap between big and second toe connected to broad tongue strap, wide shaped strap over toes, two narrow straps interweaving with tongue strap over instep, shallow sides, filled-in heel-back. 2 Man's sandal c. AD 100. Unlined thick leather sole, criss-crossed flat leather straps between shallow sides and broad adjustable tongue strap, straps from sides of filled-in heel-back. 3 Man's sandal c. 31 BC–AD 200. Thick leather sole, goatskin lining, shallow sides from filled-in heel-back to blunt toe, narrow and wide flat leather straps over toes and criss-crossed over foot to tie at ankle-level. 4 Man's sandal c. AD 200. Thick leather sole, blunt toe, leather lining, flat leather straps over toes and sides threaded through central leather-covered ring, filled-in heel-back with attached leather laces to tie around ankle and leg. 5 Man's boot c. 31 BC–AD 323. Thick leather sole, blunt toe, ankle-length pale-coloured leather upper, open on each side, contrast-colour thick leather straps from each side of front sole, bound around ankle, tied on centre front. 6 Man's hunting boot c. AD 150. Heelless thick leather sole, blunt toe, light-coloured fine leather knee-length upper, open front, criss-crossed leather thong laces from low instep over full-length inset tongue, laces bound around lower knee. 7 Soldier's boot c. AD 100–300. Unlined layered thick leather sole, open toe, broad adjustable leather tongue strap, high filled-in back, open over ankles, sides and tongue laced together with leather thong on centre front. 8 Priest's shoe c. AD 150. Heelless thin leather sole, pointed toe, embroidered fine fabric upper, low-cut front, three straps over instep, jewelled button fastenings. 9 Man's shoe c. 31 BC–AD 323. Heelless thick leather sole, pointed toe, ankle-length leather upper, high sides and heel-back, turned-down square front over instep.

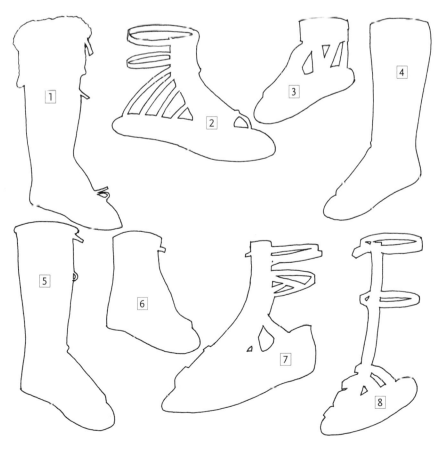

Ancient Rome 31 BC–AD 323

1 Man's riding boot c. AD 150. Heelless thick leather sole, knee-length coloured fine leather upper, embroidered decoration on back and side fronts, matching embroidery on edges of open front, criss-cross leather thong laces from low-cut front to under animal-fur cuff. 2 Senator's sandal c. AD 200. Heelless layered thick leather sole, blunt toe, leather lining, crossed flat leather straps over broad adjustable tongue strap with painted motif, two instep straps and two ankle straps fastening below. 3 Soldier's sandal c. 31 BC–AD 100. Thick leather sole, leather lining, deep strap over open toe with tongue strap over instep, four side straps attached to two buckled ankle straps. 4 Man's hunting boot c. AD 150. Unlined heelless thick leather sole, blunt toe, knee-length leather upper, contrast-colour leather band over open toe, matching inset bands at mid-calf-level and top edge binding, front opening with leather thong laces. 5 Man's hunting boot c. AD 250. Unlined heelless layered thick leather sole, blunt open toe, knee-length leather upper, open front from padded top edge to mid-calf-level, criss-crossed leather laces. 6 Soldier's boot c. AD 250. Unlined layered thick leather sole, ankle-length leather upper, flat leather laces from above open blunt toe over inset tongue to ankle-level. 7 Man's shoe c. AD 100. Heelless leather sole, blunt toe, kidskin lining, thong between big and second toe, flat leather straps threaded between scalloped sides with painted decoration and long broad tongue strap, then criss-crossed over instep to ankle and tied on centre front, filled-in heel-back. 8 Soldier's sandal c. AD 100. Unlined heelless thick leather sole, leather thong between big and second toe below knee-length flat leather tongue strap, four straps over toes and instep, single strap at mid-calf-level and buckled strap below knee.

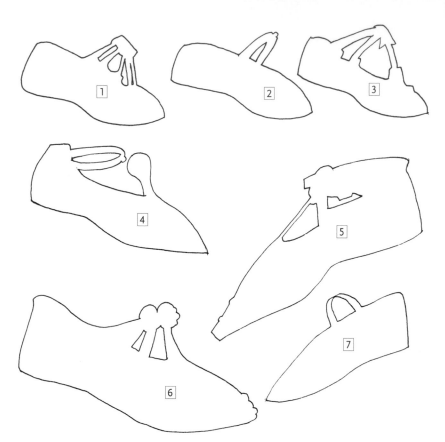

Byzantine AD 400–1100

1 Nobleman's shoe *c.* AD 400–500. Heelless thin leather sole, pointed toe, fine calfskin upper, all-over painted design with added punched hole decoration, low front and scalloped sides, high filled-in heel-back, edges bound in plain colour, matching two instep straps and adjustable split tongue strap. 2 Princess's shoe *c.* AD 400–500. Heelless leather sole, pointed toe, fine calfskin upper, kidskin lining, all-over embroidered design in gold threads, highlighted with pearls and coloured stones, instep strap with jewel button fastening. 3 Priest's shoe *c.* AD 400–500. Heelless leather sole, blunt toe, calfskin upper, low-cut front with gold plaque decoration, scalloped sides bound in contrast-colour leather, matching two instep straps and adjustable tongue strap. 4 Nobleman's shoe *c.* AD 400. Heelless thin leather sole, pointed toe, calfskin upper embroidered with gold threads and braids, matching decoration on high shaped tongue and buttoned ankle strap attached to high filled-in heel-back. 5 Emperor's shoe *c.* AD 550. Heelless thin leather sole, fine fabric lining, calfskin upper, elongated squared-off toe banded at tip with coloured stones, matching stones in buckle and clasp fastening on tapered ankle strap, open sides and low-cut shaped vamp. 6 Emperor's shoe *c.* AD 550. Heelless thin leather sole, fine fabric lining, calfskin upper, pointed toe decorated on tip with pearls, matching pearls set in clasp fastenings of tapered instep straps, open sides and low-cut vamp. 7 Princess's shoe *c.* AD 450. Heelless thin leather soles, elongated pointed toe, unlined pale-coloured calfskin upper, low-cut pointed vamp and high filled-in heel-back edged with gilded calfskin, matching instep strap and button.

Byzantine AD 400–1100

1 Priest's shoe *c.* AD 550. Leather sole, blunt toe, ankle-length fine leather upper embroidered with gold threads, set with precious stones and detail outlined with pearls, kidskin lining, ankle-level ribbon passing through concealed loops and tied at the side. 2 Emperor's shoe *c.* AD 900. Heelless thin leather sole, unlined pale-coloured calfskin upper, pointed toe decorated on tip with pearls, low sides and vamp, high filled-in heel-back, buttoned ankle strap. 3 Emperor's shoe *c.* AD 1000. Heelless thin leather sole, pointed toe, dyed calfskin upper, pale-coloured lining, bar strap and straight low-cut vamp decorated with pearls, high filled-in heel-back, tapered instep strap. 4 Empress's shoe *c.* AD 1000. Heelless thin leather sole, elongated pointed toe, unlined dyed calfskin upper, low-cut vamp edged with pearls, decoration continued around edge of high sides and filled-in heel-back, centre front clasp fastening set with coloured stones. 5 Bishop's shoe *c.* AD 550. Heelless thin leather sole, fabric lining, pale-coloured calfskin upper, elongated pointed toe with painted decoration, matching arrow-shaped tongue, long flat leather laces through holes on high sides to tie around ankle and lower leg. 6 Emperor's shoe *c.* AD 1100. Heelless thin leather sole, light-coloured ankle-length calfskin upper, slashed detail on blunt toe, inset bands of gilded leather around toes, instep and ankle, set with coloured stones. 7 Empress's shoe *c.* AD 600. Heelless thin leather sole, ankle-length gilded calfskin upper, central opening edged on each side with pearls from top to above elongated pointed toe. 8 Nobleman's boot *c.* AD 1000. Heelless thin leather sole, ankle-length calfskin upper, dark kidskin lining showing through decorative slashes on front of instep from top edge to tip of pointed toe. 9 Emperor's shoe *c.* AD 1100. Heelless thin leather sole, rich fabric upper, pointed toe decorated with gilded kidskin slashes, two matching inset gilded bands at ankle-level, jewelled band over instep above matching jewelled gold plaque.

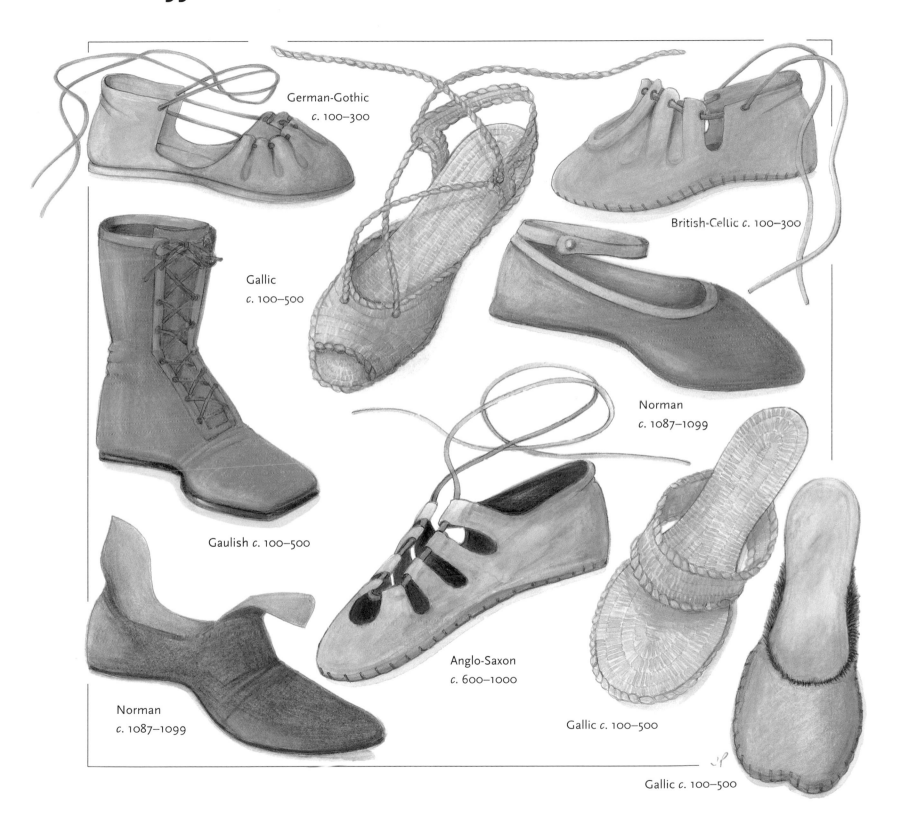

German-Gothic
c. 100–300

British-Celtic *c.* 100–300

Gallic
c. 100–500

Norman
c. 1087–1099

Gaulish *c.* 100–500

Anglo-Saxon
c. 600–1000

Norman
c. 1087–1099

Gallic *c.* 100–500

Gallic *c.* 100–500

English
c. 1140–1160

Italian c. 1140–1199

German c. 1180–1199

English c. 1150–1180

French c. 1150–1180

English c. 1120–1140

English c. 1120–1140

English
c. 1165–1185

French c. 1130–1150

Venetian *c.* 1250–1280

English *c.* 1250–1280

French *c.* 1250

French *c.* 1280–1299

Italian *c.* 1280–1299

French *c.* 1299

French *c.* 1200–1250

French c. 1300–1350

English c. 1300–1350

English c. 1377–1399

Italian c. 1375–1399

English c. 1300–1330

English c. 1350–1375

French c. 1375–1399

English c. 1375–1399

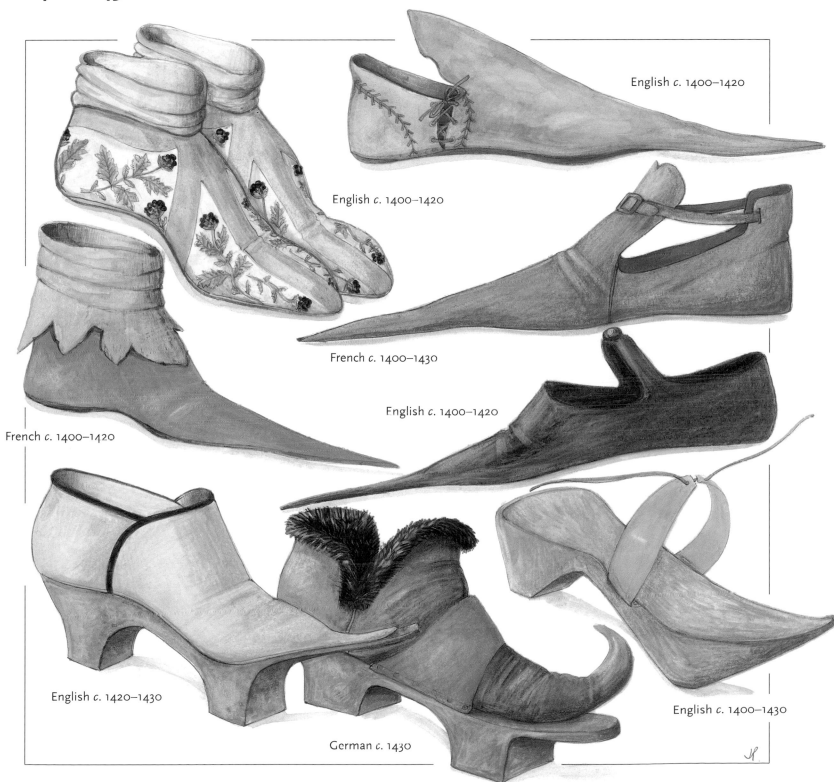

English c. 1400–1420

English c. 1400–1420

French c. 1400–1430

French c. 1400–1420

English c. 1400–1420

English c. 1420–1430

German c. 1430

English c. 1400–1430

English c. 1430–1440

English c. 1440–1450

English c. 1440–1450

French c. 1440–1450

French c. 1440–1450

German c. 1430–1450

French c. 1440–1450

1460–1480

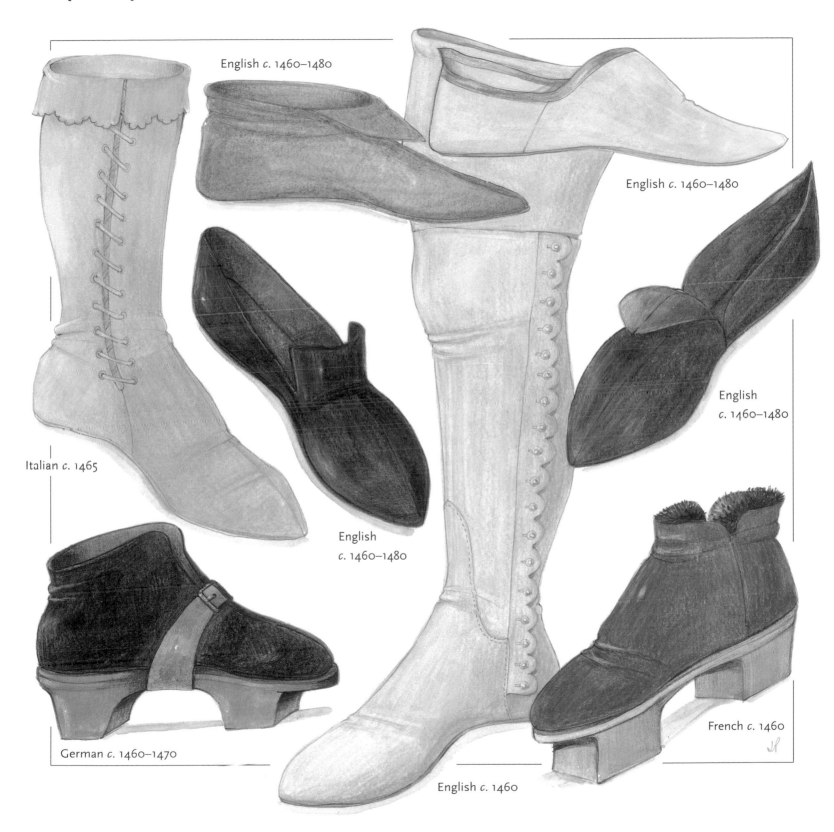

Italian c. 1465

English c. 1460–1480

English c. 1460–1480

English c. 1460–1480

English c. 1460–1480

German c. 1460–1470

English c. 1460

French c. 1460

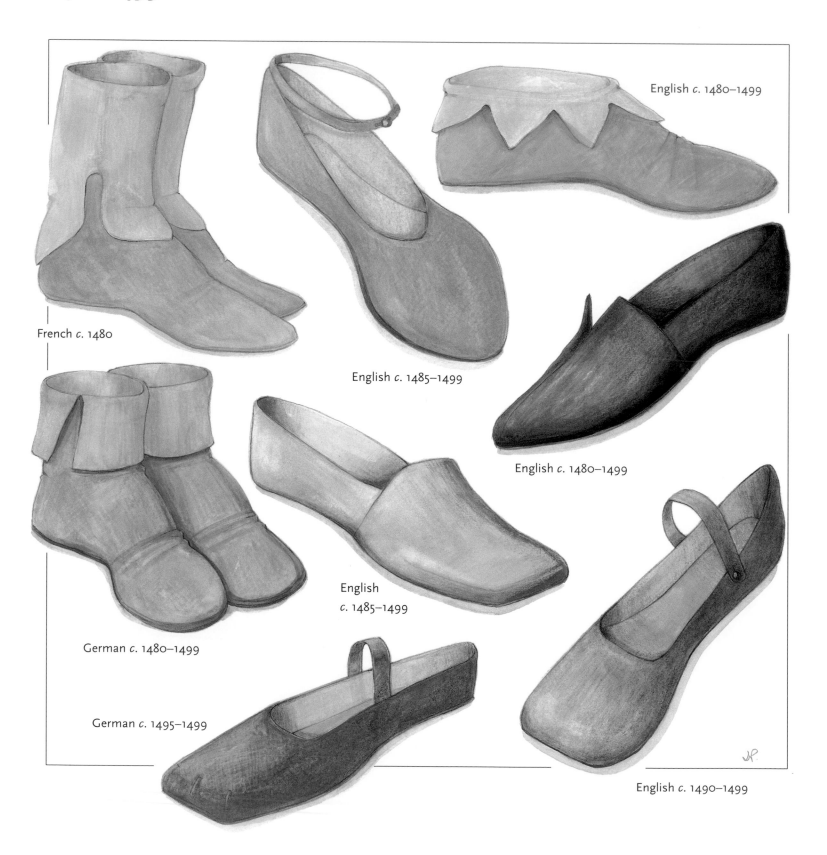

French *c.* 1480

English *c.* 1485–1499

English *c.* 1480–1499

English *c.* 1480–1499

German *c.* 1480–1499

English
c. 1485–1499

German *c.* 1495–1499

English *c.* 1490–1499

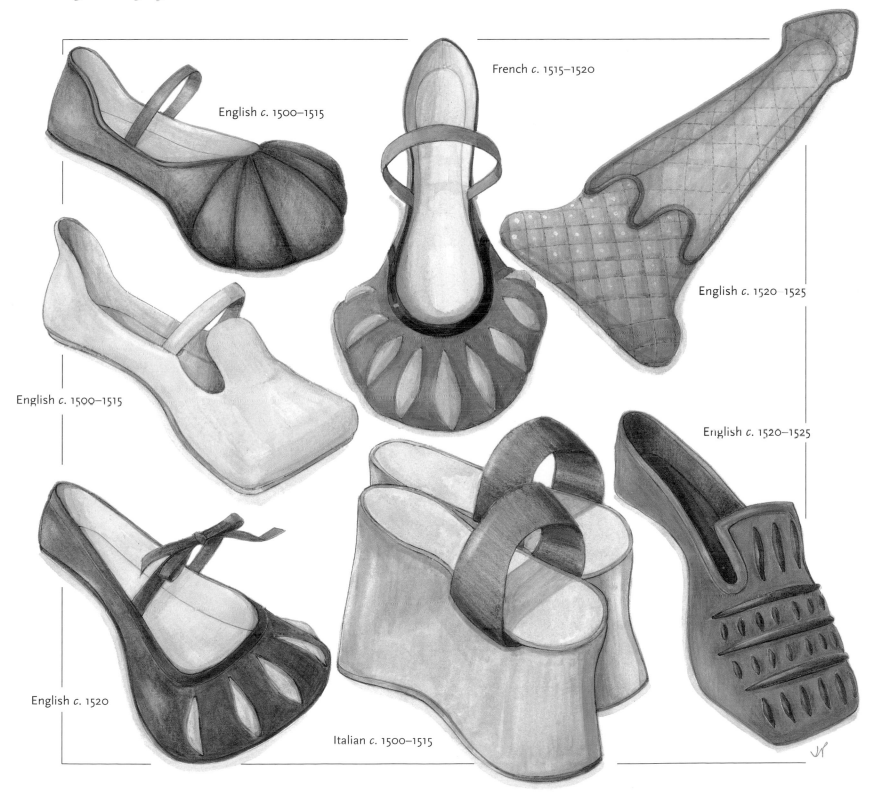

English *c.* 1500–1515

French *c.* 1515–1520

English *c.* 1520–1525

English *c.* 1500–1515

English *c.* 1520–1525

English *c.* 1520

Italian *c.* 1500–1515

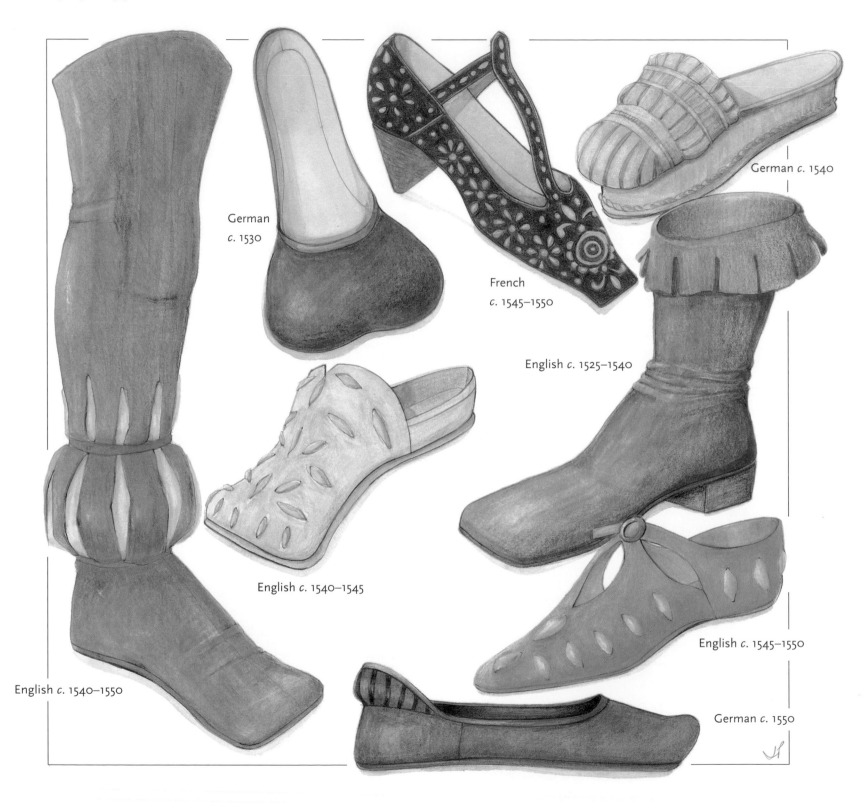

German
c. 1530

French
c. 1545–1550

German c. 1540

English c. 1525–1540

English c. 1540–1545

English c. 1540–1550

English c. 1545–1550

German c. 1550

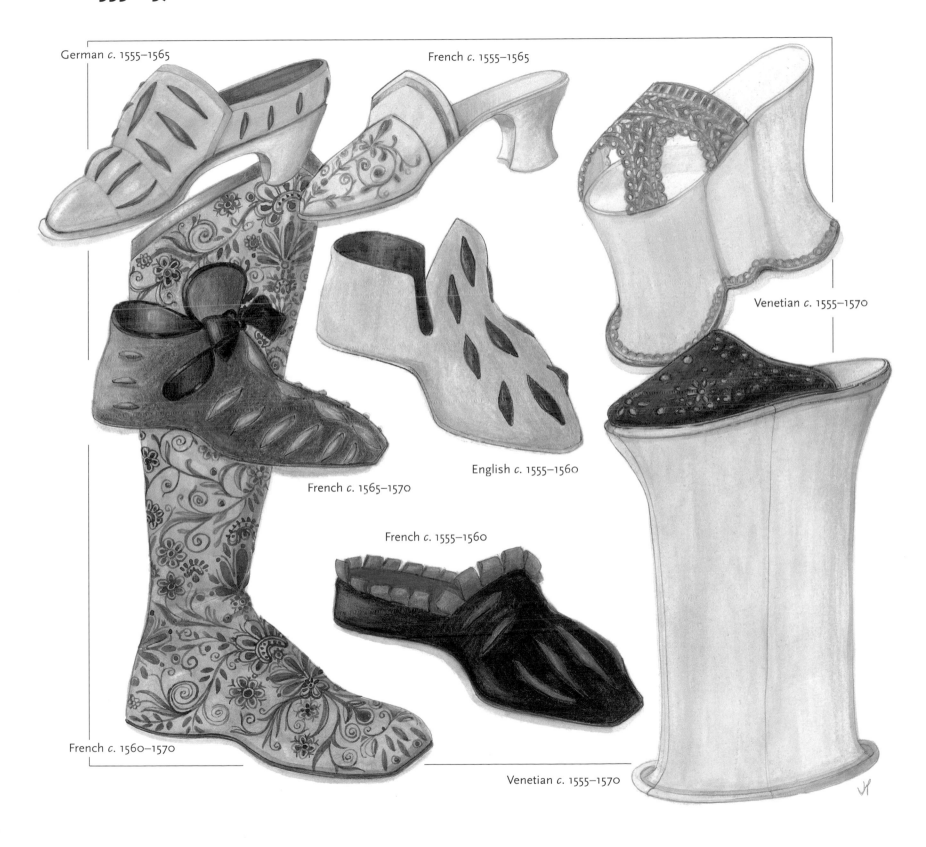

German c. 1555–1565

French c. 1555–1565

Venetian c. 1555–1570

English c. 1555–1560

French c. 1565–1570

French c. 1555–1560

French c. 1560–1570

Venetian c. 1555–1570

1575–1599

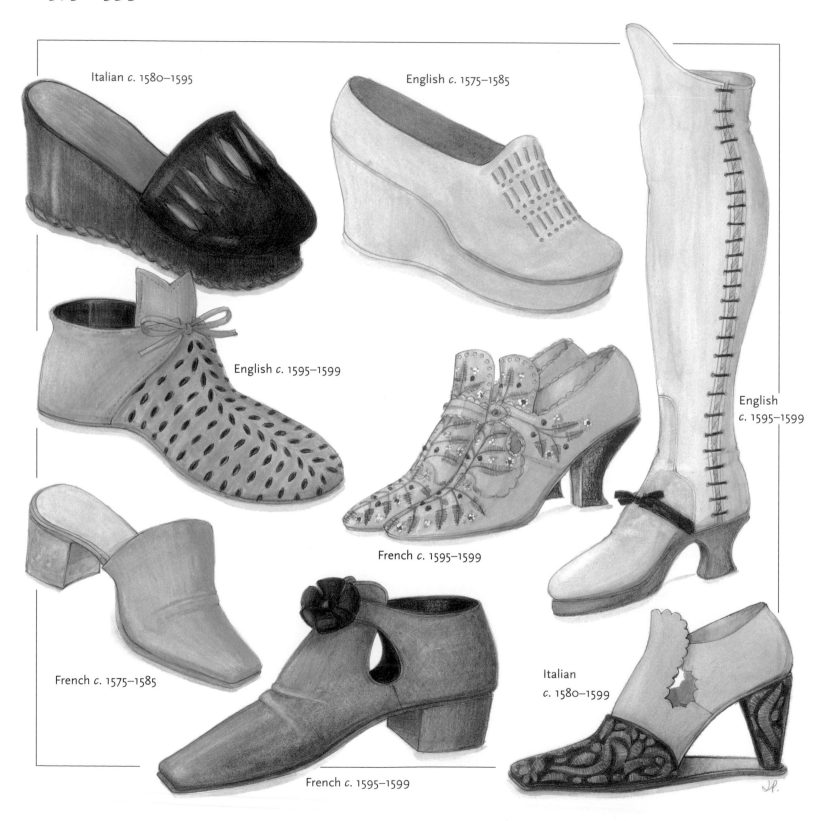

Italian *c.* 1580–1595

English *c.* 1575–1585

English *c.* 1595–1599

English *c.* 1595–1599

French *c.* 1595–1599

French *c.* 1575–1585

French *c.* 1595–1599

Italian *c.* 1580–1599

Women's shoes 1600–1650

Dutch c. 1600–1620

English c. 1625–1635

English c. 1630

English c. 1630–1640

French c. 1620–1625

Dutch c. 1630–1650

English c. 1640–1650

English c. 1640

French c. 1640–1650

Women's shoes 1650–1699

English
c. 1660–1680

English c. 1670–1690

English c. 1680–1699

English c. 1660–1685

French c. 1680–1699

French c. 1695–1699

Portuguese c. 1695

French c. 1690–1699

English c. 1690–1699

Men's shoes 1600–1699

English c. 1610–1620

English c. 1665–1675

French c. 1675–1685

French c. 1670–1680

English c. 1610–1620

English c. 1600–1615

French c. 1675–1699

French c. 1660–1670

Men's boots 1620–1699

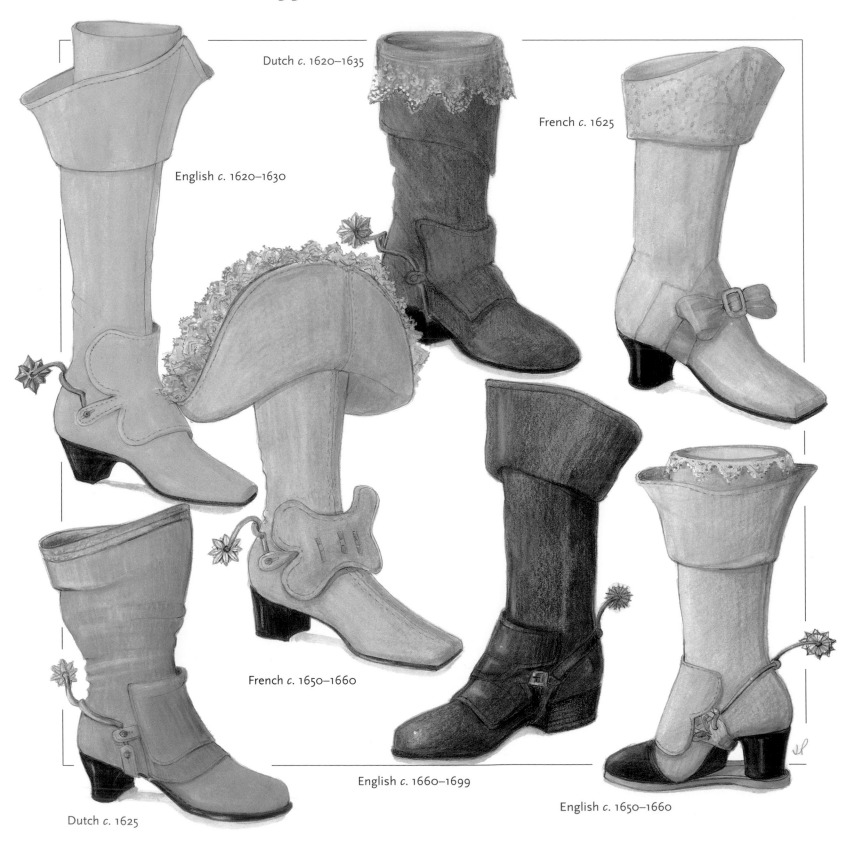

Dutch c. 1620–1635

French c. 1625

English c. 1620–1630

French c. 1650–1660

English c. 1660–1699

Dutch c. 1625

English c. 1650–1660

100–1099

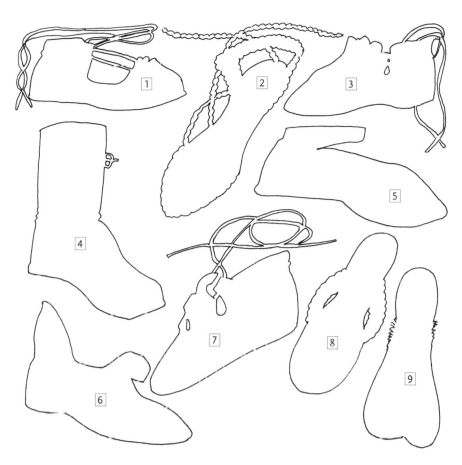

[1] German-Gothic shoe *c.* 100–300. Heelless thick leather sole, blunt toe, hide upper, top edge of low-cut front shaped with threaded leather thong, continued over low-cut open sides and through holes in top edge of filled-in heel-back, to tie around ankle. [2] Gallic sandal *c.* 100–500. Heelless woven grass sole, blunt toe, low-cut upper with open front joined to open heel-back with twisted grass straps passing over instep and open sides. [3] British-Celtic shoe *c.* 100–300. Moccasin-style heelless leather sole and upper stitched together on the outside, top edge of high-cut front shaped with threaded leather thong, continued over open sides and through holes in top edge of filled-in heel-back. [4] Gaulish boot *c.* 100–500. Heelless thick leather or wooden sole, square toe, mid-calf-length leather upper, edge of open front and top edge bound with contrast colour, matching laces over full-length tongue. [5] Norman shoe *c.* 1087–1099. Heelless thin leather sole, elongated toe, leather upper, low-cut front, edges bound with contrast colour, matching buttoned ankle strap. [6] Norman shoe *c.* 1087–1099. Heelless thin leather sole, blunt toe, dyed leather upper, low-cut sides, leaf-shaped filled-in heel-back, matching front, contrast-colour lining. [7] Anglo-Saxon shoe *c.* 600–1000. Moccasin-style heelless leather sole and upper stitched together on the outside, open design sides and front threaded with leather thong to cross over instep and tie around ankle above filled-in heel-back. [8] Gallic sandal *c.* 100–500. Heelless woven grass sole, wide blunt toe, broad strap over instep. [9] Gallic mule *c.* 100–500. Heelless thick leather sole, shaped to toes, stitched to thick fur-lined upper on the outside.

1100–1199

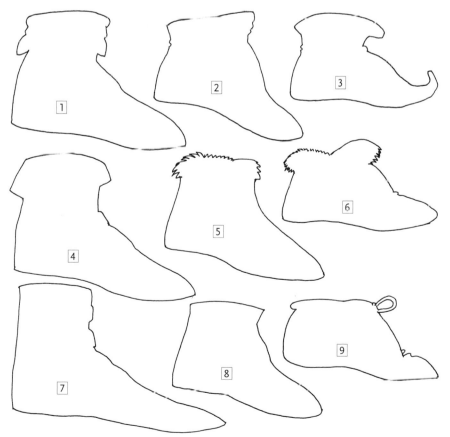

[1] English boot *c.* 1140–1160. Heelless leather sole, pointed toe, above-ankle-length leather upper, centre front slashed seam above contrast-colour lining, matching padded roll and crenellated turned-down cuff. [2] Italian ankle boot *c.* 1140–1199. Heelless thin leather sole, pointed toe, ankle-length fine brightly coloured leather upper, soft natural folds around ankle. [3] German boot *c.* 1180–1199. Heelless thin leather sole, elongated toe with turned-up pointed end, above-ankle-length fine brightly coloured upper, turned-down cuff, centre front opening and seam fastened and decorated with silver buttons graded in size. [4] English boot *c.* 1120–1140. Heelless leather sole, pointed toe, above-ankle-length leather upper, turned-down cuff, low open front, strap and buckle over instep. [5] English ankle boot *c.* 1150–1180. Heelless leather sole, pointed toe, ankle-length pale-coloured leather upper, trimmed with thin inset strips in contrasting colour, fur lining and ankle-level trim. [6] French shoe *c.* 1150–1180. Heelless leather sole, pointed toe, ankle-length fine brightly coloured leather upper, fur lining and ankle-level trim. [7] English boot *c.* 1120–1140. Thin leather sole, elongated and padded pointed toe, above-ankle-length waxed leather upper, centre front seam and opening, two strap and buckle fastenings. [8] English shoe *c.* 1165–1185. Heelless leather sole, pointed toe, open front to low instep, pale-coloured fine leather upper, contrast-colour lining, edges bound with gilded leather, matching applied strap detail, perforated decoration on sides and front. [9] French shoe *c.* 1130–1150. Fine leather sole, pointed toe, rich fabric upper embroidered with gold thread, bound edges, matching tie above front opening.

1200–1299

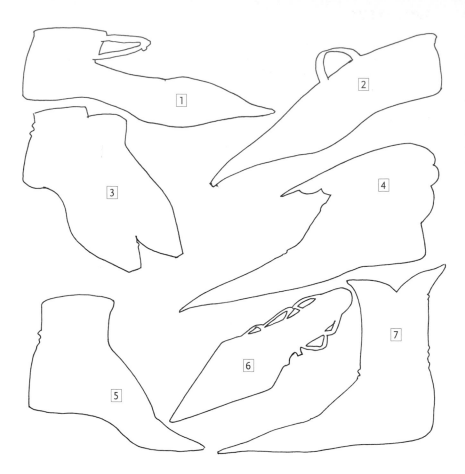

1 Venetian shoe *c.* 1250–1280. Heelless thin leather sole, long pointed toe, fine brightly coloured leather upper, low-cut pointed vamp bound with gilded leather, matching ankle strap with front button fastening. 2 English shoe *c.* 1250–1280. Heelless thin leather sole, long pointed toe with squared-off tip, fabric upper, gold thread embroidered detail under low vamp, small slashes with contrast-colour puffs, matching shoe lining, instep strap with side button fastening. 3 French ankle boots *c.* 1250. Heelless fine leather soles, narrow toes with squared-off tips, rich fabric uppers embroidered with gold threads and decorated with pearls. 4 French ankle boot *c.* 1280–1299. Heelless thin leather sole, long pointed and padded toe, fine waxed leather upper, contrast-colour lining, matching turned-down crenellated cuff, gilded leather bindings, centre front button fastening over instep. 5 French boot *c.* 1299. Heelless thin leather sole, long pointed and padded toe, fine waxed leather upper, single button fastening around ankle. 6 Italian shoe *c.* 1280–1299. Heelless thin leather sole, long pointed toe, fine leather upper, low vamp, contrast-colour lining, thin straps over instep from front, sides and side back, fastening under centre front gilded buckle. 7 French riding boot *c.* 1200–1250. Heelless leather sole, long pointed and padded toe, pale-coloured leather upper, natural creases around ankle, mid-calf-length boot-top shaped to point at centre front and back.

1300–1399

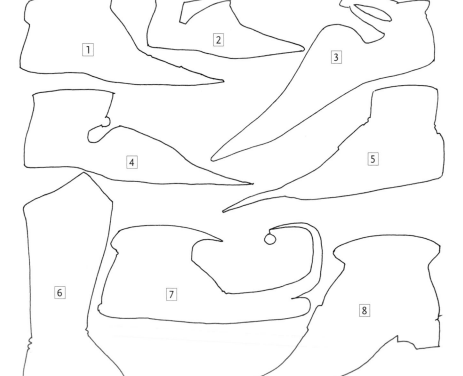

1 French ankle boot *c.* 1300–1350. Heelless thin leather sole, long pointed and padded toe, rich fabric upper decorated with criss-cross bands of gilded leather and pearl studs, ankle-level turned-down cuff. 2 English shoe *c.* 1300–1350. Heelless thin leather sole, long pointed toe, fabric upper decorated with gold thread embroidery from side back, over high instep and above padded toe, ankle strap with centre front button fastening. 3 English shoe *c.* 1377–1399. Heelless thin leather sole, long pointed toe, fine leather upper with painted and embroidered decoration over high instep and padded toe, low-cut sides, buckled instep strap. 4 English shoe *c.* 1300–1330. Heelless thin leather sole, long pointed and padded toe, fabric upper, low vamp and edges bound with gilded leather, jewelled button fastening on centre front above instep. 5 Italian boot and clog *c.* 1375–1399. Short boot with thin leather sole, long narrow pointed and padded toe, fine leather upper, side lacing to above ankle-level; carved wooden clog with filled-in heel-back, pointed front, wide leather strap over instep nailed to side edges. 6 English riding boot *c.* 1350–1375. Heelless thin leather sole, long pointed and padded toe, mid-calf-length leather upper, boot-top shaped to point at front, strap and button decorative fastening set into centre front seam. 7 French ankle boot and clog *c.* 1375–1399. Short boot with heelless thin leather sole, extended pointed piked toe with small bell decoration on tip, fine leather upper, contrast-colour lining and pointed turned-down cuff; heelless flat wooden clog with blunt toe, wide leather strap over instep nailed to side edges. 8 English boot and patten *c.* 1375–1399. Ankle boot with heelless thin leather sole, long narrow pointed toe, fine waxed leather upper, contrast-colour lining, matching turned-down cuff; wooden patten with flat sole raised on wooden block front and back, wide leather strap over instep, nailed to side edges.

1400–1430

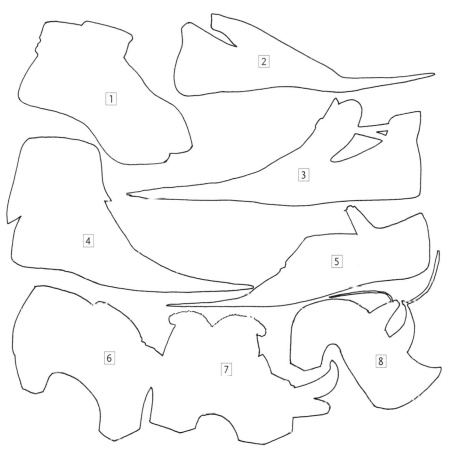

1 English ankle boots c. 1400–1420. Heelless thin leather soles, pointed toes, pale-coloured fine fabric uppers with multicoloured embroidered decoration, inset bands of gold cloth under draped ankle-level cuffs, over instep to toe and on each side front.
2 English shoe c. 1400–1420. Heelless thin leather sole, exaggerated pointed toe, fine leather upper, high pointed vamp, low-cut sides, side fastening with leather thong, matching stitched seam around filled-in heel-back and side front seams. 3 French shoe c. 1400–1430. Heelless thin leather sole, exaggerated pointed toe, fine leather upper, low-cut sides, buckled strap fastening over high shaped vamp from sides of high filled-in heel-back. 4 French boot c. 1400–1420. Heelless thin leather sole, exaggerated pointed toe, waxed leather upper, above-ankle-length pale-coloured leather cuff with fine crenellated edge, covering front of instep and back of heel. 5 Italian shoe c. 1400–1420. Heelless thin leather sole, exaggerated pointed toe, dyed and waxed leather upper, low-cut vamp, flat bar strap over instep, button fastening on centre front.
6 English shoe and patten c. 1420–1430. Heelless thin leather sole, exaggerated pointed toe, attached to carved wooden patten with front and back lift, front extended to accommodate pointed sole, pale-coloured leather upper, high vamp and filled-in heel-back, edges bound in contrast colour. 7 German shoe and patten c. 1430. Heelless thin leather sole, exaggerated pointed toe with padded piked tip, attached to carved wooden patten with front and back lift, front extended to accommodate pointed sole, dyed leather upper, high vamp and filled-in heel-back, fur lining and trim.
8 English patten c. 1400–1430. Carved wooden sole, lift to front and back, front extended to accommodate pointed toe of shoe, two flat leather straps over instep, fastening on centre front with leather thong.

1430–1450

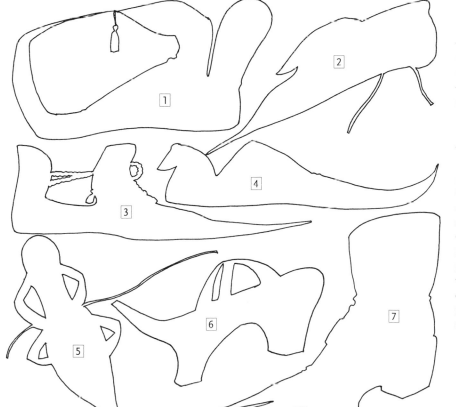

1 English ankle boot c. 1430–1440. Heelless thin leather sole, exaggerated pointed toe, pale-coloured fine leather upper, low-cut sides, ankle-length filled-in heel-back, high vamp extended into pointed turned-down cuff, tip attached to end of pointed sole by means of thin gold cord with tassel trim. 2 English shoe c. 1440–1450. Heelless thin leather sole, exaggerated pointed and padded toe, waxed fine leather upper, high vamp covered by turned-down pointed cuff, side fastening with leather thong.
3 French shoe c. 1440–1450. Heelless thin leather sole, exaggerated pointed toe, rich fabric upper, gold cord with tasselled trim threaded through loop on back of filled-in heel over low-cut sides, fastening on centre front of instep, high vamp.
4 English shoe c. 1440–1450. Heelless thin leather sole, exaggerated pointed toe with piked tip, pale-coloured leather upper, high vamp, low-cut sides, turned-down cuff on heel-back. 5 French patten c. 1440–1450. Carved flat wooden sole, elongated tip to accommodate exaggerated pointed toe of shoe, painted decoration, dyed flat leather straps, fastened over instep with fine leather thong. 6 German patten c. 1430–1450. Carved wooden sole, elongated tip to accommodate exaggerated pointed toe of shoe, lift to front and back, dyed flat leather straps crossed over instep. 7 French boot and patten c. 1440–1450. Boot with heelless thin leather sole, exaggerated pointed toe, fine leather upper, fastening with leather thong from side front to above-ankle-level; carved wooden patten, shaped sole, elongated piked tip to accommodate exaggerated pointed toe of shoe, lift to front and back, two-piece flat leather strap over instep, metal clasp fastening.

1460–1480

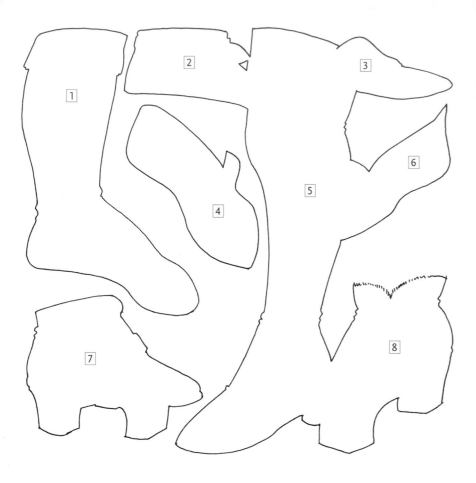

1 Italian boot c. 1465. Heelless thin leather sole, pointed toe, fine light-coloured leather upper, side fastening with leather thong, knee-level turned-down cuff with crenellated edge. 2 English shoe c. 1460–1480. Heelless thin leather sole, pointed toe, soft leather upper, high sides and back, turned-down pointed front cuff above high vamp. 3 English slipper c. 1460–1480. Heelless thin leather sole, pointed toe, fine pale-coloured leather upper, high vamp, pointed tip to heel-back, edges bound with gilded leather. 4 English slipper c. 1460–1480. Heelless thin leather sole, pointed toe, waxed dyed leather upper, high stand-up vamp, low sides and heel-back. 5 English hunting boot c. 1460. Heelless leather sole, pointed toe, waxed leather thigh-length upper, shaped vamp cut separately from leg part, button fastening with scalloped edge from above-knee-level to under ankle. 6 English slipper c. 1460–1480. Heelless thin leather sole, pointed toe, dyed leather upper, pointed tongue turned down over high vamp, shaped sides, pointed tip to heel-back. 7 German ankle boot and patten c. 1460–1470. Boot with heelless leather sole, blunt toe, ankle-length waxed leather upper, centre front opening; carved wooden patten, lift to front and back, leather securing strap over instep, metal buckle fastening. 8 French ankle boot and patten c. 1460. Boot with heelless leather sole, blunt toe, attached to carved wooden patten, lift to front and back, ankle-length waxed leather upper, sides shaped around ankle, fur lining.

1480–1499

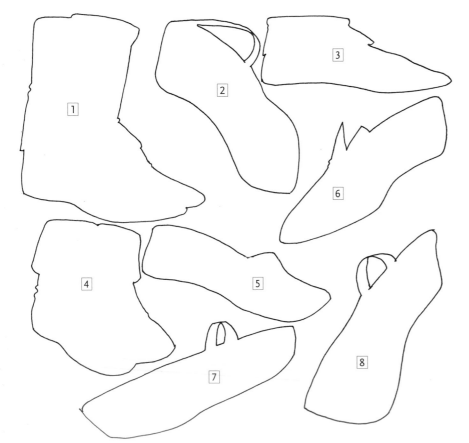

1 French boots c. 1480. Heelless thin leather soles, blunt toes, waxed soft leather uppers, deep below-knee-length pale-coloured leather turned-down cuffs, shaped over ankles, pointed over instep and heel-back. 2 English shoe c. 1485–1499. Heelless thin leather sole, blunt toe, waxed dyed leather upper, low-cut vamp, ankle strap with centre front button fastening. 3 English shoe c. 1480–1499. Heelless thin leather sole, blunt toe, cloth upper, high vamp, sides and back, pale-coloured leather turned-down cuff with pointed edge. 4 German boots c. 1480–1499. Heelless leather soles, wide blunt toes, above-ankle-length waxed leather uppers, pale-coloured leather turned-down cuffs with side slit above ankle on outside. 5 English slipper c. 1485–1499. Heelless thin leather sole, wide squared-off blunt toe, fine leather upper, high vamp, sides and heel-back. 6 English slipper c. 1480–1499. Heelless leather sole, blunt toe, waxed dyed leather upper, high vamp split on centre front seam, low sides and heel-back. 7 German shoe c. 1495–1499. Heelless leather sole, wide squared-off blunt toe, dyed leather upper, low-cut vamp, sides and heel-back, decorative slashes above toe, matching coloured fabric lining, flat leather instep strap. 8 English shoe c. 1490–1499. Heelless leather sole, wide padded blunt toe, fabric upper, low-cut vamp, fabric lining, flat instep strap with side button fastening.

1500–1525

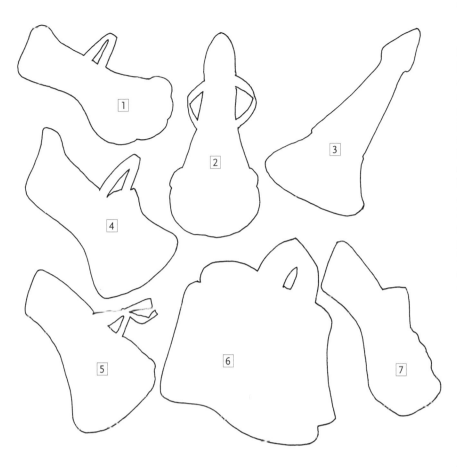

1 English nobleman's shoe *c.* 1500–1515. Heelless leather sole, velvet upper, wide blunt padded toe cut into flared panels, low-cut vamp, shallow sides and high heel-back bound with gilded kidskin, matching instep strap, silk lining. 2 French nobleman's shoe *c.* 1515–1520. Heelless leather sole, fabric upper, slashed decoration in pale-coloured taffeta above wide blunt toe, matching lining, low-cut vamp bound in contrasting colour, instep strap. 3 English nobleman's slipper *c.* 1520–1525. Heelless leather sole, exaggerated wide squared-off blunt toe, quilted leather upper, low-cut scalloped vamp, shallow sides and high heel-back bound in dark leather, quilted silk lining. 4 English gentleman's shoe *c.* 1500–1515. Heelless leather sole, wide squared-off blunt toe, pale-coloured leather upper, low-cut vamp with tab, shallow sides, high heel-back, low instep strap. 5 English nobleman's shoe *c.* 1520. Heelless leather sole, kidskin upper, slashed decoration in pale-coloured taffeta above wide padded blunt toe, matching lining, low-cut vamp, edges in contrasting colour, matching leather strap fastening over instep tied in bow on centre front. 6 Italian lady's chopines *c.* 1500–1515. High cork platforms covered in pale-coloured velvet, leather soles, wide leather strap uppers over instep, open front and back. 7 English gentleman's slipper *c.* 1520–1525. Heelless leather sole, wide squared-off blunt toe, fine kidskin upper, slashed decoration in brightly coloured silk on front, instep and high tongue, matching lining, edges bound in gilded leather.

1525–1550

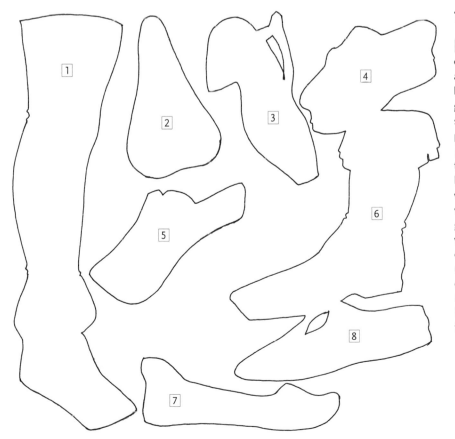

1 English gentleman's hunting boot *c.* 1540–1550. Heelless leather sole, wide squared-off blunt toe, light-coloured thigh-length upper, pale-coloured slashed decoration at ankle-level and above, fitted leg part. 2 German gentleman's slipper *c.* 1530. Heelless leather sole, wide heart-shaped blunt toe, waxed fine leather upper, edges bound in gilded leather, fabric lining. 3 French noblewoman's shoe *c.* 1545–1550. Thin leather sole, elongated squared-off toe, round wooden heel prop, dyed kidskin upper, all-over punchwork decoration, pale-coloured taffeta lining, matching T-strap fastening. 4 German lady's mule *c.* 1540. Cork platform covered in fine leather, plaited leather thong decoration above leather sole, pale-coloured kidskin upper, decorative slashes, bands and loops. 5 English nobleman's slipper *c.* 1540–1545. Heelless leather sole, wide squared-off blunt toe, light-coloured velvet upper, slashed decoration in fine silk velvet over front and high vamp, low-cut sides and back, silk lining. 6 English gentleman's riding boot *c.* 1525–1540. Thick leather sole, attached wooden heel, wide squared-off blunt toe, mid-calf-length leather upper, turned-down crenellated cuff. 7 German gentleman's slipper *c.* 1550. Heelless leather sole, waxed leather upper, turned-up blunt toe, low-cut vamp, extended high heel-back with brightly coloured slashed detail, matching lining, edges bound in gilded leather. 8 English noblewoman's shoe *c.* 1545–1550. Heelless thin leather sole, elongated blunt toe, light-coloured kidskin upper, slashed decoration on front, sides and back over silver fabric, open front and side panels under buckled bar strap.

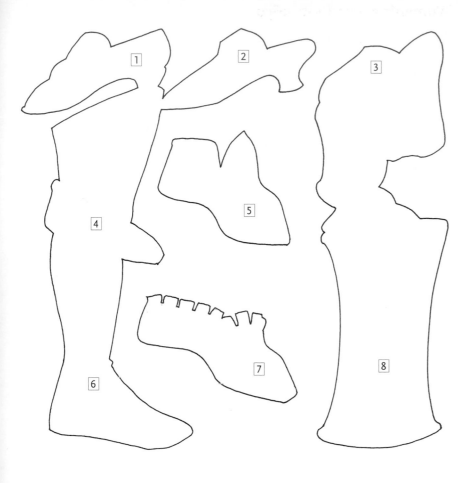

1555–1570

1 German gentleman's shoe c. 1555–1565. Wooden sole and combined high heel, blunt toe, pale-coloured leather upper, edges bound in darker colour, high vamp, front and shallow sides with slashes, dyed kidskin lining. 2 French noblewoman's mule c. 1555–1565. Thin cork sole, attached wooden heel, elongated toe, pale-coloured kidskin upper, punchwork and gold thread embroidery on front, high pointed vamp, gilded leather binding and trim, silk lining. 3 Venetian noblewoman's chopine c. 1555–1570. High platform of layered cork covered in fine pale-coloured velvet, decorated above leather sole with gold braid, matching trim on backless upper around open toe and sides. 4 French gentleman's shoe c. 1565–1570. Heelless leather sole, elongated squared-off toe, dyed kidskin upper, decorative slashes on front, over high vamp and on sides under high heel-back, coloured silk lining, front ribbon fastening over high tongue through side latchet straps. 5 English gentleman's shoe c. 1555–1560. Heelless leather sole, elongated toe, pale-coloured leather upper, decorative slashes on front and over high vamp under pointed tongue, brightly coloured silk lining, split sides, high heel-back. 6 French gentleman's court boot c. 1560–1570. Heelless leather sole, squared-off blunt toe, fitted thigh-length kidskin upper, all-over painted design, pointed top edge bound in gilded kidskin. 7 French gentleman's slipper c. 1555–1560. Heelless leather sole, elongated squared-off toe, velvet upper, decorative slashes on front and over high vamp, silk lining, matching looped trim on edges of shallow sides and heel-back. 8 Venetian woman's chopine c. 1555–1570. High platform of layered cork covered in pale-coloured kidskin, backless leather upper, all-over punchwork decoration.

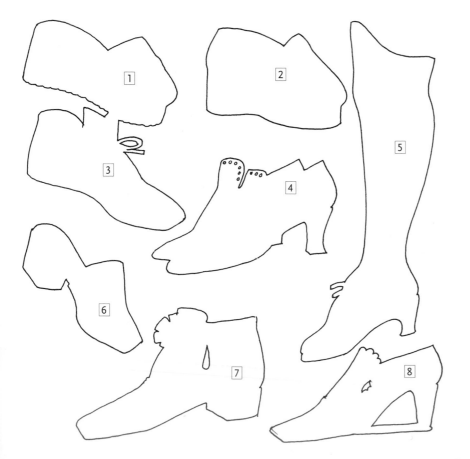

1575–1599

1 Italian gentlewoman's over-mule c. 1580–1595. Layered cork platform covered in fine leather, twisted leather thong decoration above edge of leather sole, backless leather upper, blunt toe, decorative slashes over vamp, coloured kidskin lining. 2 English gentlewoman's shoe c. 1575–1585. Layered cork sole and wedge heel, covered in pale-coloured leather, blunt toe, matching leather upper, punchwork decoration on front to under high vamp, coloured taffeta lining. 3 English lady's or gentleman's shoe c. 1595–1599. Heelless leather sole, elongated blunt toe, pale-coloured leather upper, front to under V-pointed tongue decorated with small slashes, brightly coloured silk lining, fastening on front over instep with leather thong through latchet straps. 4 French noblewoman's shoes c. 1595–1599. Leather soles, elongated toes, attached high wooden heels, pale-coloured kidskin uppers, fronts, sides, high tongues and buttoned latchet straps decorated with punchwork and coloured embroidery. 5 English noblewoman's riding boot c. 1595–1599. Thick wooden sole and combined high heel, blunt toe, fitted above-knee-length pale-coloured leather upper, side opening with coloured leather laces, matching decorative latchet straps and bow over instep. 6 French lady's or gentleman's over-mule c. 1575–1585. Leather sole, attached wooden heel, backless leather upper, high vamp, square toe. 7 French gentleman's shoe c. 1595–1599. Leather sole, square toe, attached wooden heel, leather upper, high tongue, centre fastening with ribbon rose above latchet straps, kidskin lining. 8 Italian noblewoman's shoe and clog c. 1580–1599. Clog with flat leather sole, square toe, backless, embroidered velvet upper, matching covered high wooden heel attached to fine pale-coloured leather shoe with latchet fastening under high scallop-edged tongue.

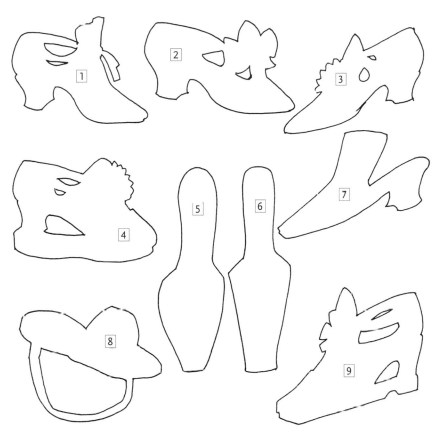

Women's shoes 1600–1650

1 Dutch noblewoman's shoe c. 1600–1620. Thin leather sole, pointed toe, red edges, matching medium-high leather-covered wooden Louis heel, fine leather upper, open sides, latchet straps fastening over high tongue with silk ribbon. 2 English woman's shoe c. 1625–1635. Fine leather sole, pointed toe, medium-high wooden Louis heel, covered in light-coloured suede, matching upper, all-over slashed decoration, open sides, latchet straps over pointed tongue, fastened with silk ribbon. 3 English noblewoman's shoe c. 1630. Fine leather sole, pointed toe, red edges, matching medium-high leather-covered wooden Louis heel, light-coloured suede upper, punchwork decoration above toe, under high vamp and on edge of heel-back, open sides, latchet straps fastening over high tongue and under large lace shoe rose.
4 French noblewoman's shoe and patten c. 1620–1625. Shoe with fine red leather sole, matching medium-high leather-covered wooden Louis heel, kidskin upper, open sides, latchet straps fastening over high tongue and under large lace shoe rose; patten with heelless thick leather sole, blunt toe, shallow sides, backless thick leather upper, slashed decoration above toe. 5 English lady's mule c. 1640. Leather sole, square toe, backless, embroidered velvet upper. 6 French lady's mule c. 1640–1650. Leather sole, flared square toe, backless kidskin upper, punchwork decoration over coloured silk lining. 7 English noblewoman's mule c. 1630–1640. Thin leather sole, square toe, red edges, matching medium-high leather-covered wooden Louis heel, backless, embroidered silk upper, high square tongue, edges bound in gold-colour silk satin.
8 English woman's patten c. 1640–1650. Heelless thick wooden sole, mounted on large flat-edged iron ring, adjustable, thick leather instep strap. 9 Dutch lady's shoe and patten c. 1630–1650. Shoe with thin leather sole, high leather-covered wooden Louis heel, matching upper, open sides, latchet straps fastening over high pointed tongue and under silk ribbon shoe rose; patten with thick, heelless wooden sole, square toe, backless, leather upper.

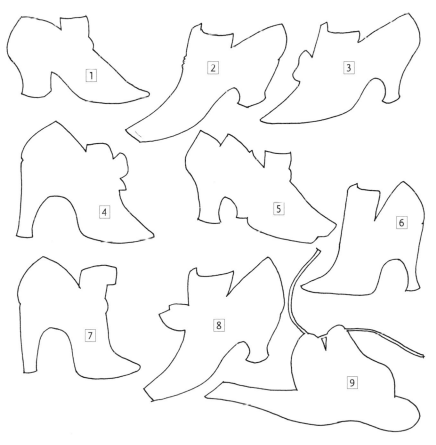

Women's shoes 1650–1699

1 English woman's shoe c. 1660–1680. Leather sole, sharp pointed toe, medium-high leather-covered wooden Louis heel, matching upper, decorative stitching over high vamp, strap and buckle fastening over high tongue. 2 English noblewoman's shoe c. 1670–1690. Leather sole, square toe, red edges, matching medium-high leather-covered wooden Louis heel, kidskin upper decorated with gold braid, matching high tongue and edges, latchet straps fastening over high vamp and under jewelled clasp.
3 English lady's shoe c. 1680–1699. Fine leather sole, sharp pointed toe, high silk-covered wooden Louis heel, silk brocade upper, matching bow trim above high vamp and under high wide tongue, edges bound in plain silk satin. 4 French noblewoman's shoe c. 1680–1699. Leather sole, pointed toe, red edges, matching slender high leather-covered wooden heel, pale-coloured kidskin upper, trimmed on front with pleated silk ribbon, matching edges and latchet straps fastening over high tongue under large ribbon bow. 5 English woman's shoes c. 1660–1685. Leather soles, square toes, high leather-covered wooden Louis heels, matching uppers, closed sides, latchet straps fastening through buckles under high tongues. 6 French noblewoman's shoe c. 1695–1699. Fine leather sole, sharp pointed toe, red edges, matching high leather-covered wooden Louis heel, silk brocade upper, fastening under high tongue, edges bound in plain silk. 7 Portuguese woman's shoe c. 1695. Leather sole, sharp pointed toe, high painted wooden heel, fabric upper, silver lace appliqué decoration, strap and buckle fastening, high turned-down tongue, edges bound in plain colour. 8 French lady's shoe c. 1690–1699. Leather sole, square toe, high velvet-covered wooden Louis heel, matching upper, gold embroidery over toe, vamp and high tongue, strap fastening on centre front under silk ribbon bow. 9 English woman's patten c. 1690–1699. Heelless thick wooden sole, elongated flared square toe, padded arch support, leather straps on each side, leather thong fastening.

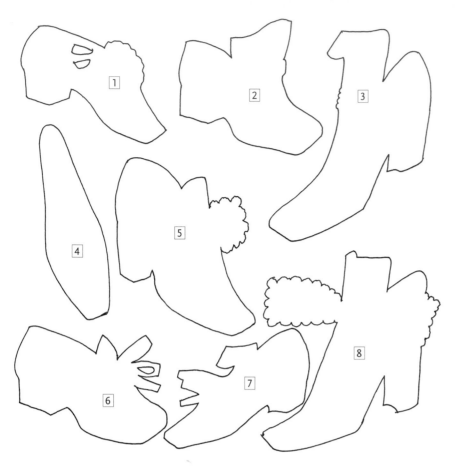

Men's shoes 1600–1699

1 English nobleman's shoe c. 1610–1620. Leather sole, square toe, red edges, matching medium-high leather-covered wooden heel, pale-coloured suede upper, punchwork decoration above toe and on heel-back, latchet straps fastening under large ruched fabric shoe rose. 2 English man's shoe c. 1665–1675. Thick leather sole, square toe, medium-high stacked leather heel, waxed and polished leather upper, strap and buckle over instep under high tongue. 3 French nobleman's shoe c. 1675–1685. Leather sole, square toe, red edges, matching high leather-covered wooden heel, pale-coloured kidskin upper, closed sides, strap and jewelled buckle fastening over instep, under high turned-down tongue, red lining. 4 English gentleman's shoe c. 1610– 1620. Pale-coloured leather upper, square toe, red edges to leather sole, open sides, latchet straps fastening under pleated taffeta shoe rose with jewelled centre. 5 French gentleman's shoe c. 1670–1680. Leather sole, square toe, high leather-covered wooden heel, matching upper, closed sides, high tongue, lace-edged stiffened taffeta bow high on instep, small looped ribbon shoe rose with jewelled centre on side front above toe. 6 English nobleman's shoe c. 1600–1615. Leather sole, square toe, red edges, matching low leather-covered wooden heel, suede upper, punchwork and slashed decoration on front, open sides, latchet straps fastening with silk ribbon bows, pointed tongue. 7 French gentleman's shoe c. 1675–1699. Thin leather sole, square toe, high leather-covered wooden heel, matching shoe lining, silk brocade upper, closed sides, latchet straps fastening with silk ribbon ties under high turned-down tongue. 8 French gentleman's shoe c. 1660–1670. Leather sole, square toe, high leather-covered wooden heel, matching toe-cap, light-coloured kidskin upper, closed sides, high tongue, strap fastening under outsized lace-edged stiffened taffeta bow with jewelled centre.

Men's boots 1620–1699

1 English nobleman's boot c. 1620–1630. Leather sole, square toe, red edges, matching medium-high leather-covered wooden heel, light-coloured leather upper, close fit over instep, ankle and leg to knee-level, wide cuff turned down and back, point on centre front, shaped spur leather over instep, spur with large rowel. 2 Dutch nobleman's boot c. 1620–1635. Leather sole, blunt toe, red edges, matching low leather-covered wooden heel, waxed leather upper, deep turned-down cuff at knee-level, point to centre front, linen boot hose with lace trim, spur leather over instep, spur with large rowel. 3 French nobleman's boot c. 1625. Red leather sole, square toe, matching medium-high leather-covered wooden Louis heel, knee-length fitted pale-coloured leather upper, deep knee-level cuff, punchwork decoration, seamed vamp, silk sash over instep, buckle and bow trim. 4 Dutch nobleman's boot c. 1625. Thick leather sole, blunt toe, red edges, matching medium-high leather-covered wooden Louis heel, light-coloured leather upper, leg widening from ankle to knee-level, edge trimmed with gold braid, large spur leather, spur with large rowel. 5 French nobleman's boot c. 1650–1660. Leather sole, square toe, red edges, matching medium-high leather-covered square wooden heel, light-coloured fine leather upper, fitted over instep, ankle and leg to knee-level, outsized turned-back cuff, extravagant lace boot hose, butterfly-shaped spur leather, spur with large rowel. 6 English man's boot c. 1660–1699. Thick leather sole, blunt toe, waxed tarred and polished leather upper, straight knee-length leg, knee-level flared cuff turned down and back, spur leather, spur with large rowel. 7 English nobleman's boot and patten c. 1650–1660. Boot with red leather sole, matching medium-high leather-covered wooden heel, pale-coloured knee-length upper, fitted leg, knee-level flared cuff turned down and back, lace-edged boot hose, butterfly-shaped spur leather, spur with large rowel; patten with heelless thick wooden sole, backless leather upper.

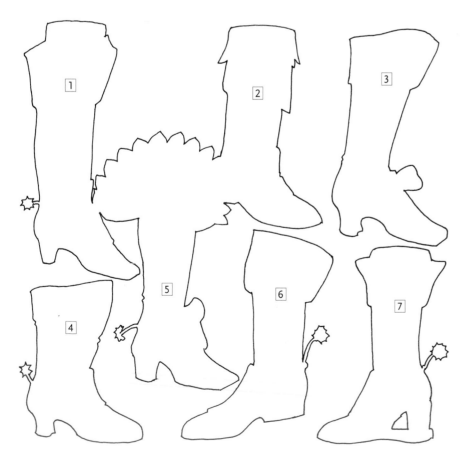

Men's shoes 1700–1799

English c. 1700–1720

English c. 1740–1750

English c. 1740–1750

French c. 1780

French c. 1790–1799

Italian c. 1750

English c. 1730–1740

English c. 1780–1795

English c. 1780–1795

Men's boots 1700–1799

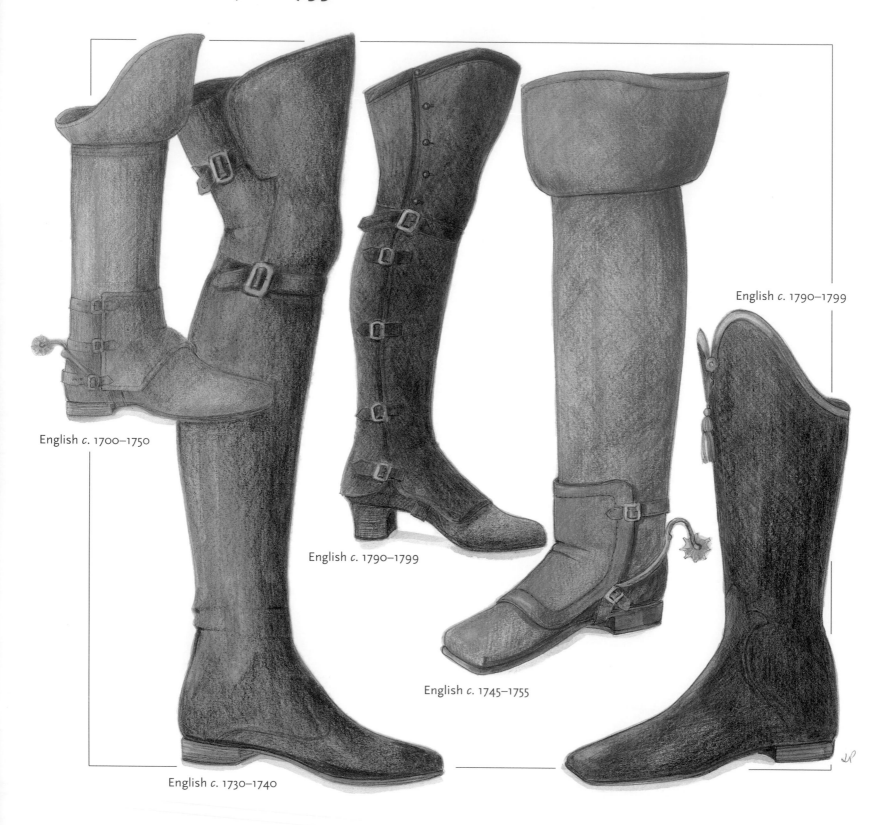

English *c.* 1700–1750

English *c.* 1730–1740

English *c.* 1790–1799

English *c.* 1745–1755

English *c.* 1790–1799

Men's boots 1790–1799

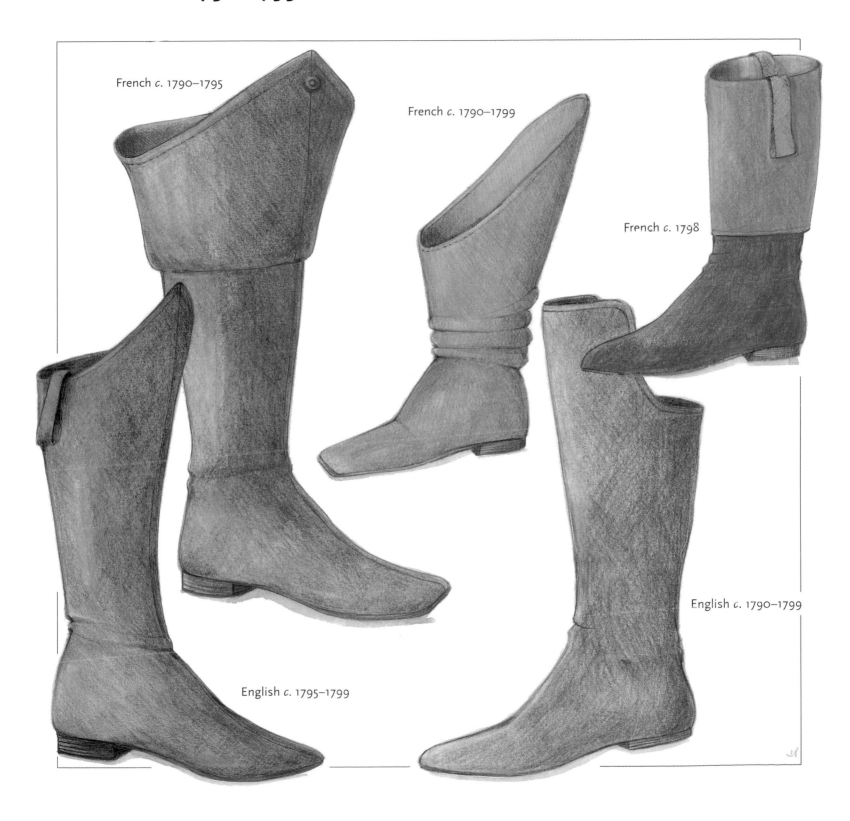

French *c.* 1790–1795

French *c.* 1790–1799

French *c.* 1798

English *c.* 1795–1799

English *c.* 1790–1799

Women's shoes 1700–1735

English c. 1730–1735

Italian c. 1700–1710

French c. 1730–1735

French c. 1720–1735

English c. 1730–1735

English c. 1700–1725

French c. 1715–1725

English c. 1730–1735

French c. 1720–1730

Women's shoes 1735–1765

Venetian *c.* 1750–1755

Venetian *c.* 1750–1760

English *c.* 1735–1750

French *c.* 1740–1750

English *c.* 1760–1765

French *c.* 1755–1760

English *c.* 1770–1775

English *c.* 1740–1750

English *c.* 1750–1760

Women's shoes 1780–1790

French *c.* 1780–1785

English *c.* 1780–1788

French *c.* 1780–1785

French *c.* 1780–1785

English *c.* 1780

English *c.* 1785–1790

English/American *c.* 1780–1790

English *c.* 1790

French *c.* 1785–1790

Women's shoes and boots 1785–1799

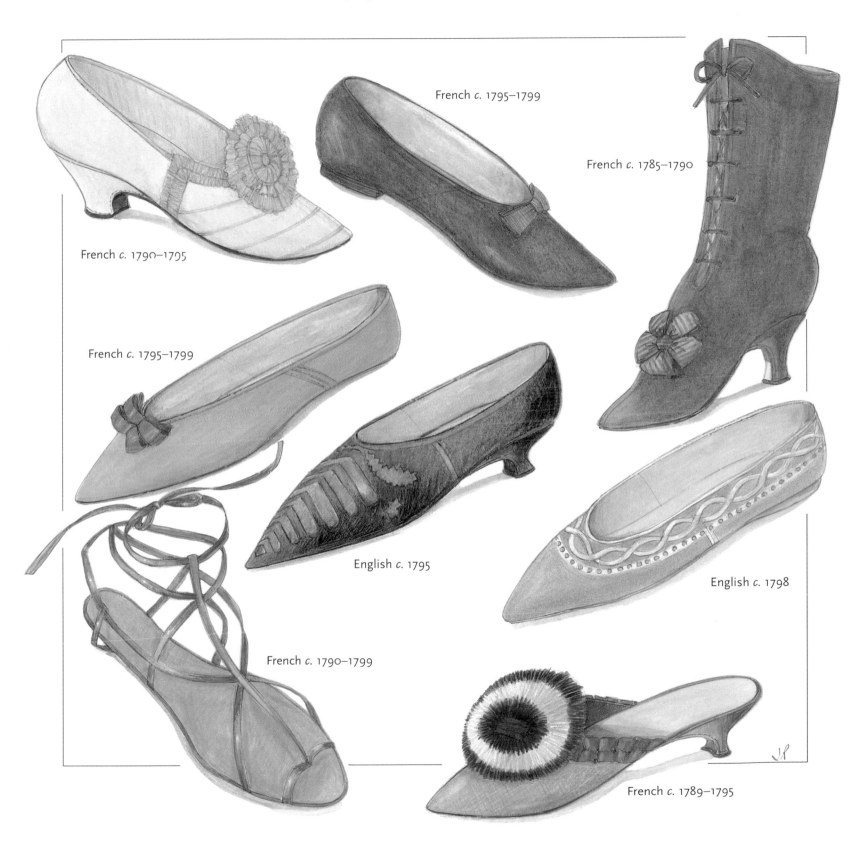

French *c.* 1790–1795

French *c.* 1795–1799

French *c.* 1785–1790

French *c.* 1795–1799

English *c.* 1795

English *c.* 1798

French *c.* 1790–1799

French *c.* 1789–1795

Men's shoes and boots 1800–1839

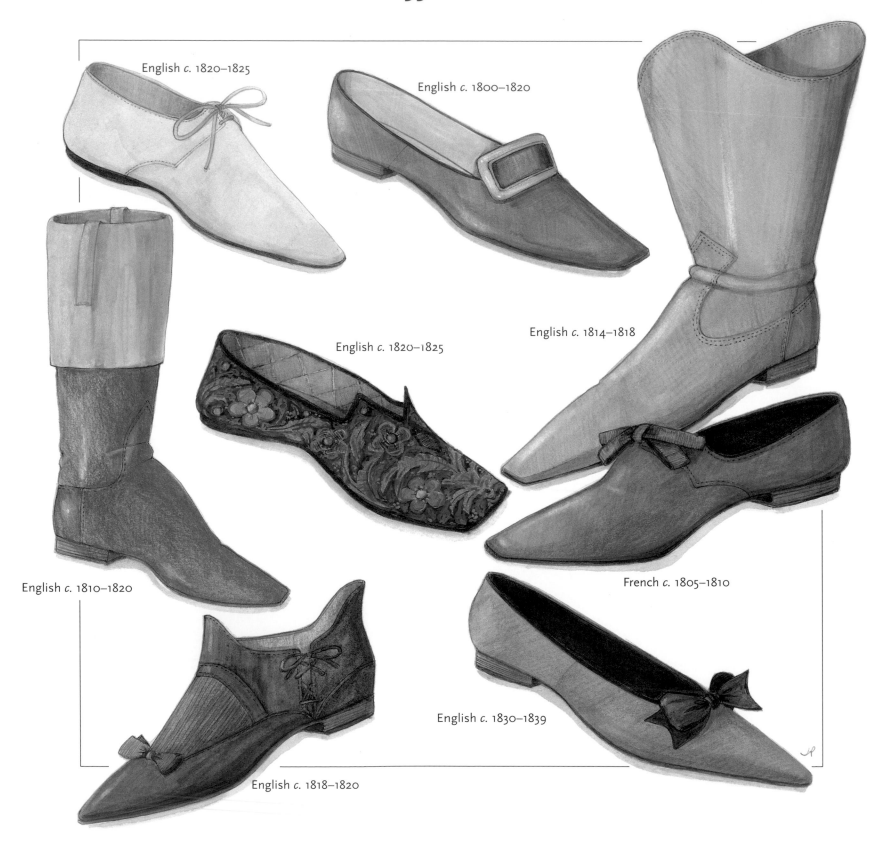

English c. 1820–1825

English c. 1800–1820

English c. 1814–1818

English c. 1820–1825

English c. 1810–1820

French c. 1805–1810

English c. 1830–1839

English c. 1818–1820

Men's shoes and boots 1840–1869

English c. 1850–1859

English c. 1855

English c. 1840–1849

English c. 1855–1860

English c. 1855–1860

English c. 1850–1860

English c. 1865–1869

Austrian c. 1840–1850

Men's shoes and boots 1870–1899

English c. 1870–1885

English c. 1890–1899

English c. 1885–1890

English c. 1880–1885

Italian c. 1885–1895

English c. 1890–1899

English c. 1880–1889

English c. 1890–1899

Women's shoes and boots 1800–1829

English c. 1820

French c. 1800–1805

English c. 1805–1815

English
c. 1810–1820

English c. 1825

English c. 1820–1829

French c. 1820

English c. 1820–1829

English c. 1800–1805

Women's shoes and boots 1830–1849

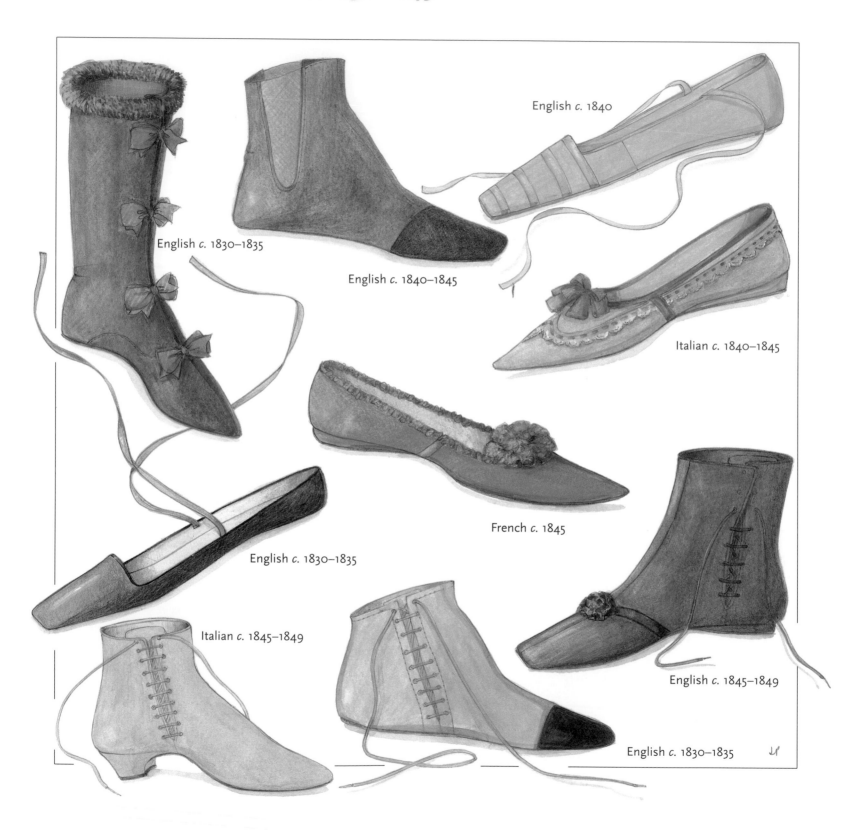

English *c.* 1830–1835

English *c.* 1840–1845

English *c.* 1840

Italian *c.* 1840–1845

French *c.* 1845

English *c.* 1830–1835

Italian *c.* 1845–1849

English *c.* 1845–1849

English *c.* 1830–1835

Women's shoes and boots 1850–1869

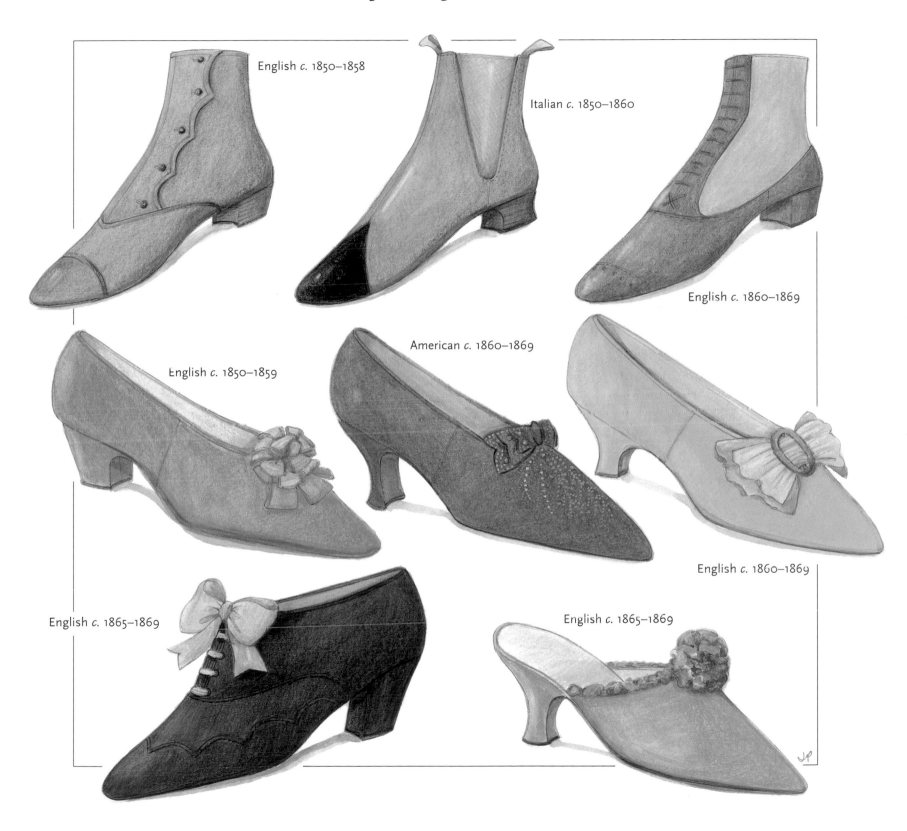

English *c.* 1850–1858

Italian *c.* 1850–1860

English *c.* 1860–1869

English *c.* 1850–1859

American *c.* 1860–1869

English *c.* 1860–1869

English *c.* 1865–1869

English *c.* 1865–1869

Women's shoes and boots 1870–1884

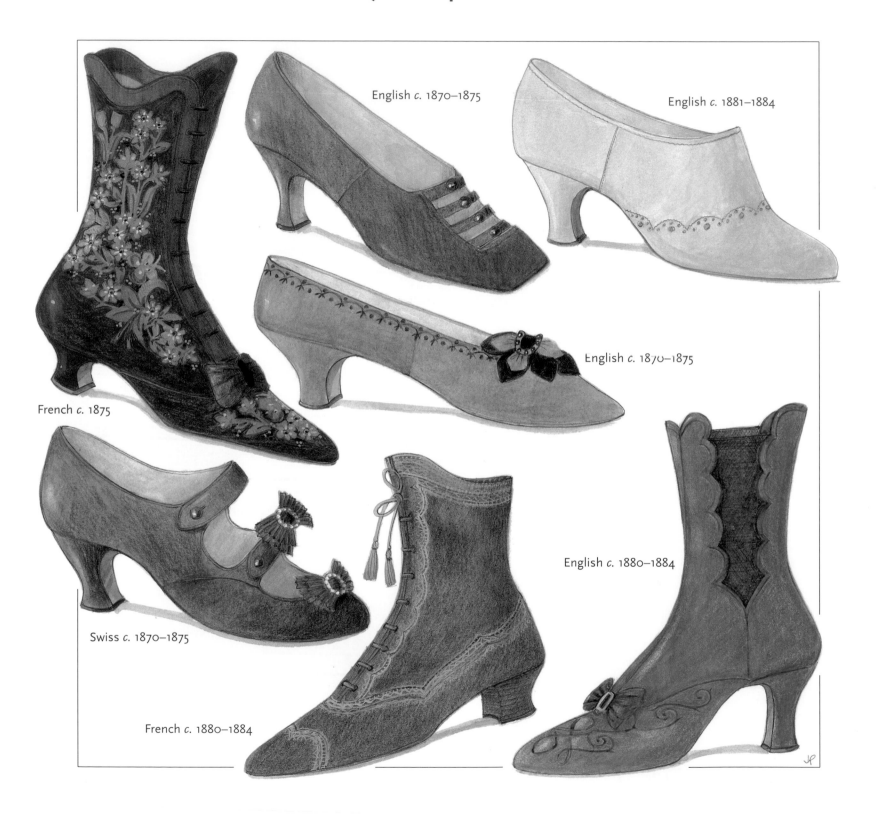

English c. 1870–1875

English c. 1881–1884

English c. 1870–1875

French c. 1875

Swiss c. 1870–1875

English c. 1880–1884

French c. 1880–1884

JP

Women's shoes and boots 1885–1899

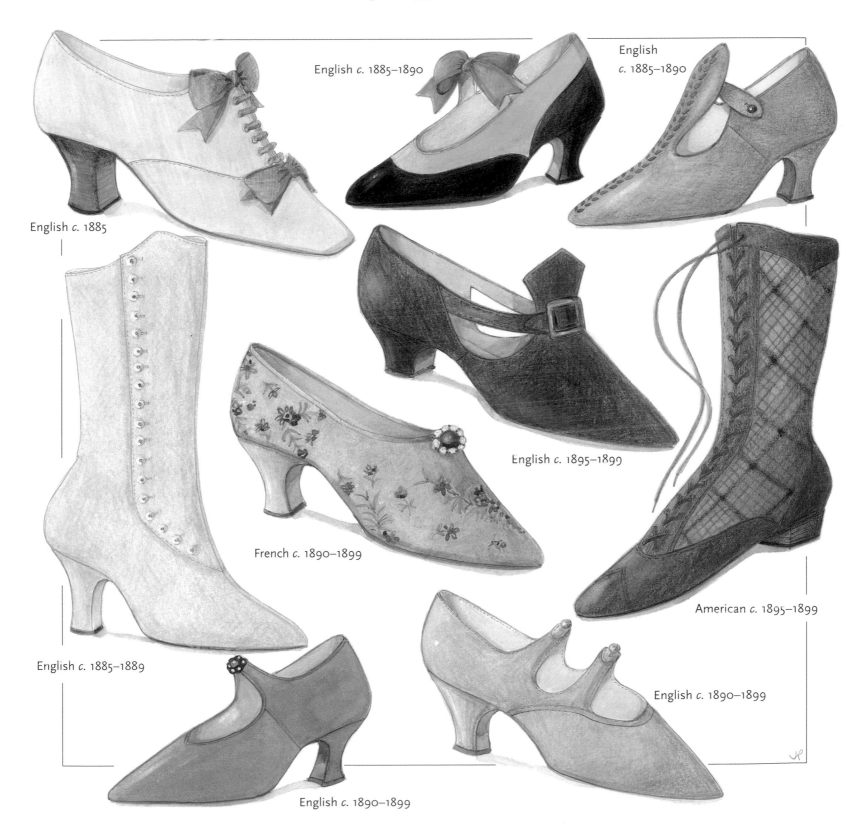

English c. 1885–1890

English
c. 1885–1890

English c. 1885

English c. 1895–1899

French c. 1890–1899

American c. 1895–1899

English c. 1885–1889

English c. 1890–1899

English c. 1890–1899

71

Women's shoes and boots 1885–1899

English *c.* 1890–1899

English *c.* 1890–1899

English *c.* 1885–1889

English *c.* 1895–1899

English *c.* 1895–1899

English *c.* 1895–1899

English *c.* 1895–1899

English *c.* 1890–1899

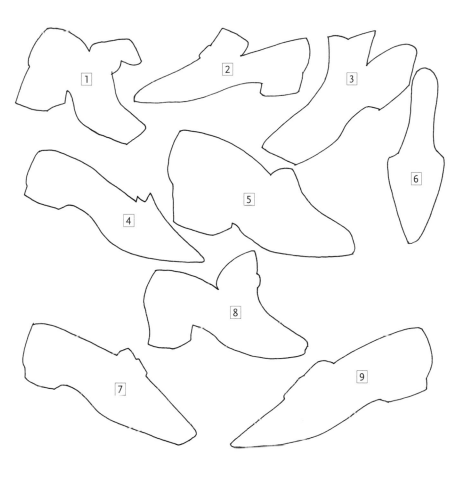

Men's shoes 1700–1799

1 English c. 1700–1720. Leather sole, square toe, medium-high leather-covered wooden heel, dyed leather upper, high vamp, extended and turned-down tongue with Cupid's-bow-shaped edge, pale-coloured linings. 2 English c. 1740–1750. Leather sole, round toe, low leather-covered wooden heel, waxed leather upper, straps with buckle fastening over instep, extended tongue. 3 English c. 1740–1750. Leather sole with red edges, wide square toe, medium-high fabric-covered wooden heel, matching backless upper, high vamp, extended tongue with Cupid's-bow-shaped edge. 4 French c. 1790–1799. Thin leather sole, pointed toe, low stacked leather heel, low-cut sides, V-shaped cut on centre front of low vamp. 5 Italian c. 1750. Leather sole, round toe, medium-high leather-covered wooden heel, waxed leather upper, straps with buckle fastening over instep, high vamp, short tongue. 6 French c. 1780. Leather sole, matching polished leather upper, pointed toe, gold braid binding around edge of high vamp, matching bow trim on centre front. 7 English c. 1780–1795. Leather sole, elongated square toe, low stacked leather heel, waxed fine leather upper, straps with large buckle fastening over low vamp, short tongue. 8 English c. 1730–1740. Thick leather sole, blunt toe, medium-high leather-covered wooden heel, straps with buckle fastening over instep, high vamp, extended tongue. 9 English c. 1780–1795. Thin leather sole, pointed toe, fine leather upper, straps with large buckle fastening over low vamp, short tongue.

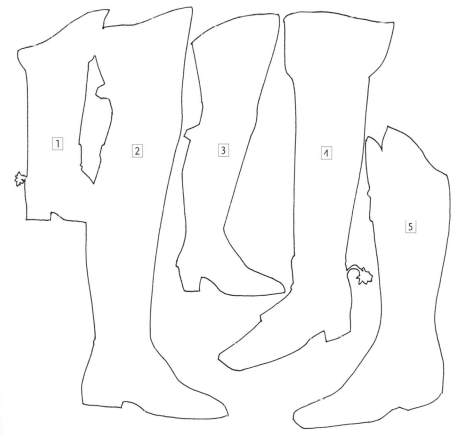

Men's boots 1700–1799

1 English army c. 1700–1750. Thick leather sole, blunt toe, low stacked leather heel, knee-length tarred and waxed leather upper, straight-cut from ankle to knee, turned-up cuff shaped to back of knee, spur leather with buckled straps, silver spur. 2 English riding c. 1730–1740. Thick leather sole, blunt toe, low stacked leather heel, thigh-length polished leather upper, decoratively shaped separate vamp, topstitched edges, fitted leg, buckled strap under knee and at thigh-level. 3 English shoe and spatterdash c. 1790–1799. Shoe with thick leather sole, blunt toe, medium-high stacked leather heel, leather upper covered by thigh-length leather spatterdash leggings, button fastening on outside from top edge to knee-level, strap with buckle fastening under knee, matching half straps and buckles to ankle-level and strap under instep of shoe, topstitched detail. 4 English army c. 1745–1755. Thick leather sole, wide square toe, low stacked leather heel, knee-length waxed leather upper, straight-cut from ankle to knee, deep turned-up cuff, spur leather with buckled straps, topstitched detail, high-set spur. 5 English civilian c. 1790–1799. Leather sole, elongated square toe, low stacked leather heel, knee-length polished fine leather upper, close-fitted to leg, decoratively shaped separate vamp, topstitched edges, top edge of boot shaped to behind knee and to V-shaped point on centre front, gold braid binding, matching tassel on centre front.

Men's boots 1790–1799

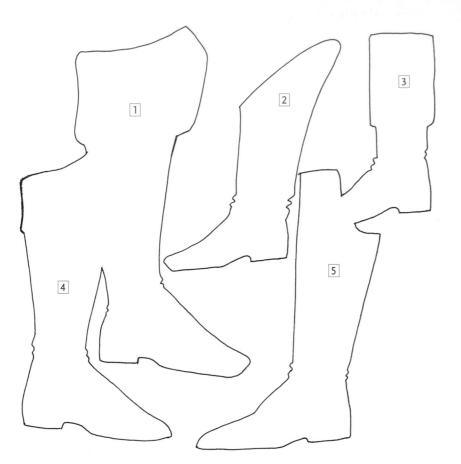

1 French c. 1790–1795. Leather sole, elongated square toe, low stacked leather heel, knee-length waxed leather upper, fitted leg, deep turned-up shaped cuff, button trim on centre front point. 2 French c. 1790–1799. Leather sole, elongated square toe, low stacked leather heel, knee-length fine leather upper, wide leg, higher at the back, natural creases around ankle. 3 French c. 1798. Thin leather sole, pointed toe, low stacked leather heel, knee-length fine leather upper, fitted leg, light-coloured turned-down cuff to ankle-level, side pulls from inside top edge. 4 English c. 1795–1799. Thin leather sole, pointed toe, low stacked leather heel, knee-length fine leather upper, fitted leg, top edge shaped behind knee to point on centre front above knee. 5 English c. 1790–1799. Thin leather sole, pointed toe, low stacked leather heel, knee-length fine leather upper, fitted leg, cut behind knee at back and above knee in tongue shape on front.

Women's shoes 1700–1735

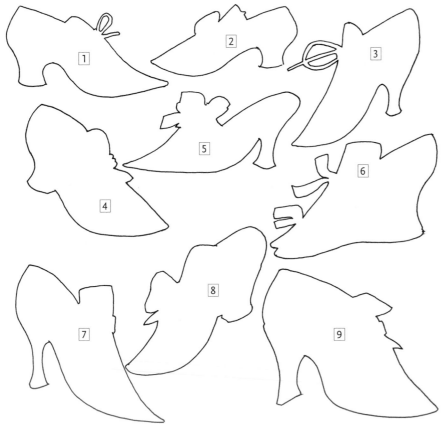

1 Italian c. 1700–1710. Leather sole, sharp pointed toe, medium-high leather-covered wooden Louis heel, pale-coloured leather upper, straps over instep fastening with ribbons, matching bindings, high vamp, short tongue. 2 English c. 1730–1735. Leather sole, sharp pointed toe, medium-high leather-covered wooden Louis heel, matching light-coloured upper, straps with coloured silk bow fastening over instep, high vamp and shaped tongue bound in contrast-colour petersham. 3 French c. 1730–1735. Leather sole, sharp pointed toe, slender high leather-covered wooden heel, matching kidskin upper, floral silk embroidery from above toe to under high tongue, matching embroidery on sides and heel-back, straps over instep fastening with ribbons. 4 English c. 1730–1735. Leather sole, sharp pointed toe, low fabric-covered wooden Louis heel, matching embroidered silk upper mounted on canvas, straps with round paste buckle fastening over instep, high tongue. 5 French c. 1720–1735. Leather sole, sharp pointed toe, slender high leather-covered wooden heel, backless velvet upper embroidered with gold threads, high vamp trimmed with frilled silk, matching bow on centre front. 6 English shoe and patten c. 1700–1725. Shoe with leather sole, pointed toe, medium-high leather-covered wooden Louis heel, embroidered silk upper, straps with ribbon fastening over instep, high tongue; patten with leather sole, arched to accommodate high heel of shoe, silk straps with ribbon tie over toes. 7 French c. 1715–1725. Leather sole, sharp pointed toe, slender high leather-covered wooden heel, matching leather upper, straps with decorative metal buckle fastening over instep, high tongue. 8 English c. 1730–1735. Leather sole, sharp pointed toe, low fabric-covered wooden heel, matching silk upper, all-over multicoloured floral embroidery, straps with silk bow fastening over instep, high tongue, contrast-colour bindings and edges. 9 French c. 1720–1730. Leather sole, sharp pointed toe, slender high leather-covered wooden heel, leather upper, straps with paste buckle fastening over instep, turned-down high tongue with Cupid's-bow-shaped edge, linings matching heel colour.

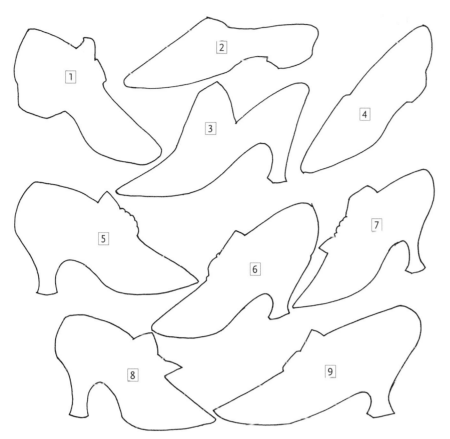

Women's shoes 1735–1765

1 English c. 1735–1750. Leather sole, elongated square toe, low leather-covered wooden heel, leather upper, straps with steel buckle fastening over instep, high tongue.
2 Venetian c. 1750–1755. Leather sole, pointed toe, low leather-covered wooden heel, backless velvet upper, embroidered with gold threads and sequins, matching sock lining. 3 French c. 1740–1750. Leather sole, sharp pointed toe, slender high fabric-covered wooden heel, matching backless satin upper, delicate floral embroidery from above toe to under point of high vamp. 4 Venetian c. 1750–1760. Leather sole, pointed toe, low fabric-covered wooden heel, matching velvet upper, embroidered with gold threads and seed pearls, low vamp and sides. 5 French c. 1755–1760. Leather sole, sharp pointed toe, medium-high fabric-covered wooden heel, matching patterned silk brocade upper, straps and paste buckle fastening over instep, short tongue. 6 English c. 1770–1775. Leather sole, sharp pointed toe, medium-high fabric-covered wedged wooden Louis heel, pale-coloured satin upper, contrast-colour straps and paste buckle fastening over instep, matching binding on short tongue, edges and heel. 7 English c. 1760–1765. Leather sole, sharp pointed toe, slender high fabric-covered wedged wooden Louis heel, matching light-coloured satin upper, straps with paste buckle fastening over instep, pointed tongue, decorative stitching. 8 English c. 1740–1750. Leather sole, sharp pointed toe, high fabric-covered wedged wooden Louis heel, matching silk grosgrain upper, multicoloured silk floral embroidery above toe, straps with metal buckle fastening over instep, high tongue. 9 English c. 1750–1760. Leather sole, sharp pointed toe, medium-high fabric-covered wedged wooden Louis heel, matching silk upper, multicoloured silk chain-stitch floral embroidery above toe, straps with metal buckle fastening above instep, short tongue.

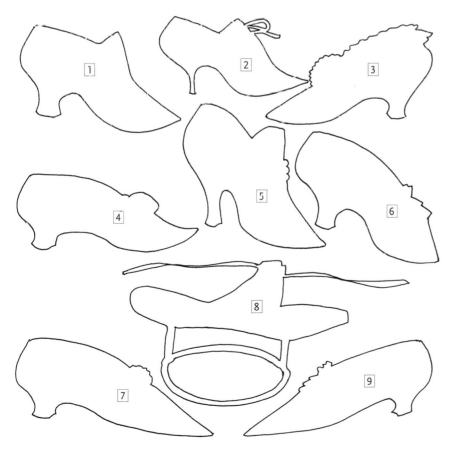

Women's shoes 1780–1790

1 English c. 1780–1788. Leather sole, sharp pointed toe, medium-high leather-covered wedged Louis heel, matching pale-coloured kidskin upper, sequin embroidery from above toe to under pointed high vamp. 2 French c. 1780–1785. Leather sole, sharp pointed toe, slender high leather-covered wooden heel, pale-coloured kidskin upper, multi-coloured floral embroidery, straps with ribbon tie over instep, short tongue.
3 French c. 1780–1785. Leather sole, sharp pointed toe, medium-high fabric-covered wedged Louis heel, matching pale-coloured satin upper, low vamp, contrast-colour pleated silk taffeta rosette, matching frill around outer edge. 4 English c. 1780. Leather sole, piked pointed toe, low leather-covered wedged wooden heel, matching polished leather upper, low vamp, fringed striped silk bow on centre front. 5 French c. 1780–1785. Leather sole, sharp pointed toe, high leather-covered wooden heel, matching embroidered upper, straps with paste buckle fastening over instep, high tongue. 6 English c. 1785–1790. Leather sole, sharp pointed toe, medium-high leather-covered wedged wooden heel, pale-coloured ribbed silk upper, sequin embroidery above toe to under pleated striped silk ribbon trim on low vamp.
7 English c. 1790. Leather sole, pointed toe, slender low fabric-covered Louis heel, matching ribbed silk upper, contrast-colour silk appliqué trim above toe, matching ruched-ribbon-covered buckle under low vamp, shoe sock and lining. 8 English/American c. 1780–1790. Thick leather sole, elongated square toe, straps with ribbon fastenings over instep, sole supported on metal struts above metal ring.
9 French c. 1785–1790. Leather sole, pointed toe, low fabric-covered wedged wooden Louis heel, matching silk satin upper, embroidered appliqué trim above toe, two-colour silk taffeta pleated ribbon trim on front of low vamp.

Women's shoes and boots 1785–1799

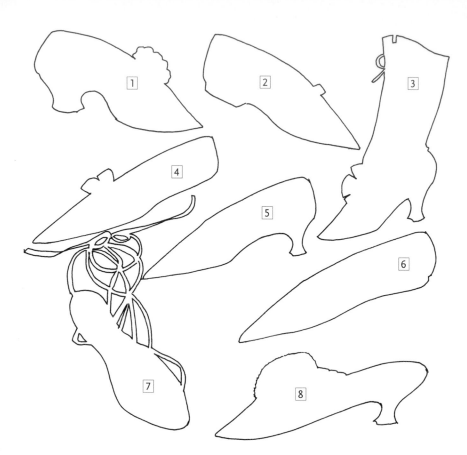

1 French *c.* 1790–1795. Leather sole, pointed toe, low leather-covered wedged wooden heel, pale-coloured silk satin upper, contrast-colour appliqué ribbon stripes on front above toe, matching ruched silk rosette and ruched trim on low vamp. 2 French *c.* 1795–1799. Leather sole, pointed toe, low stacked leather heel, fine leather upper, low vamp, contrast-colour ribbed silk ribbon bow on centre front, matching edges. 3 French *c.* 1785–1790. Riding boot with leather sole, pointed toe, medium-high leather-covered wedged wooden Louis heel, matching mid-calf-length polished upper, centre front laced fastening, striped silk rosette on low instep. 4 French *c.* 1795–1799. Heelless leather sole, pointed toe, silk satin upper, low-cut vamp, contrast-colour looped silk ribbon trim. 5 English *c.* 1795. Leather sole, pointed toe, low leather-covered wooden Louis heel, matching upper, cut-out pattern to reveal contrast-colour kidskin lining. 6 English *c.* 1798. Leather sole, shallow pale-coloured leather-covered wedge heel, leather upper, low vamp, silk and kidskin appliqué pattern, matching bound edges. 7 French *c.* 1790–1799. Sandal with heelless leather sole, gilded edges, matching narrow leather straps between big and second toe, supporting and leg binding straps. 8 French *c.* 1789–1795. Leather sole, pointed toe, low fabric-covered wedged wooden Louis heel, matching silk satin backless upper, low vamp with frilled satin ribbon edge, large tri-colour fringed ribbon rosette on centre front.

Men's shoes and boots 1800–1839

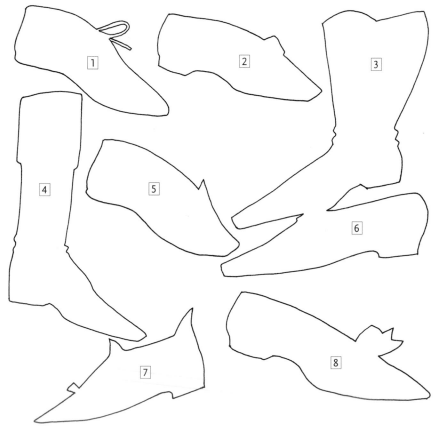

1 English *c.* 1820–1825. Dress shoe with thin coloured leather sole, rounded toe, low wedge heel, pale-coloured kidskin upper, latchet straps over high instep, fastening with silk ribbon laces, matching silk lining. 2 English *c.* 1800–1820. Thin leather sole, narrow square toe, low stacked leather heel, fine leather upper with low-cut vamp, silver buckle trim, silk-bound edges. 3 English *c.* 1814–1818. Walking boot with leather sole, narrow square toe, low stacked leather heel, mid-calf-length polished leather upper, leg flared from ankle to shaped top, topstitched edges, matching separately cut pointed vamp. 4 English *c.* 1810–1820. Leather sole, square toe, low stacked leather heel, knee-length leather upper, leg fitted from ankle to knee, deep turned-down pale-coloured matt leather cuff with pull straps, separately cut topstitched pointed vamp. 5 English *c.* 1820–1825. House slipper with leather sole, wide square toe, low leather-covered heel, silk velvet upper, multicoloured silk floral embroidery, low vamp split on centre front, edges bound in coloured silk, quilted silk lining. 6 French *c.* 1805–1810. Leather sole, narrow square toe, low stacked leather heel, fine leather upper, latchet straps fastening over high instep with silk ribbon tied in a large bow, coloured silk lining. 7 English *c.* 1818–1820. Evening shoe with thin leather sole, pointed toe, low stacked leather heel, fine leather upper with fabric insert between bow-trimmed low-cut vamp and high instep, low-cut sides with inner laced fastening, topstitched edges and detail. 8 English *c.* 1830–1839. Evening pump with thin leather sole, pointed toe, low stacked leather heel, fine polished kidskin upper with low-cut vamp, silk bow trim on centre front, matching bound edges, coloured silk lining.

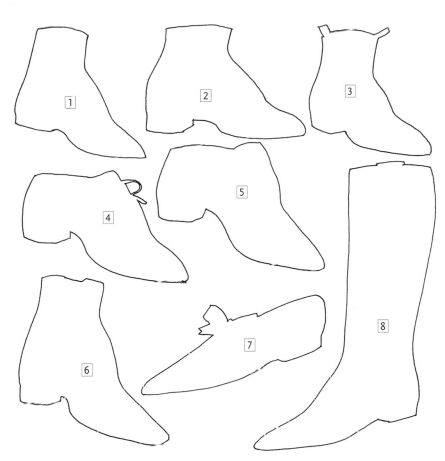

Men's shoes and boots 1840–1869

1 English c. 1840–1849. Leather sole, rounded toe, low stacked leather heel, ankle-length fine leather upper with patent leather toecap and elasticated fabric gussets. 2 English c. 1850–1859. Leather sole, round toe, medium-high stacked leather heel, leather upper with ankle-length fabric tops, side button fastening, topstitched edges and detail. 3 English c. 1855. Leather sole, round toe, medium-high stacked leather heel, leather upper, silk brocade inset from low squared-off vamp to ankle-level elasticated fabric side gussets, front and back pulls. 4 English c. 1855–1860. Leather sole, narrow square toe, medium-high stacked leather heel, patent leather upper with centre front laced fastening over instep above high tongue. 5 English c. 1855–1860. Leather sole, square toe, medium-high stacked leather heel, fine leather on front upper and thick fabric from behind heel-back to over instep with side button fastening. 6 English c. 1865–1869. Leather sole, square toe, medium-high stacked leather heel, patent leather upper, toecap with brogue detail, ankle-length matt kidskin top with elasticated fabric gussets and a simulated side button fastening. 7 English c. 1850–1860. Leather sole, pointed toe, low stacked leather heel, calfskin upper, low-cut sides, latchet straps over instep tied with ribbon laces. 8 Austrian c. 1840–1850. Leather sole, round toe, medium-high stacked leather heel, contrast-colour leather leg, fitted from ankle to knee, ribbon pulls on either side of top edge, decorative contrast-colour stitching below side ankle.

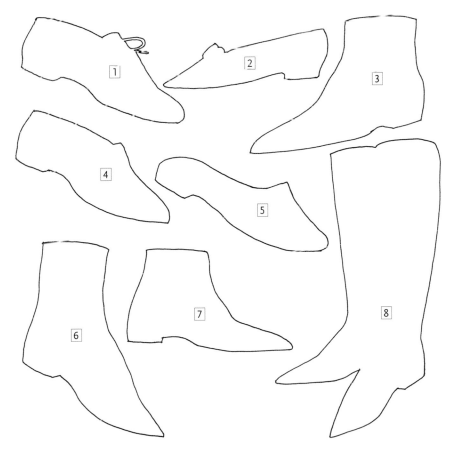

Men's shoes and boots 1870–1899

1 English c. 1870–1885. Sports shoe with thick leather sole, round toe, low stacked leather heel, pale-coloured canvas upper with polished leather toecap, heel-back and tongue under laced fastening. 2 English c. 1890–1899. Evening slipper with thin leather sole, round toe, low leather-covered heel, patent leather upper, low-cut vamp with centre front satin bow trim, matching bound edges. 3 English c. 1885–1890. Leather sole, narrow pointed toe, low stacked leather heel, calfskin upper with patent leather toecap, ankle-length light-coloured matt calfskin top, elasticated fabric side gussets and simulated side button fastening 4 English c. 1880–1885. House slipper with leather sole, round toe, low stacked leather heel, velvet upper with multicoloured floral design embroidery over front under high tongue and around sides and back, satin bound edges, quilted silk lining. 5 Italian c. 1885–1895. House slipper with thin leather sole, round toe, low heel, backless leather upper with centre front pointed vamp, embossed design of gold flowers and leaves, edges bound in coloured silk, matching lining. 6 English c. 1880–1889. Leather sole, pointed toe, low stacked leather heel, ankle-length leather upper, elasticated fabric side gussets. 7 English c. 1890–1899. Shoe with leather sole, round toe, stacked leather heel and leather upper, ankle-length spat in pale-coloured canvas, side button fastening and bar strap under foot, topstitched edges and detail. 8 English c. 1890–1899. Boots with leather soles, pointed toes, low stacked leather heels, polished leather uppers, legs fitted from ankle to knee-level, separately cut vamps, topstitched edges and detail.

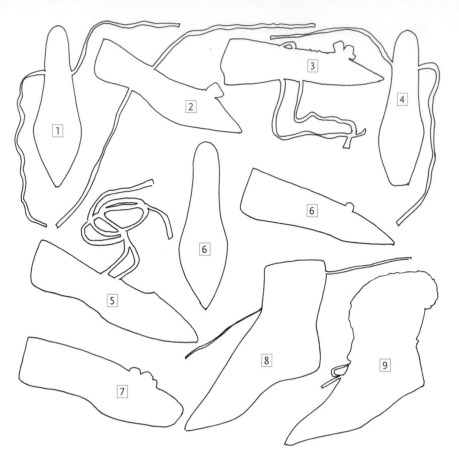

Women's shoes and boots 1800–1829

1 English c. 1820. Heelless fine leather sole, pointed toe, pale-coloured calfskin upper, low-cut vamp decorated with ruched ribbon, two long matching ties attached at sides, silk lining. 2 French c. 1800–1805. Heelless fine leather sole, round toe, pale-coloured calfskin upper printed with polka dot pattern, low-cut vamp with silk ribbon bow trim, two matching ribbon ties attached at sides, silk lining. 3 English c. 1805–1815. Fine leather sole, pointed toe, leather-covered wedge heel, matching light-coloured printed calfskin upper, low-cut vamp decorated with ruched and looped silk ribbon, two long matching ribbon ties attached at sides, silk lining. 4 English c. 1810–1820. Heelless fine leather sole, narrow square toe, brightly coloured calfskin upper, low-cut vamp with decorative gold braid 'buckle', two long silk ribbon ties attached at sides, silk lining. 5 English c. 1820–1829. Heelless fine leather sole, round toe, pale-coloured silk upper with low-cut vamp, edges bound with silk ribbon, matching applied decoration on front and sides and two long ties attached at sides, silk lining. 6 English c. 1825. Heelless fine leather soles, pointed toes, silk uppers with embroidered design in coloured and silver threads, low-cut vamps, jewelled button trimmings. 7 French c. 1820. Heelless fine leather sole, wide square toe, calfskin upper, low-cut vamp decorated with contrast-colour looped silk ribbon on centre front, matching bound edges. 8 English c. 1820–1829. Heelless fine leather sole, pointed toe, above-ankle-length calfskin upper seamed over instep and toe, side laced fastening. 9 English c. 1800–1805. Heelless leather sole, pointed toe, ankle-length pale-coloured calfskin upper, fur-trimmed top edge and part lining, centre front laced opening.

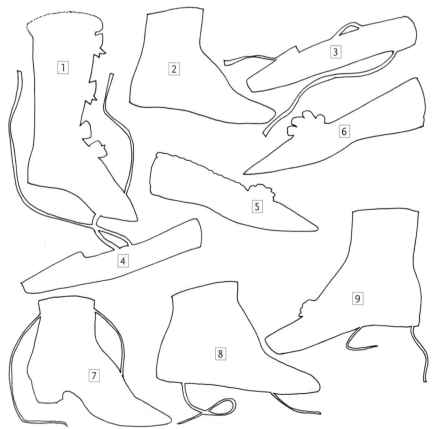

Women's shoes and boots 1830–1849

1 English c. 1830-1835. Heelless leather sole, pointed toe, below-knee-length fine leather upper with fitted leg to fur-trimmed top, centre front opening with four ribbon fastenings over full-length tongue. 2 English c. 1840–1845. Heelless fine leather sole, wide square toe, ankle-length calfskin upper with patent leather toecap and elasticated side gussets. 3 English c. 1840. Heelless fine leather sole, square toe, pale-coloured matt calfskin upper, banded over front under low-cut square vamp with satin ribbon, two long matching ties attached at sides, fabric lining. 4 English c. 1830–1835. Heelless fine leather sole, wide square toe, silk upper with low-cut square vamp, satin bound edges, two long matching ribbon ties attached at sides, fabric lining. 5 French c. 1845. Fine leather sole, pointed toe, low leather-covered wedge heel, matching upper with ruched silk rosette on low-cut vamp, matching edges, silk lining. 6 Italian c. 1840–1845. Fine leather sole, pointed toe, low leather-covered wedge heel, silk upper with contrast-colour looped silk ribbon trim on low-cut vamp, matching bound edges, seams and fine ribbon running through narrow scalloped lace trim, silk lining. 7 Italian c. 1845–1849. Leather sole, round toe, low silk-covered wooden heel, matching ankle-length upper, inner side opening with lacing over full-length tongue. 8 English c. 1830–1835. Heelless fine leather sole, round toe, matt calfskin upper with patent leather toecap, inner side opening with lacing over full-length tongue. 9 English c. 1845–1849. Fine leather sole, wide square toe, low silk-covered wedge heel, matching ankle-length upper, applied satin ribbon and ruched rosette below instep, inner side opening with lacing over full-length tongue.

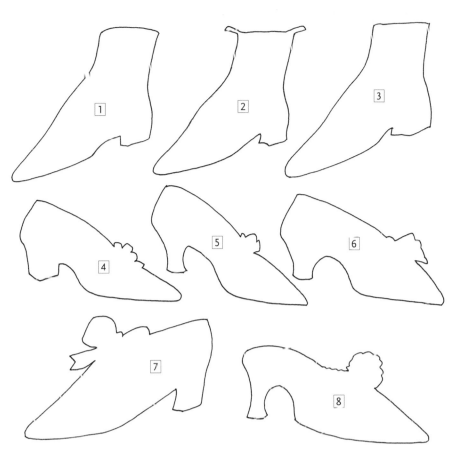

Women's shoes and boots 1850–1869

1 English c. 1850–1858. Leather sole, pointed toe, low stacked leather heel, ankle-length calfskin upper, scalloped side button fastening with topstitched edges, matching toecap. 2 Italian c. 1850–1860. Leather sole, pointed toe, shaped stacked leather heel, ankle-length calfskin upper with V-shaped patent leather toecap, elasticated fabric side gussets, front and back pull tapes. 3 English c. 1860–1869. Leather sole, round toe, leather-covered heel, matching calfskin upper, toecap with brogue detail, ankle-length canvas sides and back, laced fastening through eyelets set in faced leather opening. 4 English c. 1850–1859. Leather sole, almond-shaped toe, medium-high leather-covered heel, matching calfskin upper, low-cut vamp trimmed with looped velvet ribbon, matching bound edges. 5 American c. 1860–1869. Leather sole, pointed toe, high Louis heel, silk upper, front embroidered with beads, matching double bow above low-cut vamp, fabric lining. 6 English c. 1860–1869. Leather sole, pointed toe, medium-high silk-covered heel, matching upper, low-cut vamp trimmed with taffeta ribbon threaded through gold-coloured oval buckle, silk lining. 7 English c. 1865–1869. Leather sole, pointed toe, medium-high leather-covered heel, matching calfskin upper, scalloped and topstitched wing-shaped seam, front fastening over high instep with wide silk ribbon. 8 English c. 1865–1869. House slipper with fine leather sole, pointed toe, high silk-covered Louis heel, matching backless upper, edge of vamp trimmed with ruched fine silk and rosette on centre front, silk lining.

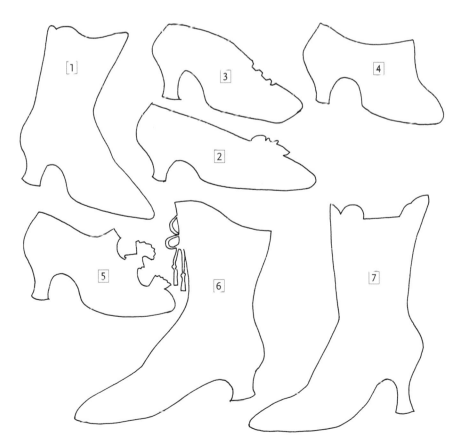

Women's shoes and boots 1870–1884

1 French c. 1875. Leather sole, pointed toe, medium-high silk-covered Louis heel, matching mid-calf-length upper, multicoloured floral embroidery on fitted leg and over toe, wide self-colour silk bindings, matching facings of laced centre front opening and flat bow on instep. 2 English c. 1870–1875. Leather sole, pointed toe, medium-high silk-covered Louis heel, matching upper, low-cut vamp with two-colour rosette and buckle trim, embroidered decoration under bound edges. 3 English c. 1870–1875. Leather sole, wide square toe, high leather-covered Louis heel, matching calfskin upper, low-cut vamp with four decorative straps. 4 English c. 1881–1884. Leather sole, pointed toe, high suede-covered heel, matching upper, perforated decoration below scalloped and pinked wing seam under high vamp. 5 Swiss c. 1870–1875. Leather sole, round toe, high leather-covered Louis heel, matching upper with two side-buttoned straps over instep, lower strap decorated with pleated silk bow and paste buckle, matching decoration on low-cut vamp. 6 French c. 1880–1884. Leather sole, pointed toe, low stacked heel, ankle-length calfskin upper with toecap edges in lace, matching decoration on curved top edge, seams on each side of laced front fastening and over instep to heel-back. 7 English c. 1880–1884. Leather sole, pointed toe, high silk-covered Louis heel, matching mid-calf-length upper with embroidery over toe extending to sides, fitted leg, satin-bound scalloped top edge, matching edges of elasticated side gussets and buckled bow over low vamp.

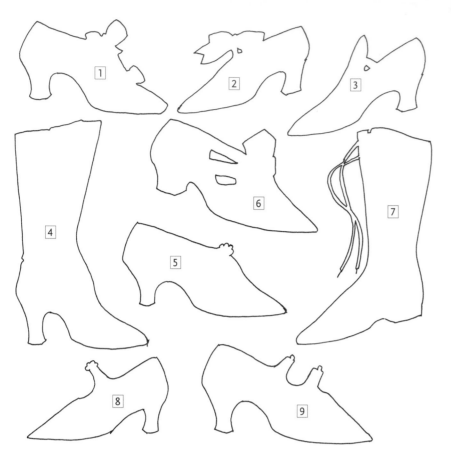

Women's shoes and boots 1885–1899

1 English *c.* 1885. Leather sole, square toe, high stacked leather heel, pale-coloured doeskin upper with ribbon laces through centre front, matching bow trim on low vamp. 2 English *c.* 1885–1890. Leather sole, pointed toe, high leather-covered Louis heel, matching lower part of calfskin upper, pale-coloured calfskin top, matching bar strap with centre front ribbon bow fastening. 3 English *c.* 1885–1890. Leather sole, pointed toe, leather-covered Louis heel, matching calfskin upper with T-strap, threaded contrast-colour leather thong from point of toe to tip of strap, side button fastening. 4 English *c.* 1885–1889. Leather sole, pointed toe, high leather-covered heel, matching mid-calf-length dyed calfskin upper with pearl button side fastening from shaped boot top to centre of high instep. 5 French *c.* 1890–1899. Leather sole, pointed toe, low satin-covered Louis heel, matching upper with multicoloured silk floral embroidered decoration, jewelled button trim on centre front of low-cut vamp. 6 English *c.* 1895–1899. Leather sole, pointed toe, low leather-covered heel, matching calfskin upper with low-cut sides, strap and buckle fastening over high pointed tongue. 7 American *c.* 1895–1899. Leather sole, round toe, low stacked leather heel, mid-calf-length leather upper with toe-cap, top shaped towards knee, centre front laced opening, sides of fitted leg from top to over side-front instep panelled with checked wool tweed. 8 English *c.* 1890–1899. Leather sole, pointed toe, high silk-covered Louis heel, matching upper, single bar strap over instep, fastening with jewelled button on centre front. 9 English *c.* 1890–1899. Leather sole, pointed toe, high leather-covered heel, matching gilded kidskin upper with two bar straps over instep, fastening on centre front with gold-coloured ball buttons.

Women's shoes and boots 1885–1899

1 English *c.* 1890–1899. Leather sole, pointed toe, high fabric-covered Louis heel, matching silk velvet upper with low-cut vamp and single bar strap over instep, ribbon bow fastening on centre front. 2 English *c.* 1890–1899. Leather sole, pointed toe, high leather-covered Louis heel, matching light-coloured calfskin upper with low-cut vamp and single narrow strap over instep, side button fastening. 3 English *c.* 1885–1889. Leather sole, pointed toe, low satin-covered heel, mid-calf-length contrast-colour satin upper covered with lace, satin bindings and edges, matching ribbon laces in front opening. 4 English *c.* 1895–1899. Leather sole, pointed toe, high stacked leather heel, leather front upper to low W-shaped wing seam, pale-coloured doeskin to mid-calf-length, side button fastening from top edge to side instep. 5 English *c.* 1895–1899. Leather sole, pointed toe, high leather-covered heel, matching heel-back, front upper, edges and detail on pale-coloured doeskin upper, scalloped side-front opening fastened with contrast-colour buttons in sets of two. 6 English *c.* 1895–1899. Leather sole, pointed toe, high gilded-leather-covered heel, brocade upper with low-cut vamp, small gold-coloured buckle trim on centre front. 7 English *c.* 1895–1899. Leather sole, pointed toe, high leather-covered heel, matching calfskin upper with strap and buckle fastening over high pointed tongue. 8 English *c.* 1890–1899. Leather sole, pointed toe, low leather-covered heel, matching patent leather upper striped in contrast-colour grosgrain ribbon, matching bound edges, low vamp trimmed with two-colour ribbon bow.

Men's shoes and boots 1900–1909

English c. 1903–1905

English c. 1900–1906

American c. 1900–1909

English c. 1905–1909

American c. 1905

English c. 1900–1909

English c. 1900–1909

English c. 1900–1909

Women's shoes and boots 1900–1905

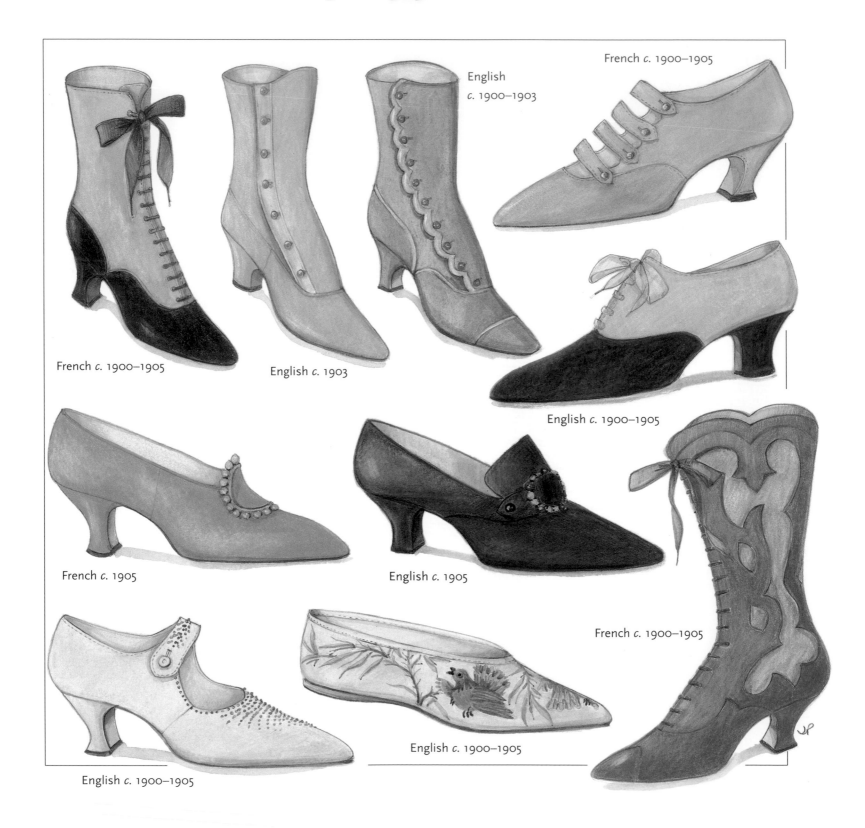

English c. 1900–1903

French c. 1900–1905

French c. 1900–1905

English c. 1903

English c. 1900–1905

French c. 1905

English c. 1905

French c. 1900–1905

English c. 1900–1905

English c. 1900–1905

Women's shoes and boots 1905–1909

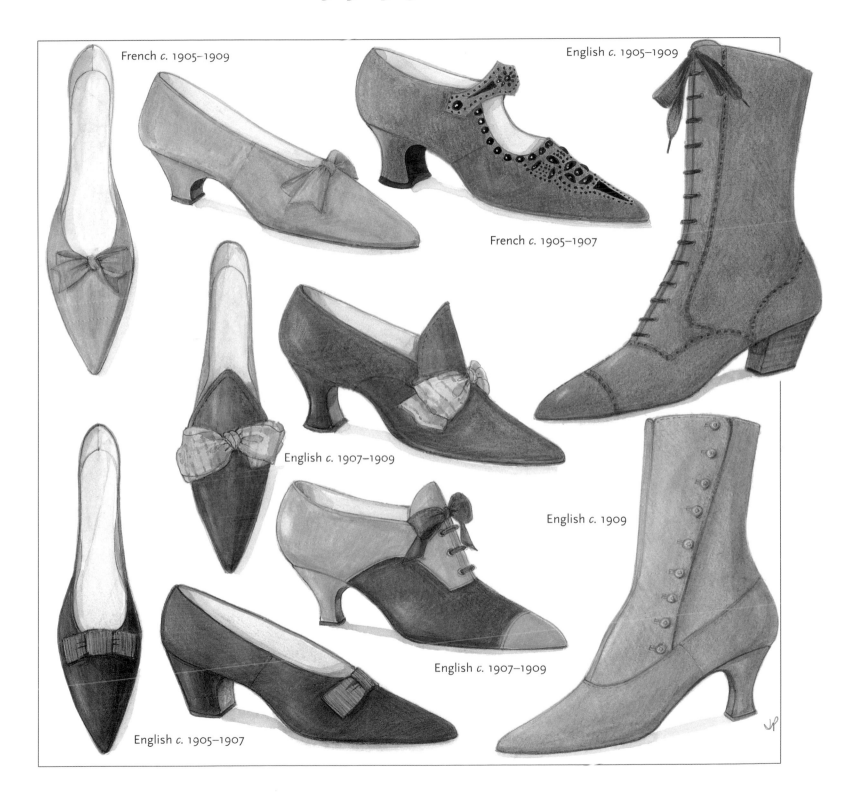

French c. 1905–1909

English c. 1905–1909

French c. 1905–1907

English c. 1907–1909

English c. 1909

English c. 1907–1909

English c. 1905–1907

Men's shoes and boots 1910–1919

American *c.* 1910–1919

English *c.* 1910–1919

English *c.* 1910–1919

English *c.* 1912–1915

English *c.* 1915–1919

American *c.* 1913–1919

American *c.* 1915–1919

English *c.* 1910–1919

Women's shoes and boots 1910–1914

English *c.* 1910

English *c.* 1910–1914

English *c.* 1910–1912

American *c.* 1910–1914

English *c.* 1910

American *c.* 1914

English *c.* 1914

French *c.* 1914

Women's shoes and boots 1915–1919

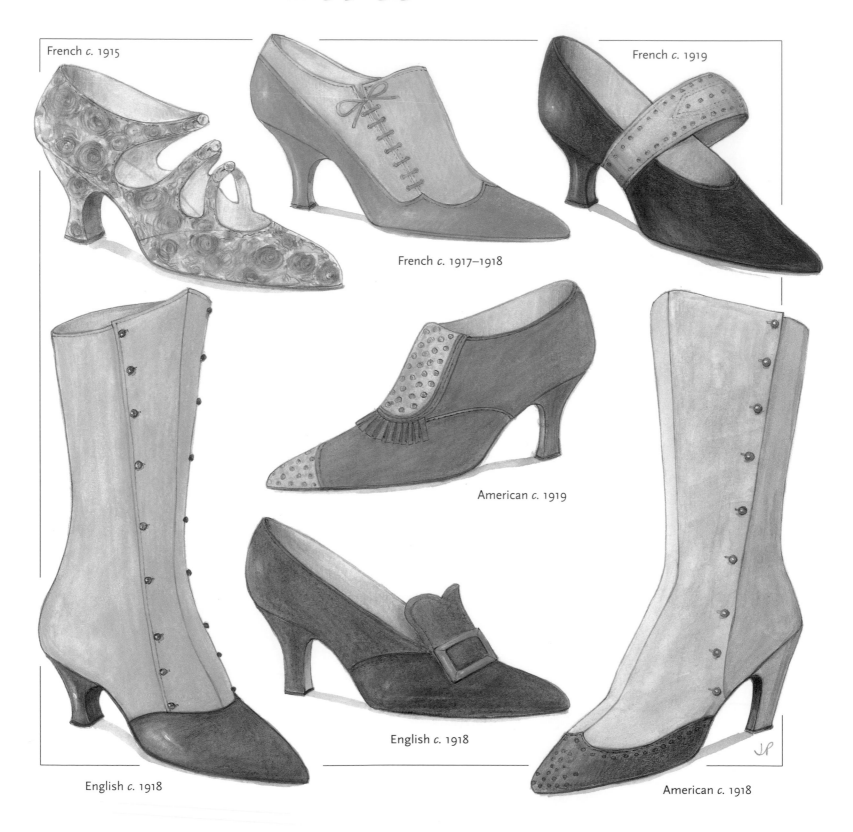

French *c.* 1915

French *c.* 1917–1918

French *c.* 1919

American *c.* 1919

English *c.* 1918

English *c.* 1918

American *c.* 1918

Men's shoes 1920–1929

American c. 1925

American c. 1928

American c. 1928–1929

French c. 1925–1926

English c. 1926

English c. 1928

English c. 1926–1928

English c. 1920–1922

American c. 1923

Women's boots 1920–1929

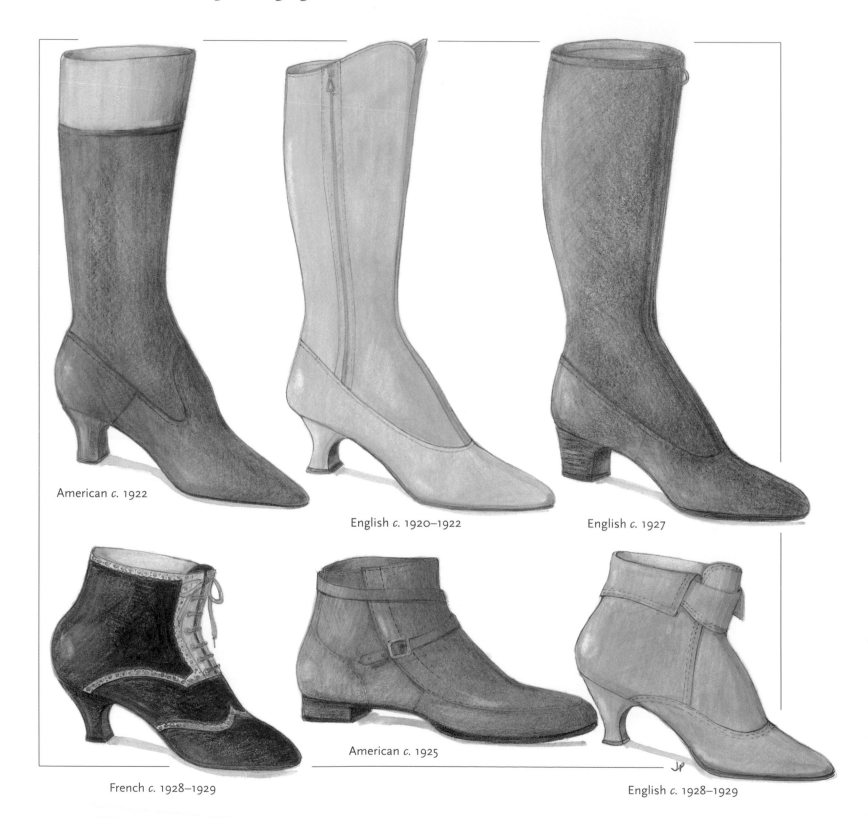

American *c.* 1922

English *c.* 1920–1922

English *c.* 1927

French *c.* 1928–1929

American *c.* 1925

English *c.* 1928–1929

Women's shoes 1920–1923

English *c.* 1920–1922

American *c.* 1920

English *c.* 1920–1921

English *c.* 1920–1922

English *c.* 1922

American *c.* 1922–1923

English *c.* 1920–1923

French *c.* 1922–1923

English *c.* 1921–1922

Women's shoes 1924–1926

American c. 1924

English c. 1924

French c. 1925

French c. 1924–1926

English c. 1925

French c. 1925

English c. 1925–1926

English c. 1925

Women's shoes 1927–1929

English c. 1927–1928

English c. 1929

American c. 1928–1929

American c. 1927–1929

American c. 1928–1929

English c. 1929

English c. 1927–1929

French c. 1928–1929

French c. 1929

Men's shoes 1930–1939

English c. 1930–1939

English c. 1938

English c. 1930–1939

English c. 1935

English
c. 1938–1939

English
c.1938

English c. 1935–1939

American c. 1937

American c. 1936–1939

English c. 1935–1939

English c. 1937–1939

English c. 1937–1939

Women's shoes 1930–1932

American *c.* 1932

English *c.* 1932

Swiss *c.* 1930

English *c.* 1932

English *c.* 1932

American *c.* 1931

American *c.* 1930

French *c.* 1932

Women's shoes 1933–1934

American c. 1933

English c. 1934

English c. 1934

English c. 1934

American c. 1934

English c. 1933

Swiss c. 1934

Austrian c. 1934

Women's shoes 1935–1936

French c. 1935–1936

American c. 1935

French c. 1936

English c. 1936

English c. 1935

American c. 1936

English c. 1935

English c. 1936

English c. 1936

Women's shoes and boots 1937–1939

English *c.* 1937

English *c.* 1937

English *c.* 1938

French *c.* 1939

American *c.* 1939

English *c.* 1938

English *c.* 1939

American *c.* 1938

American *c.* 1939

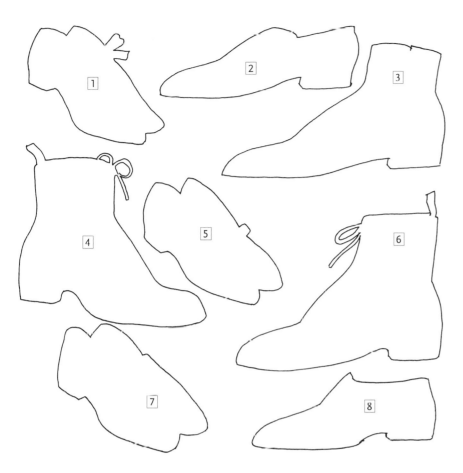

Men's shoes and boots 1900–1909

1 English c. 1903–1905. Leather soles, pointed toes, low stacked leather heels, calfskin uppers, toecaps with punched holes on seam edges matching other edges and seams, ribbon laces. 2 English c. 1900–1906. Leather sole, pointed toe, low stacked leather heel, calfskin upper, toecap with punched holes on seam edge, low-cut vamp, light-coloured matt kidskin ankle-length infill with side button fastening. 3 American c. 1900–1909. Leather sole, pointed toe, low stacked leather heel, calfskin upper, toecap with punched holes on seam edge, low-cut vamp, ankle-length pale-coloured matt kidskin infill with side press-stud fastening. 4 American c. 1905. Leather sole, blunt toe, high stacked leather heel, ankle-length leather upper, raised box toecap with punched holes on seam edge, laced over instep with hooks above, back pull tape. 5 English c. 1905–1909. Evening slippers with leather soles, pointed toes and low stacked leather heels, patent leather uppers, low-cut vamps decorated with flat petersham ribbon bows. 6 English c. 1900–1909. Cricket boot with leather sole, pointed toe and low stacked leather heel, ankle-length pale-coloured matt calfskin upper, toecap with punched holes on seam edge, laced over instep to ankle, back pull tape. 7 English c. 1900–1909. Leather soles, pointed toes, low stacked leather heels, suede uppers laced over instep. 8 English c. 1900–1909. Leather sole, pointed toe, low stacked leather heel, leather upper, toecap with punched holes on seam edge, topstitched strap over toes under laced fastening.

Women's shoes and boots 1900–1905

1 French c. 1900–1905. Leather sole, pointed toe, high patent-leather-covered Louis heel, matching upper with low-cut vamp, mid-calf-length matt kidskin infill, fastened from instep over full-length tongue with silk ribbon lace. 2 English c. 1903. Leather sole, pointed toe, low calfskin-covered heel, matching light-coloured upper with side button fastening from low vamp through contrast-colour strap. 3 English c. 1900–1903. Leather sole, pointed toe, high calfskin-covered Louis heel, matching mid-calf-length upper, edge of toecap piped with contrast colour, repeated on seams and on scalloped edge of side button fastening. 4 French c. 1900–1905. Leather sole, pointed toe, high silk-grosgrain-covered Louis heel, matching upper with low-cut vamp and four bar straps with button fastenings. 5 French c. 1905. Leather sole, pointed toe, high suede-covered Louis heel, matching upper, low-cut vamp trimmed with jewelled buckle. 6 English c. 1905. Leather sole, pointed toe, high calfskin-covered Louis heel, matching upper, low-cut vamp, buttoned bar strap with jewelled buckle over high tongue. 7 English c. 1900–1905. Leather sole, pointed toe, dark-coloured calfskin-covered heel, matching front part of upper, pale-coloured matt calfskin back part from wing seam under laced ribbon fastening to heel-back. 8 English c. 1900–1905. Leather sole, pointed toe, high calfskin-covered Louis heel, matching upper with bead trim under and around low vamp, repeated on buttoned bar strap. 9 English c. 1900–1905. House slipper with leather sole, pointed toe and small wedge heel, imported silk-satin upper with multicoloured silk embroidery. 10 French c. 1900–1905. Leather sole, pointed toe, high calfskin-covered Louis heel, matching mid-calf-length upper, inset gold-coloured calfskin side panels, front laced ribbon fastening from low vamp to scalloped top.

Women's shoes and boots 1905–1909

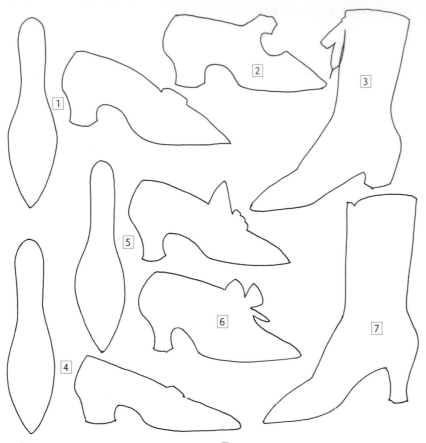

1 French c. 1905–1909. Evening shoes with leather soles, pointed toes and low silk-satin-covered heels, matching uppers, low-cut vamp trimmed with self-fabric bows. 2 French c. 1905–1907. Evening shoe with leather sole, pointed toe and thick low calfskin-covered Louis heel, matching upper, jet bead trim under and around low-cut vamp, repeated on shaped bar strap with jet button fastening. 3 English c. 1905–1909. Leather sole, pointed toe, medium-high stacked leather heel, mid-calf-length calfskin upper, toecap with punched holes on seam edge, repeated on other decorative seams, fastened over full-length tongue with wide ribbon lace. 4 English c. 1905–1907. Leather soles, pointed toes, low kidskin-covered heels, matching polished uppers, low-cut vamps trimmed with contrast-colour petersham ribbon bows. 5 English c. 1907–1909. House shoes with leather soles, pointed toes and high velvet-covered Louis heels, matching uppers trimmed with large striped silk taffeta bows set under high pointed tongues. 6 English c. 1907–1909. Leather sole, pointed toe, high calfskin-covered Louis heel, matching upper with contrast-colour inset panel from above toecap to under wing-shaped seam, fastening with wide silk ribbon lace over high instep with full-length pointed tongue. 7 English c. 1909. Leather sole, pointed toe, high calfskin-covered Louis heel, matching mid-calf-length upper, side button fastening from high vamp to under topstitched top edge, stitching repeated on other seams and edges.

Men's shoes and boots 1910–1919

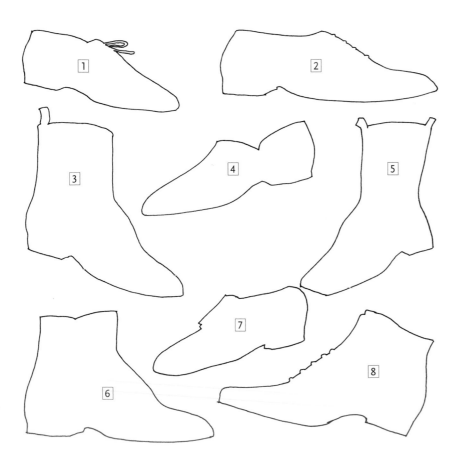

1 American c. 1910–1919. Leather sole, pointed toe, low stacked leather heel, pale-coloured polished calfskin upper, toecap with punched holes on seam edge, contrast-colour matt calfskin inset top with polished calfskin strap on each side of laced fastening. 2 English c. 1910–1919. Leather sole, pointed toe, low stacked leather heel, pale-coloured matt calfskin upper, contrast-colour polished calfskin winged toecap with punched holes on seam edge, matching heel-back seam, outer top edge and edge of shaped facings of laced fastening. 3 English c. 1912–1915. Leather sole, pointed toe, low stacked leather heel, polished calfskin upper with toecap, ankle-length cloth top with scallop-edged side button fastening, back pull tape. 4 English c. 1910–1919. House slipper with leather sole, pointed toe and low stacked leather heel, calfskin upper with high vamp and low sides. 5 English c. 1915–1919. Leather sole, square toe, low stacked leather heel, calfskin upper, toecap with punched holes on seam edge, matching seam from low vamp to heel-back, ankle-length top with elasticated gussets, front and back pull tapes. 6 American c. 1915–1919. Leather sole, pointed toe, low stacked leather heel, calfskin upper with toecap, ankle-length cloth top with side button fastening. 7 American c. 1913–1919. Leather sole, blunt toe, low stacked leather heel, calfskin upper, wing seam with punched holes on edge, matching other seams, laced fastening under extended turned-down fringed tongue. 8 English c. 1910–1919. Leather sole, square toe, low stacked leather heel, ankle-length calfskin upper with toecap, laced over instep with hooks above.

Women's shoes and boots 1910–1914

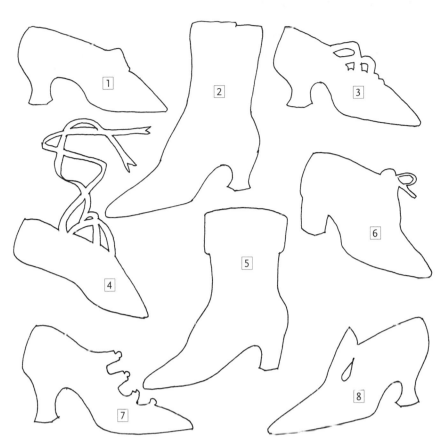

1 English c. 1910–1912. Leather sole, pointed toe, high calfskin-covered Louis heel, matching upper, low-cut vamp trimmed with jewelled square buckle. 2 English c. 1910. Leather sole, pointed toe, high calfskin-covered Louis heel, matching upper, mid-calf-length pale-coloured matt calfskin top with side button fastening. 3 English c. 1910–1914. Leather sole, pointed toe, medium-high calfskin-covered Louis heel, matching upper, low-cut vamp with scalloped front edge decorated with punched holes, crossed straps over instep, button fastening on one side. 4 American c. 1910–1914. Tango dancing pump with heelless thin leather sole, fine kidskin upper, low-cut vamp trimmed with a tiny bow matching colour of long ribbon ankle ties extending from each side of front and through metal rings on sides. 5 English c. 1910. Leather sole, pointed toe, thick medium-high calfskin-covered heel, matching upper with shaped toecap, ankle-length cloth top with side button fastening, deep Persian lamb cuff. 6 American c. 1914. Leather sole, pointed toe, medium-high stacked leather heel, polished calfskin upper, toecap with punched holes on seam edge, matching heel-back, top outer edge and strap on each side of laced fastening, pale-coloured matt calfskin panels on each side front. 7 English c. 1914. Leather sole, pointed toe, high calfskin-covered Louis heel, matching upper, low-cut vamp trimmed with gold-coloured glass button, repeated as fastenings and trim on three bar straps. 8 French c. 1914. Leather sole, pointed toe, high velvet-covered Louis heel, matching upper, wing seam and T-strap edged with lines of machine embroidery in contrasting colours.

Women's shoes and boots 1915–1919

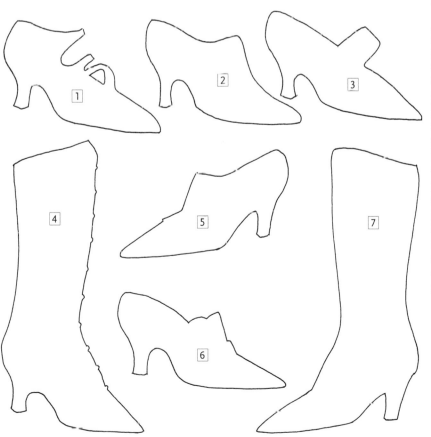

1 French c. 1915. Leather sole, pointed toe, high fabric-covered Louis heel, matching printed silk upper, low-cut vamp and two bar straps over instep fastened with self-covered buttons on centre front, matching ankle strap. 2 French c. 1917–1918. Leather sole, pointed toe, slender high calfskin-covered Louis heel, matching upper with low-cut scalloped vamp, pale-coloured calfskin infill, high instep, side laced fastening. 3 French c. 1919. Leather sole, pointed toe, high calfskin-covered Louis heel, matching upper with low-cut vamp, wide contrast-colour bar strap over instep with punched hole decoration. 4 English c. 1918. Leather sole, pointed toe, high calfskin-covered Louis heel, matching wing-shaped part of front upper, mid-calf-length light-coloured suede top with mock double-breasted button fastening. 5 American c. 1919. Leather sole, pointed toe, slender high calfskin-covered Louis heel, matching upper, contrast-colour calfskin toecap with all-over punched hole decoration, repeated on deep turned-down fringed tongue above high vamp. 6 English c. 1918. Leather sole, pointed toe, straight high calfskin-covered heel, matching upper, low-cut vamp decorated with large plain metal buckle under high Cupid's-bow-shaped tongue. 7 American c. 1918. Leather sole, pointed toe, straight high suede-covered heel, matching mid-calf-length upper with side button fastening, wing-shaped contrast-colour calfskin toecap decorated with punched hole pattern.

Men's shoes 1920–1929

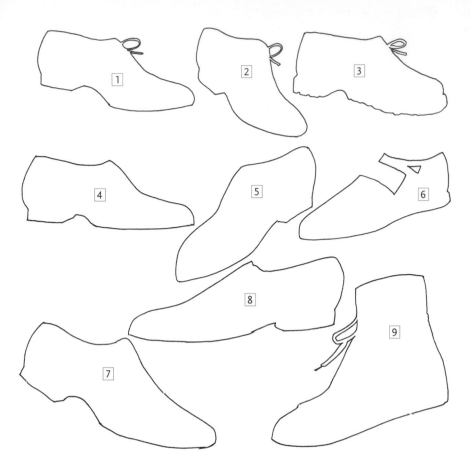

1 American c. 1925. Leather sole, pointed toe, low stacked leather heel, calfskin upper, toecap, decorative strap over toes, facings each side of laced fastening following same shape, heel-back, top outside edge and tongue all in dark colour, pale-colour infills.
2 American c. 1928. Leather sole, blunt toe, low stacked leather heel, pale-coloured calfskin upper with contrast-colour extended facings on each side of laced fastening.
3 American c. 1928–1929. Crepe sole with blunt toe and combined low heel, synthetic leather-look upper, wing seam with punched hole decoration matching other seams, laced fastening. 4 English c. 1926. Leather sole, blunt toe, low stacked leather heel, calfskin upper, toecap with punched hole pattern and edging, mock reptile panels, laced fastening. 5 French c. 1925–1926. Leather sole, pointed toe, low stacked leather heel, pale-coloured calfskin upper with dark-coloured calfskin inset from above wing seam to under laced fastening, dark colour repeated on heel-back. 6 English c. 1928. Beach sandal with thick rubber sole and combined low heel, moulded rubber upper with open sides, filled-in heel-back and buckled ankle strap. 7 English c. 1920–1922. Leather sole, pointed toe, low stacked leather heel, polished dark calfskin upper with white calfskin infill on sides between edges of filled-in heel-back and top edge of wing seam, punched hole decoration, laced fastening above dark tongue. 8 English c. 1926–1928. Leather sole, pointed toe, low stacked leather heel, calfskin toecap, facings of laced fastening, matching tongue, decorative side straps and lower part of heel-back. 9 American c. 1923. Sports boot with moulded rubber sole and combined heel, matching blunt toecap and ankle guard, ankle-length canvas upper, leather facings to laced fastening over full-length canvas tongue.

Women's boots 1920–1929

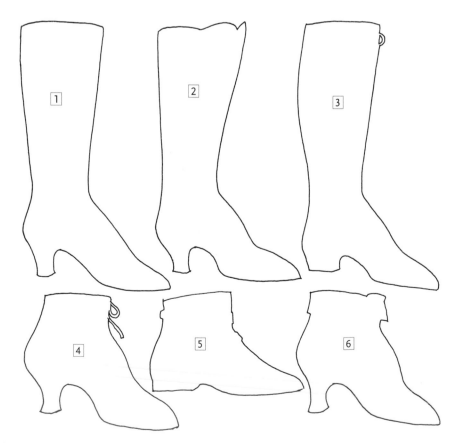

1 American c. 1922. Leather sole, pointed toe, high calfskin-covered heel, matching upper with seamed golosh and high pointed tongue over high instep, knee-length fitted leg with matt calfskin contrast-colour deep cuff. 2 English c. 1920–1922. Leather sole, pointed toe, high calfskin-covered Louis heel, matching upper with seamed and topstitched golosh, long fitted leg shaped over knee at front, side zip fastening. 3 English c. 1927. Leather sole, blunt toe, medium-high stacked leather heel, calfskin upper with seamed and topstitched golosh, knee-length fitted leg, centre front zip fastening. 4 French c. 1928–1929. Leather sole, pointed toe, high calfskin-covered Louis heel, matching ankle-length upper, wing seam with punched hole decoration highlighted in pale colour, repeated on other seams, edges and facings to laced fastening above dark tongue. 5 American c. 1925. Riding boot with leather sole, blunt toe and low stacked leather heel, ankle-length calfskin upper with stitched apron front, single narrow strap from centre of heel-back crossed over instep and buckled on one side above concealed zip fastening. 6 English c. 1928–1929. Leather sole, pointed toe, high calfskin-covered Louis heel, matching ankle-length upper with topstitched wing seam, matching edges of high tongue, wide turned-down cuff and centre front collar.

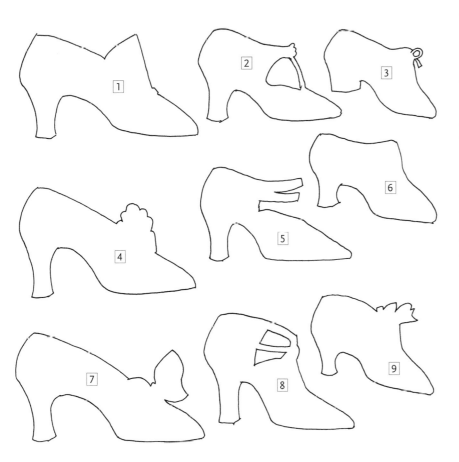

Women's shoes 1920–1923

1 English c. 1920–1922. Leather sole, pointed toe, high calfskin-covered heel, matching upper with decorative strap and buckle trim under high tongue, punched decoration on centre of tongue, matching design above toe, topstitched edges and seams. 2 American c. 1920. Leather sole, pointed toe, high calfskin-covered heel, matching upper with open sides, low-cut vamp with openwork decoration over brightly coloured kidskin lining, repeated around top outside edge and on upper part of T-strap with jewelled buckle fastening on centre front. 3 English c. 1920–1921. Leather sole, pointed toe, low calfskin-covered heel, matching upper with full brogue decoration, laced fastening over high instep. 4 English c. 1920–1922. Leather sole, pointed toe, high calfskin-covered heel, matching upper, low-cut vamp with high fan-shaped quilted tongue under plain metal buckle. 5 English c. 1922. Leather sole, pointed toe, high calfskin-covered heel, matching upper with low-cut vamp, open sides and two ankle straps with side button fastenings. 6 American c. 1922–1923. Leather sole, pointed toe, medium-high calfskin-covered Louis heel, matching upper, high vamp trimmed with stripes of contrast-colour grosgrain ribbon, elasticated side gussets. 7 English c. 1920–1923. Leather sole, pointed toe, high calfskin-covered heel, matching upper, low-cut vamp with large silk taffeta bow trim. 8 French c. 1922–1923. Leather sole, pointed toe, high fabric-covered heel, matching silk-satin upper with open sides, contrast-colour cross-over straps with single side button fastening attached to high vamp. 9 English c. 1921–1922. Leather sole, pointed toe, high suede-covered heel, matching upper with satin ribbon laced fastening over high pointed tongue.

Women's shoes 1924–1926

1 American c. 1924. Leather sole, pointed toe, high suede-covered heel, matching upper heel-back and wide bar strap with jewelled half-buckle, patent leather front upper. 2 English c. 1924. Leather sole, pointed toe, low patent-leather-covered heel, matching upper, low-cut vamp trimmed with wide gold-coloured kidskin, matching bar strap with single side button fastening and matching edges of heel-back. 3 French c. 1925. Leather sole, pointed toe, high gold-coloured kidskin heel, matching double T-straps, bindings and trim on open-sided brocade upper. 4 French c. 1924–1926. Leather sole, pointed toe, high silk-covered heel, matching open-sided upper, low vamp trimmed with gold-coloured silk brocade, repeated on heel-back, on buttoned ankle strap and behind heel. 5 English c. 1925. Leather sole, pointed toe, low velvet-covered heel, matching open-sided upper, low-cut vamp bound and trimmed with gold-coloured kidskin, matching three-strand bar strap and bound heel-back. 6 French c. 1925. Leather sole, pointed toe, high silk-covered heel, matching open-sided upper, low-cut vamp trimmed and bound with gold-coloured kidskin, repeated on two link straps and heel-back. 7 English c. 1925–1926. Leather sole, pointed toe, high lizard-skin-covered heel, matching open-sided upper, low-cut vamp and T-strap with side button fastening. 8 English c. 1925. Leather sole, pointed toe, low reptile-skin-covered heel, matching toecap, wide bindings and trim on matt calfskin upper.

Women's shoes 1927–1929

1 English c. 1927–1928. Leather sole, pointed toe, high hand-painted-calfskin heel, matching open-sided upper, low-cut vamp with plain-coloured bound edge, matching vertical linking straps to ankle strap with buckled fastening and edges of heel-back.
2 English c. 1929. Leather sole, pointed toe, straight high suede-covered heel, matching upper, edges bound in contrast-colour calfskin, laced fastening over matching high pointed tongue and apron front. 3 American c. 1928–1929. Leather sole, pointed toe, high gold calfskin-covered heel, open-sided velvet upper, gold calfskin open toe strap cut in one with scalloped central strap with cut-out decoration, repeated on edge of heel-back, velvet ankle strap with metal buckle. 4 American c. 1927–1929. Leather sole, pointed toe, high calfskin-covered heel, matching open-sided upper, edges of low-cut vamp piped in contrast colour, repeated on scalloped upper edges of heel-back, ankle strap and inset decoration above toes. 5 American c. 1928–1929. Leather sole, pointed toe, high silk-covered Louis-style heel, matching open-sided upper, buttoned T-strap above joined shaped straps over toes with open centres, edges piped in gold kidskin. 6 English c. 1929. Leather sole, pointed toe, high calfskin-covered heel, open-sided calfskin upper with low-cut vamp, scalloped top edge to heel-back and buckled ankle strap, contrast-colour calfskin scalloped toecap and matching base to heel-back. 7 English c. 1927–1929. Leather sole, pointed toe, high calfskin-covered heel, matching upper, low-cut vamp trimmed with metal buckle. 8 French c. 1928–1929. Leather sole, pointed toe, high calfskin-covered heel, matching upper, wide contrast-colour suede strap over instep with punched hole decoration. 9 French c. 1929. Leather sole with pointed toe and high glacé-kid-covered Louis-style heel, matching upper, inset bands of contrast-colour calfskin with punched hole decoration above low-cut vamp and behind heel back.

Men's shoes 1930–1939

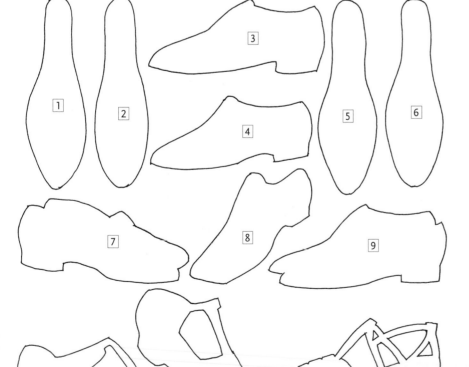

1 English c. 1938. Leather sole, pointed toe, low stacked leather heel, matt suede upper with calfskin toecap, facings to laced fastening and tongue, punched hole decoration to edges and seams. 2 English c. 1930–1939. Leather sole, pointed toe, low stacked leather heel, calfskin upper with laced fastening above winged seam, punched hole decoration on edge, matching pattern above toe. 3 English c. 1930–1939. Leather sole, blunt toe, low stacked leather heel, textured calfskin upper with toecap and laced fastening. 4 English c. 1935. Leather sole, pointed toe, low stacked leather heel, canvas upper, calfskin toecap, heel-back, strap under matching facings of laced fastening. 5 English c. 1938–1939. Moulded rubber sole with blunt toe and combined low heel, calfskin upper with laced fastening above apron front. 6 English c. 1938. Leather sole, blunt toe, low stacked leather heel, calfskin upper with wrap-over buckled strap. 7 English c. 1935–1939. Leather soles, blunt toes, low stacked leather heels, suede uppers with shaped straps over high tongues, apron fronts, topstitched edges and detail. 8 American c. 1937. Leather sole, square toe, low stacked leather heel, suede upper with wing seam from above toe, laced fastening, topstitched edges and detail. 9 American c. 1936–1939. Leather soles, pointed toes, low stacked leather heels, glacé kid uppers with contrast-colour calfskin panels set between wing seams, heel-backs and laced fastenings. 10 English c. 1935–1939. Leather sole, blunt toe, low stacked leather heel, calfskin open-sided upper with cut-out pattern on sides of front and buckled T-strap. 11 English c. 1937–1939. Crepe sole with blunt toe and combined low heel, open-sided matt calfskin upper with cut-out pattern on front and buckled T-strap. 12 English c. 1937–1939. Leather sole, blunt toe, low stacked leather heel, open-sided calfskin upper with narrow central strap running from piked toe under wrap-over front with cut-out decoration on one side to buckled bar strap over instep, matching strap around heel secured by single vertical strap from behind heel.

Women's shoes 1930–1932

1 English c. 1932. Leather sole, blunt toe, high stacked leather heel, calfskin upper, low-cut vamp with fringed calfskin tongue, punched hole decoration and trim.
2 American c. 1932. Leather sole, blunt toe, high stacked leather heel, matt calfskin upper with punched hole decoration, matching trim on contrast-colour polished calfskin heel-back and strap over toes. 3 English c. 1932. Leather sole, blunt toe, high calfskin-covered heel, matching upper, high flared tongue with topstitched trim from under narrow strap with punched hole decoration over low-cut vamp. 4 Swiss c. 1930. Leather sole, pointed toe, high gold calfskin-covered heel, coloured calfskin upper with low-cut sides and vamp, gold calfskin buttoned T-strap, matching straps over front with decorative embroidered spots between straps, strap detail repeated on heel-back.
5 American c. 1931. Leather sole, pointed toe, slender high velvet-covered heel, matching sideless upper with fine silk cord threaded through channels on top outside edges of cut-out sides of heel-back, crossed over instep and continued through channels on vamp edges with matching cut-out detail, cord tied on front at ankle-level. 6 English c. 1932. Leather sole, pointed toe, high matt-calfskin-covered heel, matching upper, low-cut vamp and shaped sides with contrast-colour piping, polished calfskin motif on side-front of heel-back and on edge of front laced ankle strap. 7 American c. 1930. Beach sandal with crepe sole comprised of blunt toe and combined low heel, crossed striped canvas straps over instep, matching cut-away heel-back and side-buttoned ankle strap. 8 French c. 1932. Leather sole, pointed toe, slender high matt-calfskin-covered heel, matching upper with low-cut vamp and front edge of heel-back trimmed with snakeskin, matching connecting strap between open side and buckled ankle strap.

Women's shoes 1933–1934

1 American c. 1933. Leather sole, blunt toe, high silk-covered heel, matching front upper trimmed with narrow straps of gold-coloured kidskin, matching buckled T-strap and heel strap. 2 English c. 1934. Leather sole, blunt toe, high calfskin-covered heel, matching upper with low-cut scalloped vamp, narrow straps over instep tied with leather-trimmed laces, punched hole decoration on edges and detail. 3 English c. 1934. Leather sole, blunt toe, high calfskin-covered heel, matching upper from heel-back to low-cut vamp, matt calfskin front under scalloped wing seam, piped edges and seams in contrast colour. 4 English c. 1934. Crepe sole with blunt toe and combined low heel, calfskin upper with punched hole decoration and cut-out detail on sides and front over coloured lining, tasselled leather laces through scalloped front edges.
5 American c. 1934. Leather soles, blunt toes, high silver calfskin heels, embroidered brocade uppers with silver and gold calfskin asymmetric sunray striped trim on outer edge from back to low-cut vamp on one side and from front heel-back over open side to vamp on the other. 6 English c. 1933. Heelless leather and rope sole, wide spotted cotton strap over instep, matching carrier above with ribbon lace, metal ring on each side of sole to secure ribbon for fastening around ankle. 7 Swiss c. 1934. Leather sole, blunt toe, low stacked leather heel, striped canvas crossed straps over instep, matching side carriers and buckled ankle strap. 8 Austrian c. 1934. Hinged wooden sole with pointed toe and combined medium-high heel, striped canvas strap over toes with bound edges and cord fastening, matching side carriers and buckled ankle strap.

Women's shoes 1935–1936

1 American c. 1935. Leather sole, blunt toe, gold slender high calfskin-covered heel, matching asymmetric strap over toes, bar strap over instep and narrow heel strap. 2 French c. 1935–1936. Leather sole, blunt toe, slender high calfskin-covered heel, matching upper, low-cut vamp trimmed with large snakeskin buckle. 3 French c. 1936. Leather sole, blunt toe, slender high silk-grosgrain-covered heel, matching sideless upper, low-cut vamp with cut-out side detail, wide ankle strap with large jewelled buckle. 4 American c. 1936. Leather sole, blunt toe, slender high brocade-covered heel, matching ankle-length upper, cut-out detail over instep with button trim, open toe, buckle fastening behind heel at ankle-level. 5 English c. 1936. Leather sole, blunt toe, thick high calfskin-covered heel and matching platform, upper with low-cut vamp edged in silver and gold calfskin, repeated on cross-over buckled ankle strap. 6 English c. 1935. Leather sole, blunt toe, high calfskin-covered heel, matching front upper with all-over punched hole decoration under wing seam, matt calfskin to heel-back. 7 English c. 1935. Leather sole, blunt toe, high calfskin-covered heel, matching upper, contrast-colour flared tongue set under narrow strap on low-cut vamp narrowing to toe end. 8 English c. 1936. Leather sole, blunt toe, low stacked leather heel, matt calfskin sideless upper with topstitched vertical strap over open toe and under matching horizontal strap joining combined buckled T-strap, filled-in heel-back. 9 English c. 1936. Leather sole, blunt toe, high stacked leather heel, calfskin upper with low-cut vamp and inset serpentine panel of matt calfskin on front and sides.

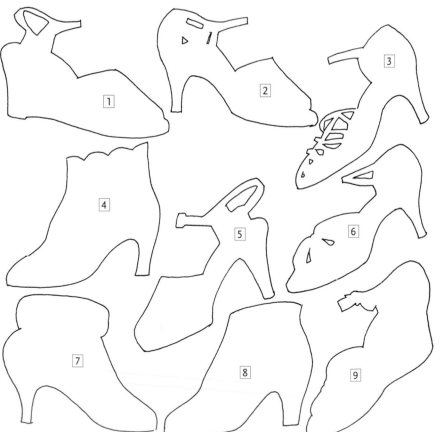

Women's shoes and boots 1937–1939

1 English c. 1937. Leather sole, blunt toe, high calfskin-covered wedge heel and matching platform, sideless upper with low-cut vamp and open toe, buckled ankle strap through side carriers. 2 English c. 1937. Leather sole, blunt toe, high gold calfskin-covered heel and matching platform, sideless upper comprised of silver calfskin side straps attached to central panel of joined gold calfskin straps, silver calfskin heel-back with cut-out side panels and buckled ankle strap. 3 English c. 1938. Leather sole, blunt toe, slender high silver calfskin-covered heel and matching platform, sideless upper with fine straps over toes, filled-in heel-back and buckled ankle strap. 4 French c. 1939. Leather sole, blunt toe, high calfskin-covered heel, matching upper with low-cut vamp seam, matt calfskin boot top with scalloped edge and side button fastening. 5 American c. 1939. Leather sole, blunt toe, high suede-covered heel and matching deep platform with contrast-colour inset piping, sideless upper with low-cut vamp and two-colour buckled ankle strap through wide side carriers. 6 English c. 1938. Leather sole, blunt toe, slender high silk-covered heel and matching deep platform, sideless upper with two wide straps ruched together under central knot, filled-in heel-back and buckled ankle strap. 7 English c. 1939. Leather sole, blunt toe, high suede-covered heel, matching ankle-length upper with dyed Persian lamb cuff and side zip fastening. 8 American c. 1938. Leather sole, blunt toe, thick calfskin-covered heel and matching deep platform, ankle-length suede upper with decorative strap and buckle on side-back top edge and concealed side zip fastening. 9 American c. 1939. Leather sole, blunt toe, high silk-covered wedge heel and matching platform, sideless upper, front with low-cut vamp and open toe ruched in centre under narrow self-fabric strap, ruching repeated under decorative bow fastening on filled-in heel-back.

Men's shoes 1940–1949

English c. 1945–1949

English c. 1945–1949

American c. 1946–1949

American c. 1945–1949

English c. 1940–1949

American c. 1940–1949

English c. 1946–1949

American c. 1948

English c. 1943–1949

French c. 1943–1946

American c. 1948

Women's shoes and boots 1940–1942

American *c.* 1942

English *c.* 1940

English *c.* 1940–1941

English *c.* 1940–1942

English *c.* 1940

English *c.* 1942

English *c.* 1942

English *c.* 1942

American *c.* 1941

Women's shoes 1943–1944

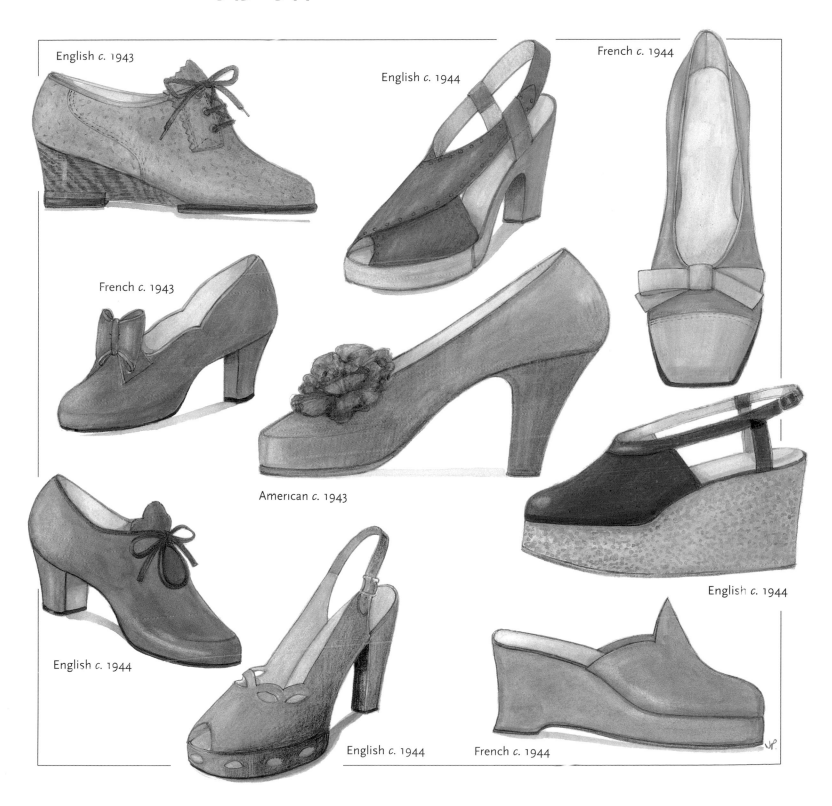

English c. 1943

English c. 1944

French c. 1944

French c. 1943

American c. 1943

English c. 1944

English c. 1944

English c. 1944

French c. 1944

Women's shoes 1945–1946

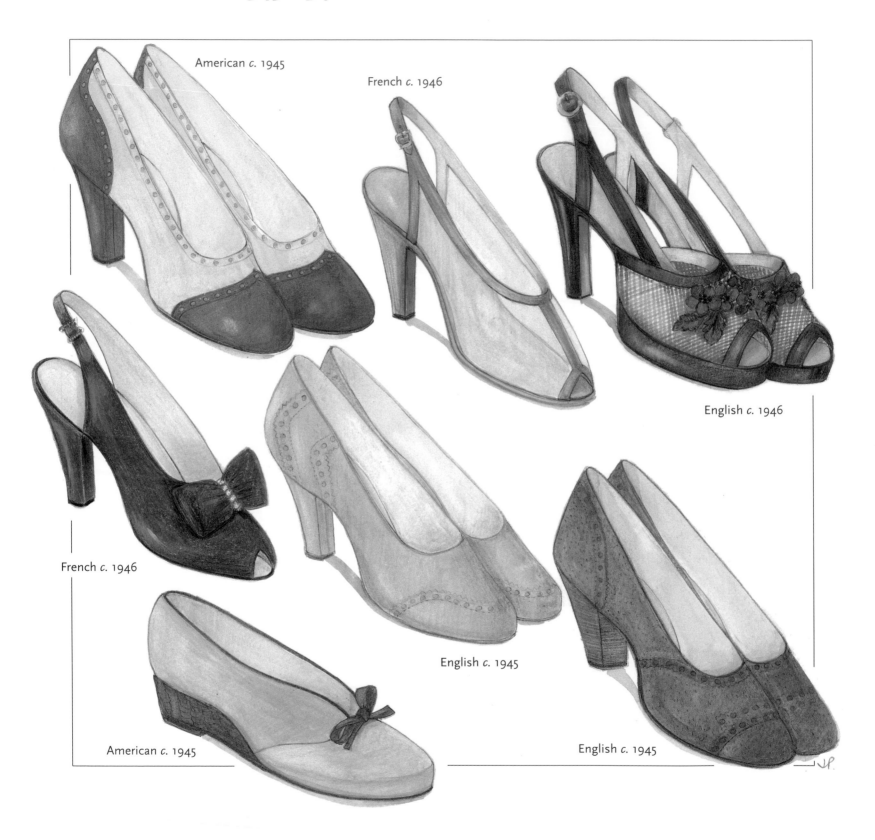

American *c.* 1945

French *c.* 1946

English *c.* 1946

French *c.* 1946

English *c.* 1945

American *c.* 1945

English *c.* 1945

Women's shoes 1947–1949

English *c.* 1947

English *c.* 1949

American *c.* 1948

English *c.* 1949

American *c.* 1949

English *c.* 1948

English *c.* 1947

French *c.* 1949

English *c.* 1949

Men's shoes 1950–1959

English *c.* 1950–1955

English *c.* 1957–1959

English *c.* 1950–1955

American *c.* 1956–1959

English *c.* 1950–1953

English
c. 1950–1953

English *c.* 1959

English *c.* 1959

American *c.* 1956–1959

Women's shoes 1950–1952

English c. 1950

English c. 1952

English c. 1952

French c. 1952

American c. 1952

English c. 1950

American c. 1951

English c. 1950

English c. 1952

Women's shoes and boots 1953–1954

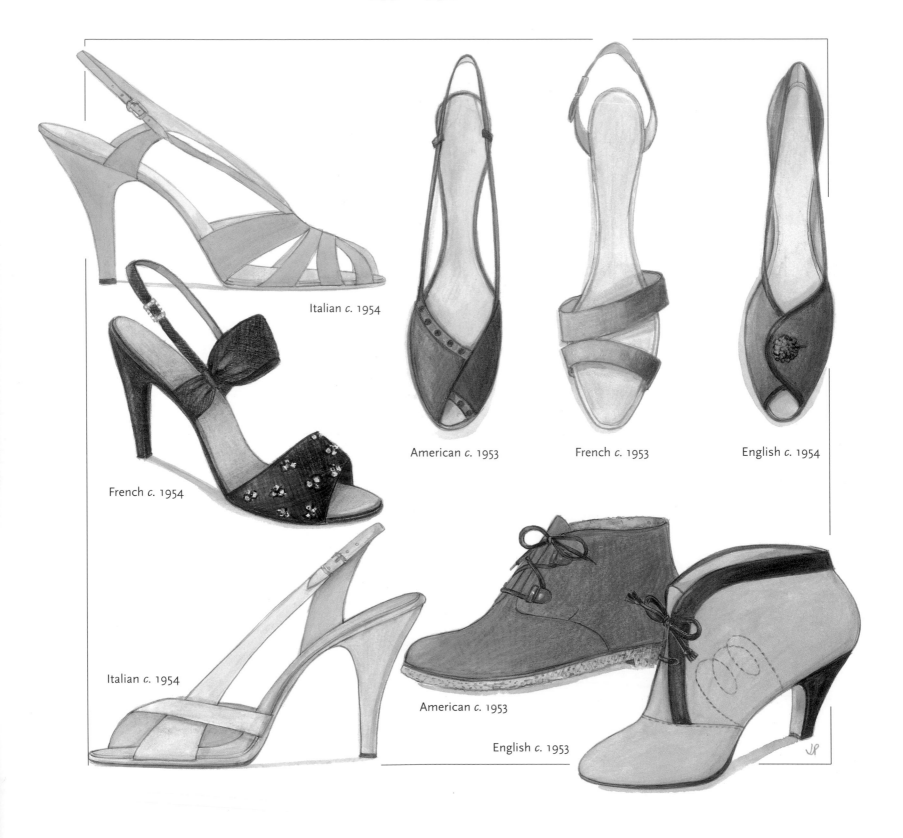

Italian *c.* 1954

French *c.* 1954

Italian *c.* 1954

American *c.* 1953

French *c.* 1953

English *c.* 1954

American *c.* 1953

English *c.* 1953

Women's shoes 1955–1956

American *c.* 1955

English *c.* 1956

American *c.* 1955

Italian *c.* 1955

English *c.* 1956

Italian *c.* 1956

English *c.* 1955

Italian *c.* 1955

Women's shoes 1957–1959

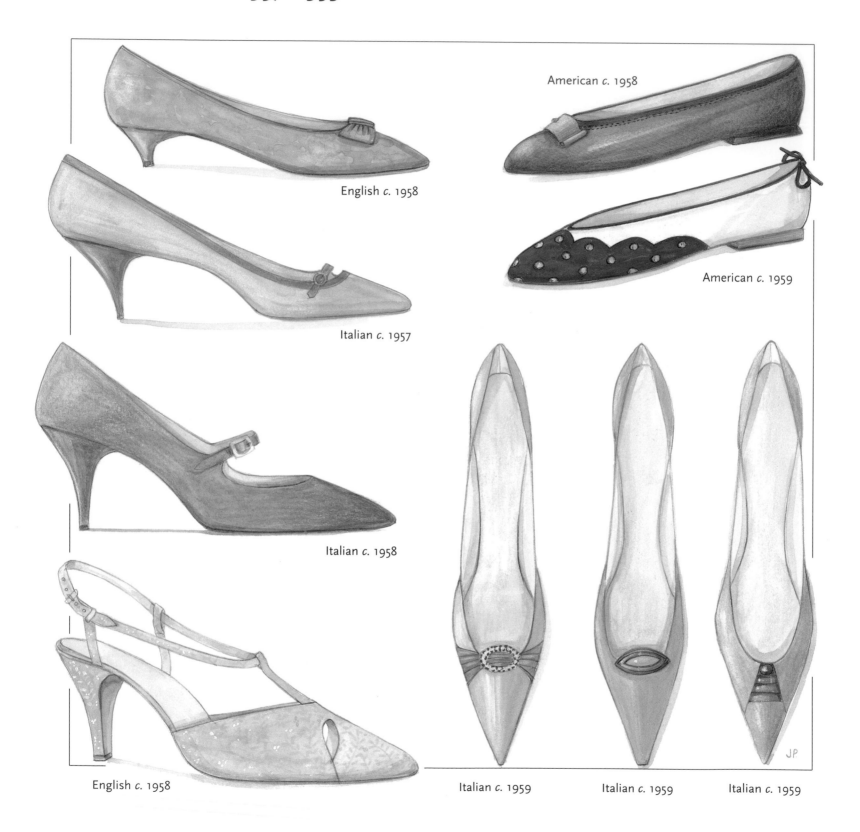

American c. 1958

English c. 1958

Italian c. 1957

American c. 1959

Italian c. 1958

English c. 1958

Italian c. 1959

Italian c. 1959

Italian c. 1959

Men's shoes and boots 1960–1969

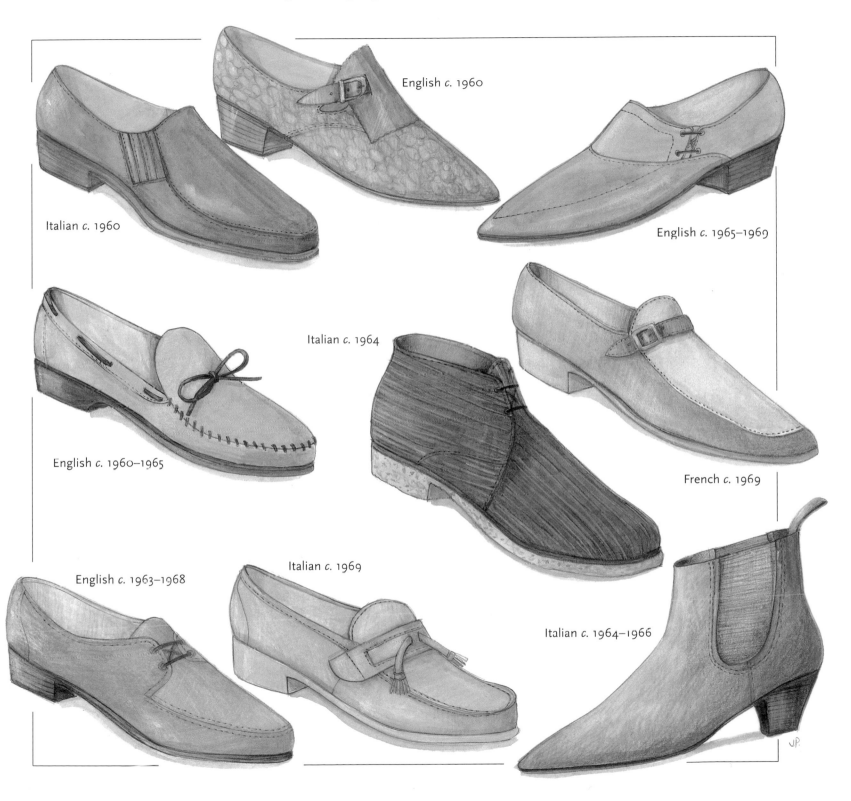

English c. 1960

Italian c. 1960

English c. 1965–1969

Italian c. 1964

English c. 1960–1965

French c. 1969

English c. 1963–1968

Italian c. 1969

Italian c. 1964–1966

Women's shoes 1960–1962

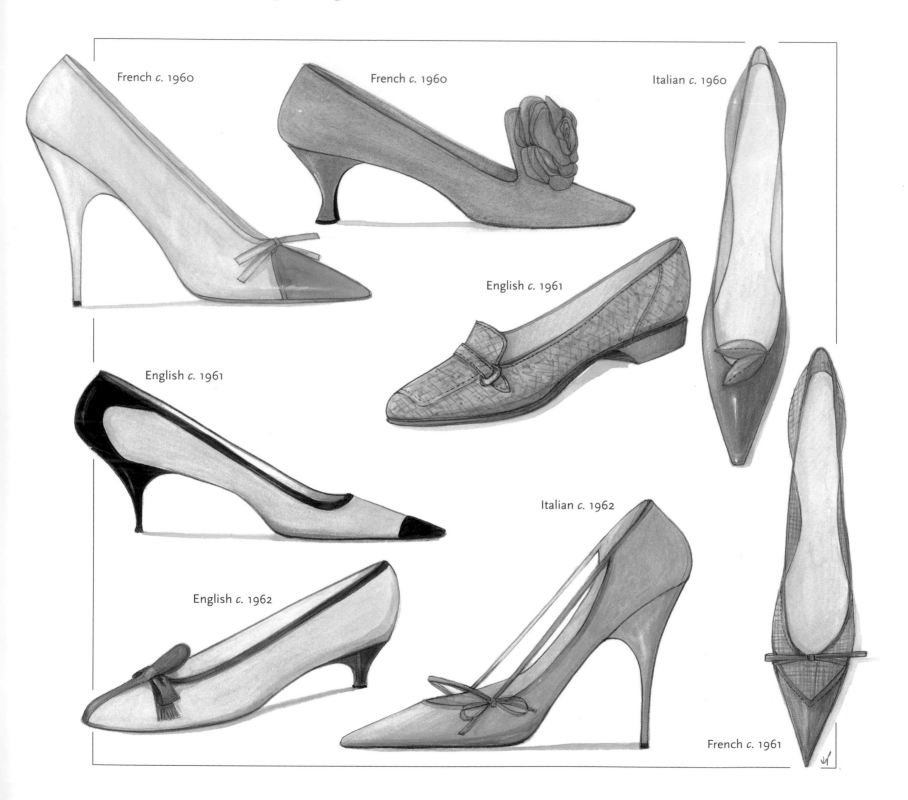

French *c.* 1960

French *c.* 1960

Italian *c.* 1960

English *c.* 1961

English *c.* 1961

Italian *c.* 1962

English *c.* 1962

French *c.* 1961

Women's shoes 1963–1964

English *c.* 1964

French *c.* 1963

English *c.* 1964

Italian *c.* 1963

English *c.* 1964

English *c.* 1963

French *c.* 1963

English *c.* 1963

Italian *c.* 1964

Women's shoes 1965–1966

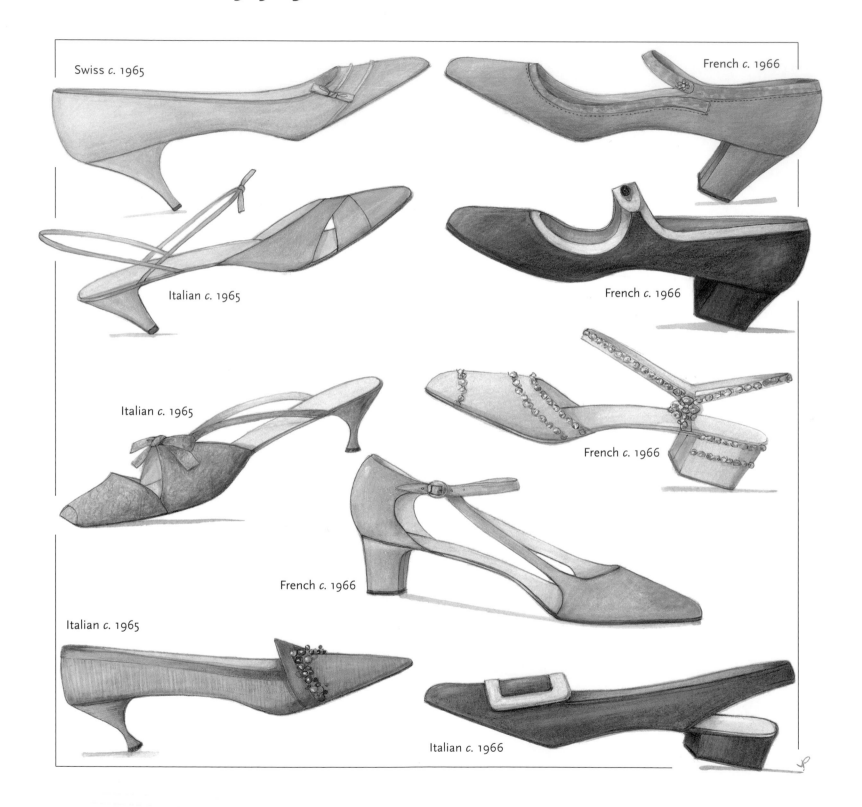

Swiss *c.* 1965

French *c.* 1966

Italian *c.* 1965

French *c.* 1966

Italian *c.* 1965

French *c.* 1966

French *c.* 1966

Italian *c.* 1965

Italian *c.* 1966

Women's shoes 1967–1969

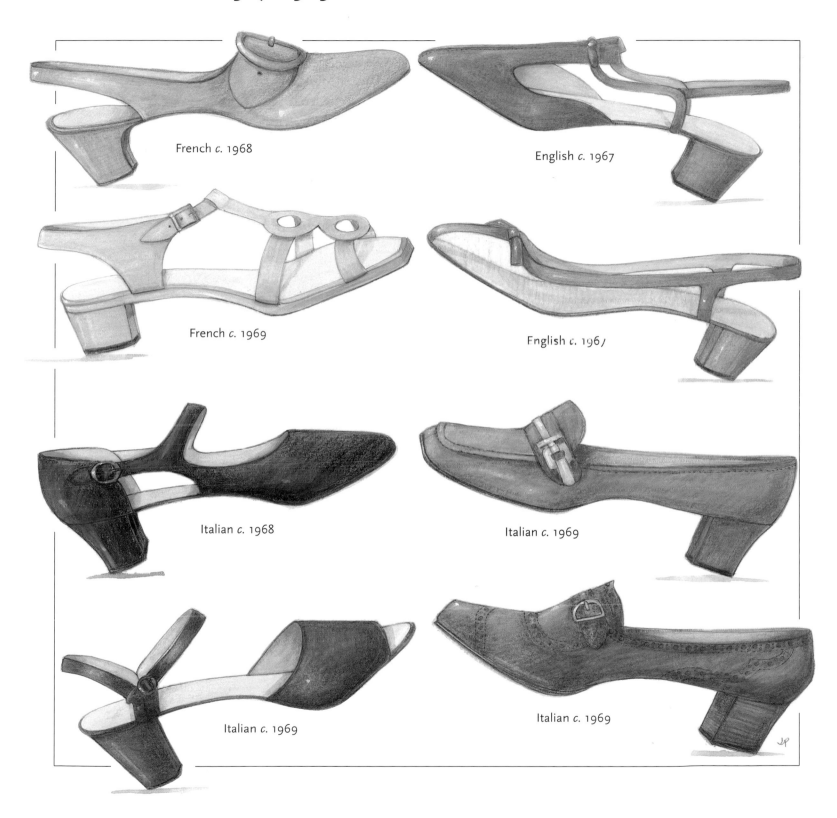

French c. 1968

English c. 1967

French c. 1969

English c. 1967

Italian c. 1968

Italian c. 1969

Italian c. 1969

Italian c. 1969

Women's boots 1960–1969

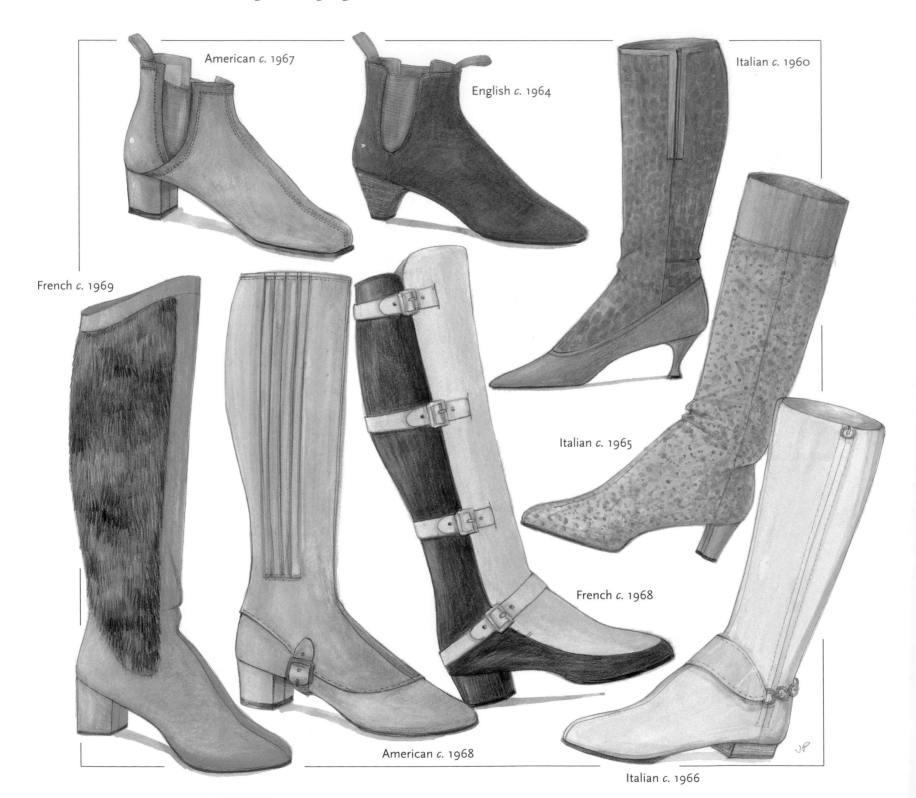

American *c.* 1967

English *c.* 1964

Italian *c.* 1960

French *c.* 1969

Italian *c.* 1965

French *c.* 1968

American *c.* 1968

Italian *c.* 1966

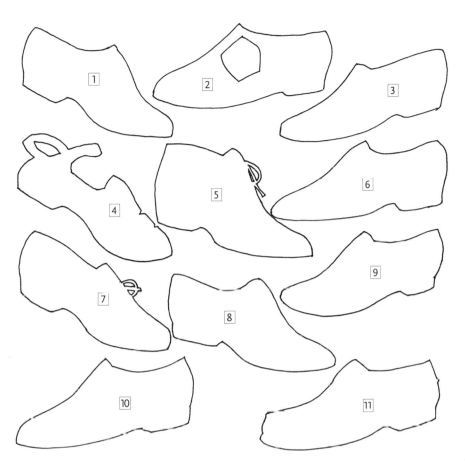

Men's shoes 1940–1949

1 English c. 1945–1949. Leather sole, blunt toe, low stacked leather heel, grained calfskin upper with apron front under laced fastening, topstitched edges and detail.
2 English c. 1945–1949. Crepe sole with blunt toe and combined low heel, sideless calfskin upper, openwork design over front on buckled T-strap and on side heel-back.
3 American c. 1946–1949. Leather sole, blunt toe, low stacked leather heel, calfskin upper with contrast-colour apron front, combined tongue and bound edges, topstitched detail. 4 American c. 1945–1949. Leather sole, blunt toe, low stacked leather heel, sideless calfskin upper with open toe and cut-out design on sides, decorative buckled strap threaded through short tongue, matching ankle strap.
5 American c. 1940–1949. Crepe sole with blunt toe and combined low heel, ankle-length suede upper, laced fastening above high tongue, topstitched edges and detail.
6 English c. 1940–1949. Leather sole, blunt toe, low stacked leather heel, textured calfskin upper, toecap with perforated detail, laced fastening. 7 American c. 1948. Leather sole, blunt toe, low stacked leather heel, calfskin upper with combined apron front and tongue, sides with threaded leather thong, matching bow trim on front.
8 English c. 1943–1949. Leather sole, blunt toe, low stacked leather heel, calfskin upper, plain front, laced above high tongue. 9 American c. 1946–1949. Leather sole, blunt toe, low stacked leather heel, calfskin upper, snakeskin front under wing seam, matching heel-back, laced fastening. 10 French c. 1943–1946. Rubber sole with blunt toe and combined low heel, calfskin upper with perforated decoration on side panels, laced fastening. 11 American c. 1948. Rubber sole with blunt toe and combined low heel, suede upper with raised and topstitched seam on apron front, matching dart on heel-back, laced fastening.

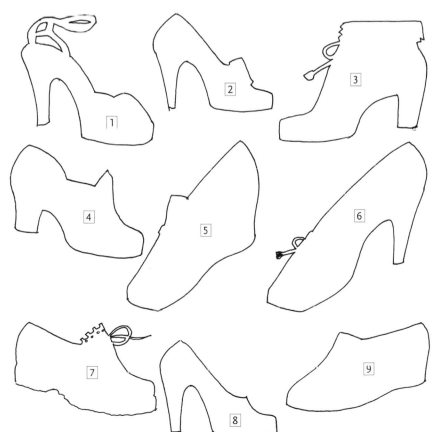

Women's shoes and boots 1940–1942

1 American c. 1942. Leather sole, blunt toe, high suede-covered heel and deep platform, matching sideless upper, low-cut V-shaped vamp, cut-out side detail and open toe, side carriers with buckled ankle strap. 2 English c. 1940. Leather sole, blunt toe, high calfskin-covered heel and decorative brass studded tongue on high vamp, suede upper with box toe. 3 English c. 1940–1941. Leather sole with blunt toe, medium-high suede-covered heel, matching lower part of upper and ankle-length cuff, each with crenellated edges, and laces above pale-coloured leather body. 4 English c. 1940. Leather sole, blunt toe, medium-high calfskin-covered heel, matching nail-decorated platform and upper with elasticated side panels. 5 English c. 1940–1942. Leather sole with square toe, calfskin-covered wedge heel and combined platform, matching elongated turned-down tongue stitched down over box toe, contrast-colour leather body and buckled strap over instep. 6 English c. 1942. Leather sole, square toe, high calfskin-covered heel, matching upper with bow trim on pale-coloured calfskin combined tongue and apron front, pale-coloured inset side panels. 7 English c. 1942. Crepe sole with blunt toe and combined low heel, calfskin upper with apron front, crenellated edges and perforated decoration, matching tongue under leather laces, topstitched edges and detail. 8 English c. 1942. Leather sole with blunt toe, high calfskin-covered heel, matching upper with high vamp, outer edges bound with snakeskin, deep box toe. 9 American c. 1941. Leather sole, blunt toe, calfskin-covered wedge heel and combined platform, matching piped edges and fringed laces on side opening of contrast-colour calfskin upper.

Women's shoes 1943–1944

1 English c. 1943. Leather sole, blunt toe, high polished wood wedge heel, textured calfskin upper, high tongue with crenellated edge, matching edges of facings to laced fastening. 2 English c. 1944. Hinged wooden platform sole and combined high heel, wide calfskin straps from front sides, crossing over instep, forming open toe, narrowing through side carriers to behind heel, perforated decoration. 3 French c. 1944. Leather sole with square toe, pale-coloured calfskin box toecap, bow trim and piped edges, contrast-colour matt calfskin body. 4 French c. 1943. Leather sole with blunt toe, high suede-covered heel, matching upper with box toe, scalloped edges and edges of large stand-up bow piped with contrast colour. 5 American c. 1943. Leather sole with blunt toe, high calfskin-covered heel and matching shallow platform, upper with box toe and large rosette above low-cut vamp. 6 English c. 1944. Leather sole, blunt toe, high cork wedge heel and combined platform, sideless calfskin upper, stitched strap over edge of high vamp, through side carriers to buckled fastening on heel-back. 7 English c. 1944. Leather sole, blunt toe, medium-high suede-covered heel, matching upper with box toe, keyhole opening above high tongue with scalloped edge, contrast-colour calfskin bow tie and piping. 8 English c. 1944. Leather sole, blunt toe, high suede-covered heel and platform with cut-out leaf-shapes, repeated under low-cut scalloped vamp of matching upper, open toe and buckled heel strap. 9 French c. 1944. Leather sole, blunt toe, high calfskin-covered wedge heel and combined platform, matching backless upper with high pointed vamp.

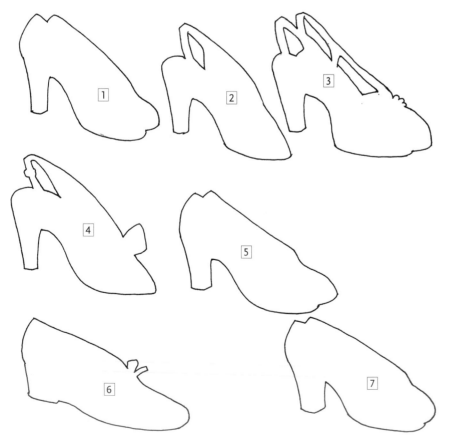

Women's shoes 1945–1946

1 American c. 1945. Leather soles, blunt toes, high calfskin-covered heels, matching toecaps with perforated decoration on pointed seam edges, repeated on shaped heel-backs, contrast-colour suede bodies. 2 French c. 1946. Leather sole, blunt toe, high gold calfskin-covered heel, clear plastic backless upper with open toe, edges bound in gold calfskin, matching buckled heel strap. 3 English c. 1946. Leather soles, blunt toes, high calfskin-covered heels, matching wide bindings, buckled heel straps and decorative flowers on centre front of nylon mesh uppers. 4 French c. 1946. Leather sole, blunt toe, high velvet-covered heel, matching upper with open toe, large bow with jewelled centre set on low-cut vamp, side-buckled heel strap. 5 English c. 1945. Leather soles, blunt toes, high calfskin-covered heels, matching uppers, low-cut vamps with perforated decoration and topstitched detail. 6 American c. 1945. Leather sole with blunt toe, snakeskin-covered low wedge heel and fine platform, contrast-colour suede upper with box toe, high sides piped in calfskin to match colour of snakeskin, matching bow on centre front of low-cut vamp. 7 English c. 1945. Leather soles, blunt toes, high stacked leather heels, textured calfskin uppers, low-cut vamps, heel-backs and mock toecaps decorated with perforations and topstitching.

Women's shoes 1947–1949

1 English c. 1947. Leather sole, blunt toe, high calfskin-covered heel, matching upper with lines of decorative topstitching on sides and under low-cut vamp. 2 English c. 1949. Leather sole, blunt toe, high suede-covered heel and matching upper, low-cut vamp in-filled with two straps set under three buckled bar straps. 3 American c. 1948. Leather sole, blunt toe, low suede-covered wedge heel and combined platform, matching sideless upper with low-cut heart-shaped vamp, buckled ankle strap threaded through high wing-shaped heel-back. 4 English c. 1949. Leather sole, blunt toe, small calfskin-covered heel combined with wedge and platform, matching straps over instep form open toe, threaded T-strap connected to buckled heel strap. 5 American c. 1949. Leather sole, blunt toe, low calfskin-covered heel, matching upper with low-cut vamp in-filled with criss-crossed straps to ankle-level, side buckle fastening. 6 English c. 1947. Leather sole, blunt toe, high gold calfskin-covered heel, matching sideless upper with open toe, side carriers for flared ankle strap with buckle fastening. 7 French c. 1949. Leather sole, blunt toe, high gold calfskin-covered heel, matching filled-in heel-back, buckled instep strap and centre front retaining strap over gold mesh cross straps. 8 English c. 1948. Leather sole, blunt toe, low suede-covered heel and combined platform, matching plain upper with high vamp and buckled heel strap. 9 English c. 1949. Leather sole, blunt toe, high suede-covered heel, matching ankle-length upper, wing-shaped heel-back, cut-out decoration on sides, open front above low-cut vamp laced together with silk ribbon bow.

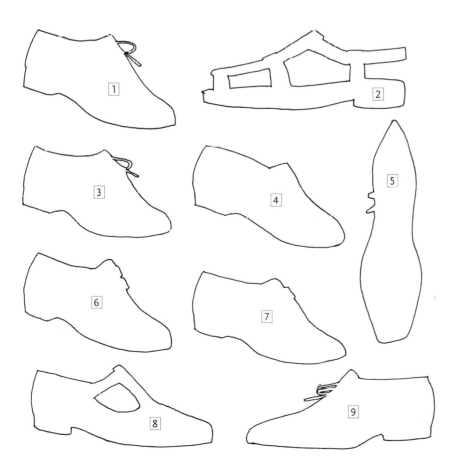

Men's shoes 1950–1959

1 English c. 1950–1955. Crepe sole with blunt toe and combined low heel, calfskin upper, front part under laced fastening comprised of interwoven strips of calfskin, heel-back, tongue and bound edges in matching colour, side panels in contrast colour. 2 English c. 1957–1959. Rubber sole with blunt toe and combined low heel, upper comprised of calfskin straps over toes and instep, through carriers to buckled fastening. 3 English c. 1950–1955. Rubber sole with blunt toe and combined low heel, calfskin upper with mock toecap, heel-back and facings, perforated and stitched detail, laced fastening. 4 American c. 1956–1959. Leather sole, blunt toe, low stacked leather heel, calfskin upper with contrast-colour apron front and combined tongue. 5 English c. 1959. Leather sole, asymmetric square toe, calfskin upper with plain front, laced fastening through two eyelets. 6 English c. 1950–1953. Crepe sole with blunt toe and combined low heel, textured calfskin upper with apron front and two buckled straps over instep. 7 English c. 1950–1953. Rubber sole with blunt toe and combined low heel, calfskin upper with apron front and single buckled strap over instep, topstitched edges and detail. 8 English c. 1959. Leather sole, blunt toe, low stacked leather heel, calfskin upper with open sides and apron front with panel of interwoven strips of calfskin at base of buckled T-strap. 9 American c. 1956–1959. Crepe sole with blunt toe and combined low heel, suede upper with plain front, high sides and laced front fastening through two eyelets.

Women's shoes 1950–1952

1 English *c.* 1950. Leather sole, blunt toe, slender high calfskin-covered heel, matching sideless upper, low-cut vamp edged with patent leather, matching bow trim. 2 English *c.* 1952. Leather sole, blunt toe, low suede-covered heel, matching upper with apron front, low-cut vamp with self-fabric bow trim. 3 English *c.* 1952. Leather sole with almond-shaped toe, slender high kidskin-covered heel, matching upper comprised of fine criss-crossed straps from shallow sides over toes and instep to buckled heel strap. 4 French *c.* 1952. Leather sole, almond-shaped toe, slender high calfskin-covered heel, matching upper with cut-away sides and low-cut vamp trimmed with self-fabric rouleau bow on centre front. 5 American *c.* 1952. Leather sole, blunt toe, high patent-leather-covered heel, matching backless upper with low-cut pointed vamp edged with suede, matching trim over open toe, elasticated bar strap over instep. 6 American *c.* 1951. Leather sole, blunt toe, low calfskin-covered wedge heel, matching upper comprised of fine straps crossed over toes, decorated with three multicoloured calfskin flowers, heel strap and buckled ankle strap. 7 English *c.* 1950. Rubber sole with blunt toe, medium-high canvas-covered wedge heel, matching sideless upper with low-cut vamp, open toe and single strap from side front, across instep, behind heel to side back. 8 English *c.* 1950. Leather sole, almond-shaped toe, high suede-covered heel and fine platform, matching upper with open toe and openwork above to low-cut vamp, trimmed in contrast colour, filled-in sides forming buckled heel strap. 9 English *c.* 1952. Leather sole, almond-shaped toe, high calfskin-covered heel, matching upper with wide straps crossed over from each side forming open toe, filled-in sides and heel-back.

Women's shoes and boots 1953–1954

1 Italian *c.* 1954. Leather sole, almond-shaped toe, slender high calfskin-covered heel, matching upper comprised of flared straps over toes to low-cut vamp, side carriers and narrow heel strap with buckle fastening. 2 American *c.* 1953. Leather sole, almond-shaped toe, slender high calfskin-covered heel, matching upper with open toe and asymmetric low-cut vamp trimmed on opposite edges in contrast-colour perforated binding, narrow strap from side front, through side carriers and behind heel. 3 French *c.* 1953. Leather sole, almond-shaped toe, slender high calfskin-covered heel, matching upper comprised of two asymmetrically set calfskin straps over toes, buckled heel strap. 4 English *c.* 1954. Leather sole, almond-shaped toe, slender high calfskin-covered heel, matching upper with mock wrap-over front forming open toe, contrast-colour binding, decorative button trim on centre front. 5 French *c.* 1954. Leather sole, almond-shaped toe, slender high velvet-covered heel, matching sideless upper with low-cut vamp and open toe scattered with crystal beads, narrow heel strap with jewelled buckle, attached to wide bar strap over instep. 6 Italian *c.* 1954. Leather sole, almond-shaped toe, slender high calfskin-covered heel, matching upper comprised of straps of various widths over toes and a single asymmetric strap from side front through carrier to side back, side buckle fastening on ankle. 7 American *c.* 1953. Crepe sole with blunt toe and combined low heel, ankle-length suede upper with plain front and laced fastening through hooks over extended tongue, lambswool lining. 8 English *c.* 1953. Leather sole, almond-shaped toe, suede-covered high heel, matching wide binding on edge of ankle-length contrast-colour upper, laced fastening, decorative stitching on sides and front.

Women's shoes 1955–1956

1 American c. 1955. Leather sole, almond-shaped toe, slender high sparkly plastic-covered heel, matching backless upper with low-cut vamp, wide open toe and bar strap over instep with jewelled buckle fastening. 2 English c. 1956. Leather sole, blunt toe, low textured calfskin-covered heel, matching upper with outside topstitched centre seam from front of toe to top of tongue, laced fastening. 3 American c. 1955. Leather sole, almond-shaped toe, slender high cotton-gingham-covered heel, matching sideless upper with upward pointed edge to low-cut vamp and downward pointed edge to wide open toe, buckled heel strap. 4 Italian c. 1956. Leather sole, almond-shaped toe, high calfskin-covered stiletto heel, matching upper with asymmetric low-cut vamp, cut-out detail and open toe edged in contrast colour. 5 English c. 1956. Leather sole, square toe, medium-high stacked leather heel, calfskin upper with upward pointed edge to low-cut vamp, perforated and topstitched decoration on front and sides. 6 Italian c. 1955. Leather sole, almond-shaped toe, high calfskin-covered stiletto heel, matching upper with wrap-over effect and cut-out design on front, forming low-cut pointed vamp and V-shaped open toe, low sides, topstitched edges and detail. 7 Italian c. 1955. Leather sole, almond-shaped toe, low calfskin-covered heel, matching upper with low-cut vamp and asymmetric wrap-over effect with single button trim on one side, topstitched edges and detail. 8 English c. 1955. Leather sole, almond-shaped toe, slender medium-high calfskin-covered heel, matching trim under oval brass buckle on low-cut vamp, contrast-colour calfskin body with open toe and buckled heel strap, brightly coloured inner lining.

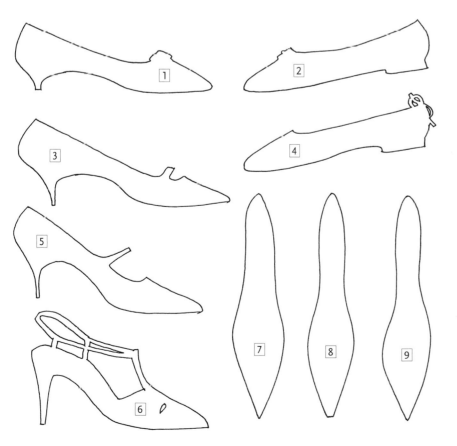

Women's shoes 1957–1959

1 English c. 1958. Leather sole, pointed toe, low patterned silk-covered spike heel, matching upper with low-cut vamp and self-fabric ruched bow trim on centre front. 2 American c. 1958. Leather sole, pointed toe, flat flared calfskin-covered heel, matching upper with metal buckle trim on low-cut vamp. 3 Italian c. 1957. Leather sole, pointed toe, medium-high calfskin-covered stiletto heel, matching buckled bar strap above very low-cut vamp and outside edges of contrast-colour pearlized calfskin upper. 4 American c. 1959. Leather sole, pointed toe, low stacked leather heel, pale-coloured calfskin upper with low-cut vamp, contrast-colour front with perforated pattern and scalloped wing seam, matching bow trim on heel-back and bound outer edges. 5 Italian c. 1958. Leather sole, long pointed toe, high gold calfskin-covered stiletto heel, matching upper with low-cut vamp and buckled bar strap over instep. 6 English c. 1958. Leather sole, pointed toe, silk-brocade-covered stiletto heel, matching sideless upper with low-cut vamp and keyhole detail on side fronts, fine T-strap, ankle and heel straps, buckled fastening. 7 Italian c. 1959. Leather sole, long sharp pointed toe, high pale-coloured patent-leather stiletto heel, matching upper with very low-cut vamp, pleated silk ribbon threaded through jewelled oval buckle. 8 Italian c. 1959. Leather sole, elongated narrow square toe, high pearlized calfskin-covered stiletto heel, matching upper, very low-cut vamp trimmed with matt metal buckle. 9 Italian c. 1959. Leather sole, long sharp pointed toe, high pearlized calfskin-covered stiletto heel, matching upper, contrast-colour pleated calfskin panel and covered button trim under very low-cut vamp.

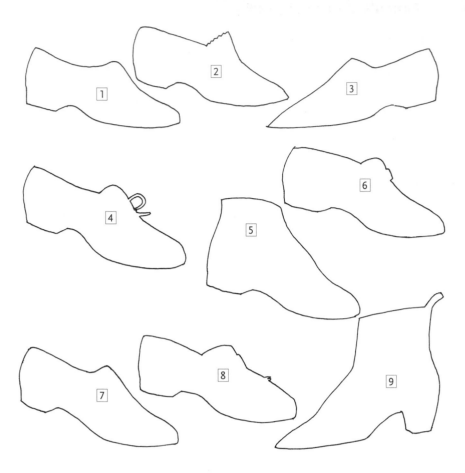

Men's shoes and boots 1960–1969

1 Italian c. 1960. Leather sole, blunt toe, low stacked leather heel, calfskin upper with topstitched apron front and elasticated side gussets. 2 English c. 1960. Leather sole, pointed toe, medium-high stacked leather heel, mock snakeskin upper, calfskin strap with buckle fastening threaded through matching tongue set on outside above low-cut vamp. 3 English c. 1965–1969. Leather sole, long pointed toe, medium-high shaped stacked leather heel, calfskin upper with mock apron front, side laced fastening, topstitched seams and decoration. 4 English c. 1960–1965. Rubber sole with blunt toe and combined low heel, mock suede upper with apron front decorated with contrast-colour leather-look thonging, matching detail on side edges and bow trim under high tongue. 5 Italian c. 1964. Crepe sole with blunt toe and combined low heel, ankle-length cotton cord upper with leather lining, laced fastening over high tongue. 6 French c. 1969. Rubber sole with square toe and combined low heel, calfskin upper with buckled strap over contrast-colour tongue and apron front. 7 English c. 1963–1968. Leather sole, blunt toe, low stacked leather heel, suede upper with apron front and laced fastening over tongue, topstitched edges and detail. 8 Italian c. 1969. Rubber sole with blunt toe and combined low heel, calfskin upper, apron front with raised seam, buckled strap with knotted tasselled thong detail over tongue, topstitched edges and detail. 9 Italian c. 1964–1966. Leather sole, pointed toe, high tapered stacked leather heel, ankle-length calfskin upper with deep elasticated side gussets, pull tape from edge of heel-back.

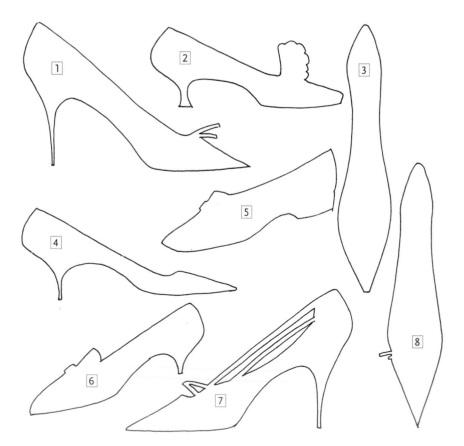

Women's shoes 1960–1962

1 French c. 1960. Leather sole, sharp pointed toe, high calfskin-covered stiletto heel, matching upper, low-cut vamp trimmed with self-fabric rouleau bow, deep toecap in contrast colour. 2 French c. 1960. Leather sole, square toe, high fabric-covered Louis-style heel, matching upper with low-cut vamp and high tongue decorated with self-fabric rose. 3 Italian c. 1960. Leather sole, narrow chisel-shaped toe, high calfskin-covered stiletto heel, coloured glacé kid upper with very low-cut vamp in-filled with self-fabric leaves. 4 English c. 1961. Leather sole, long pointed toe, medium-high calfskin-covered stiletto heel, matching toecap, heel-back and trim of contrast-colour calfskin upper. 5 English c. 1961. Rubber sole with almond-shaped toe and combined low heel, textured calfskin upper with stitched apron front and buckled strap over high tongue. 6 English c. 1962. Leather sole, almond-shaped toe, low calfskin-covered heel, matching centre front strap from tip of toe and combined decorative tongue with threaded fringed bow and bindings on contrast-colour calfskin upper. 7 Italian c. 1962. Leather sole, sharp pointed toe, high calfskin-covered stiletto heel, matching upper with very low-cut vamp, low sides, rouleau bar strap over toes, matching side straps and single bow trim on one side. 8 French c. 1961. Leather sole, sharp pointed toe, high calfskin-covered stiletto heel, gold calfskin upper with very low-cut vamp and matching rouleau bow trim on centre front and binding on edges of gold mesh sides and upper front.

Women's shoes 1963–1964

1 English c. 1964. Leather sole, blunt toe, low leather-covered heel, matching upper, low-cut vamp and bar strap with rouleau bow fastening. 2 English c. 1964. Leather sole, blunt toe, medium-high stacked leather heel, calfskin upper, apron front with raised seam running from top of high flared tongue to tip of toe, stitched edges and detail. 3 French c. 1963. Leather sole, almond-shaped toe, flat leather heel, calfskin upper, edges of low-cut sides and square vamp threaded with elastic. 4 Italian c. 1963. Leather sole, almond-shaped toe, low parti-coloured calfskin-covered heel, matching upper with low-cut straight vamp. 5 English c. 1964. Leather sole, long almond-shaped toe, thick high silk-covered heel, matching upper with low-cut V-shaped vamp and wide bar strap over instep, jewelled buckled fastening. 6 English c. 1963. Leather sole, long almond-shaped toe, thick medium-high calfskin-covered heel, matching bindings and bow trim of heel-back strap on contrast-colour upper. 7 French c. 1963. Leather sole, square toe, thick high calfskin-covered heel, matching back part and tongue of upper, contrast-colour suede front and bow trim. 8 English c. 1963. Leather sole, almond-shaped toe, medium-high patent-leather-covered stiletto heel, matching front upper with open toe, contrast-colour bindings and buckled heel strap. 9 Italian c. 1964. Leather sole, sharp pointed toe, high calfskin-covered stiletto heel, matching front upper with cut-out side detail and contrast-colour button trim, colour repeated on toecap, sides and heel-back.

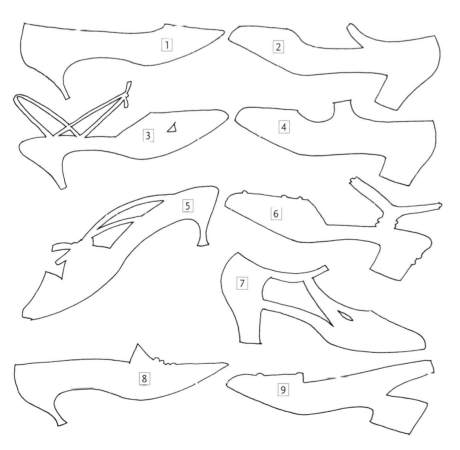

Women's shoes 1965–1966

1 Swiss c. 1965. Leather sole, pointed toe, medium-high calfskin-covered stiletto heel, matching upper, low-cut vamp above contrast-colour piped seams and small bow trim on one side. 2 French c. 1966. Leather sole, elongated blunt toe, thick medium-high calfskin-covered heel, matching upper with low-cut vamp, edges and buttoned bar strap in mock lizard skin. 3 Italian c. 1965. Leather sole, almond-shaped toe, low calfskin-covered heel, matching front upper with stitched strap detail open on sides, fine heel and instep straps. 4 French c. 1966. Leather sole, blunt toe, low calfskin-covered heel, matching upper, low-cut vamp, contrast-colour buttoned bar strap and outside edges. 5 Italian c. 1965. Leather sole, narrow square toe, medium-high silk-covered Louis-style stiletto heel, matching backless upper, two-part split front, filled-in open toe and bow trim on centre front vamp with thin straps to side-back. 6 French c. 1966. Leather sole, blunt toe, thick low silver calfskin-covered heel trimmed with crystal beads, matching front upper, bar and joined heel straps. 7 French c. 1966. Leather sole, almond-shaped toe, thick medium-high calfskin-covered heel, matching sideless upper with low-cut vamp, buckled bar strap connected to side straps. 8 Italian c. 1965. Leather sole, sharp pointed toe, medium-high silk-covered Louis-style stiletto heel, matching upper, wide self-colour satin bound to edges, pointed vamp with bead trim. 9 Italian c. 1966. Leather sole, blunt toe, thick low calfskin-covered heel, matching upper with large buckle trim above low-cut vamp and wide heel strap.

Women's shoes 1967–1969

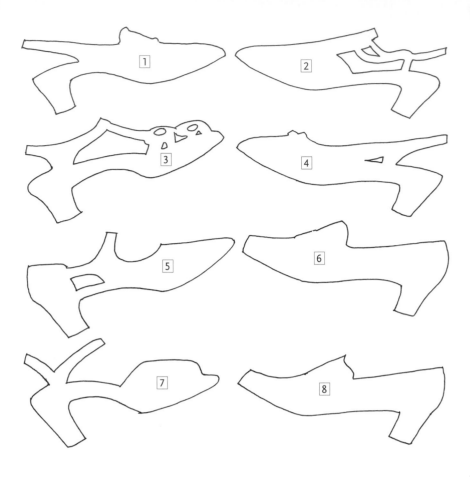

1 French c. 1968. Leather sole, blunt toe, thick low calfskin-covered heel, matching upper with outsized strap and buckle fastening over instep and wide heel strap.
2 English c. 1967. Leather sole, almond-shaped toe, thick low calfskin-covered heel, matching upper with T-strap set into low-cut vamp, narrow heel and side straps.
3 French c. 1969. Leather sole, square toe, thick low calfskin-covered heel, matching shallow platform and upper, straps over toes with cut-out detail, T-strap and buckled ankle strap. 4 English c. 1967. Leather sole, almond-shaped toe, thick low calfskin-covered heel, matching heel strap, centre front bow trim on low-cut vamp and bindings on clear plastic upper. 5 Italian c. 1968. Leather sole, almond-shaped toe, thick low suede-covered heel, matching sideless upper with low-cut vamp, wide bar strap and buckled side strap. 6 Italian c. 1969. Leather sole, square toe, thick low calfskin-covered heel, matching upper, wide strap with linked chain decoration set between apron front and tongue, topstitched edges and detail. 7 Italian c. 1969. Leather sole, almond-shaped toe, thick high calfskin-covered heel, matching sideless upper with low-cut vamp and open toe, buckled bar strap and combined heel strap. 8 Italian c. 1969. Leather sole, wide square toe, medium-high stacked leather heel, calfskin upper with buckled bar strap over high tongue, shaped toecap and heel-back, edges and detail decorated with mock perforations.

Women's boots 1960–1969

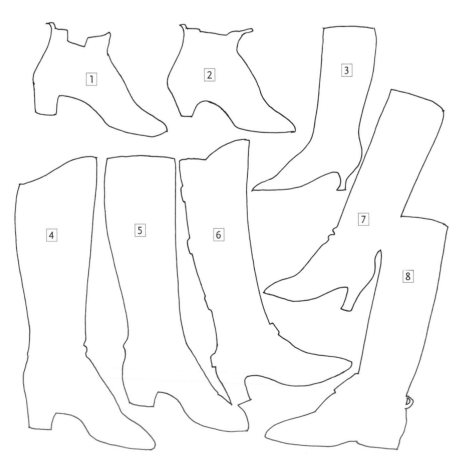

1 American c. 1967. Leather sole, square toe, thick low calfskin-covered heel, matching ankle-length upper with wrap-over sides under deep elasticated gussets, topstitched edges and detail, back pull tape. 2 English c. 1964. Leather sole, almond-shaped toe, medium-high shaped stacked leather heel, ankle-length calfskin upper with elasticated side gussets, front and back pull tapes on top edge. 3 Italian c. 1960. Leather sole, pointed toe, medium-high calfskin-covered Louis-style stiletto heel, matching shoe and trim on knee-length mock snakeskin upper, concealed elasticated gusset. 4 French c. 1969. Leather sole, blunt toe, thick low calfskin-covered heel, matching above-knee-length upper with fur side panels. 5 American c. 1968. Above-knee-length suede legging with buckled strap under instep, shaped to fit over shoe or short boot, elasticated side panels from top edge to ankle-level. 6 French c. 1968. Leather sole, blunt toe, thick low calfskin-covered heel, matching back part of above-knee-length upper, front part and four buckled straps in contrast colour. 7 Italian c. 1965. Leather sole, almond-shaped toe, thick high calfskin-covered heel, matching deep knee-level cuff above straight-cut textured calfskin leg. 8 Italian c. 1966. Leather sole, blunt toe, low stacked leather heel, knee-length calfskin upper with straight-cut leg, side zip fastening, decorative spur leathers with chain around heel-back.

Men's shoes and boots 1970–1979

Italian *c.* 1970–1972

Italian *c.* 1974–1976

Italian *c.* 1972–1973

Italian *c.* 1977–1979

Italian *c.* 1977–1979

English *c.* 1975

English *c.* 1972

Italian *c.* 1977

Italian *c.* 1978

Women's shoes and boots 1970–1972

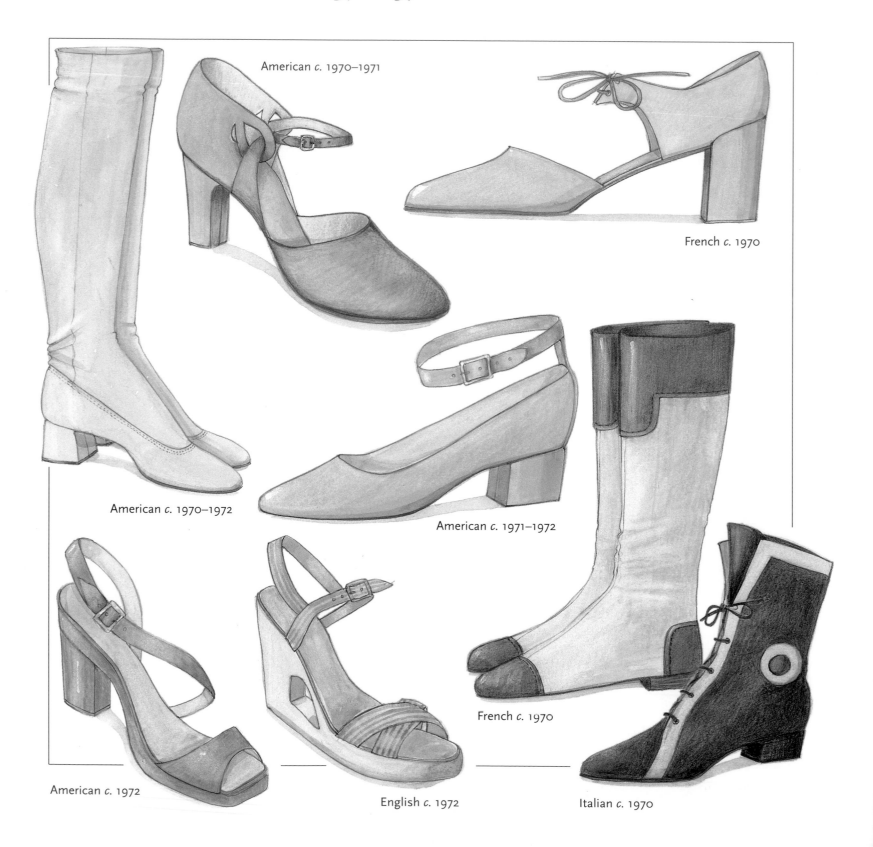

American *c.* 1970–1971

French *c.* 1970

American *c.* 1970–1972

American *c.* 1971–1972

American *c.* 1972

English *c.* 1972

French *c.* 1970

Italian *c.* 1970

Women's shoes and boots 1973–1974

English *c.* 1973

French *c.* 1973

German *c.* 1973

German *c.* 1974

French *c.* 1974

English *c.* 1973

Italian *c.* 1974

French *c.* 1974

Women's shoes and boots 1975–1976

English *c.* 1975

English *c.* 1975–1976

Italian *c.* 1976

English *c.* 1975

English *c.* 1975

Italian *c.* 1976

Italian *c.* 1976

Women's shoes and boots 1977–1979

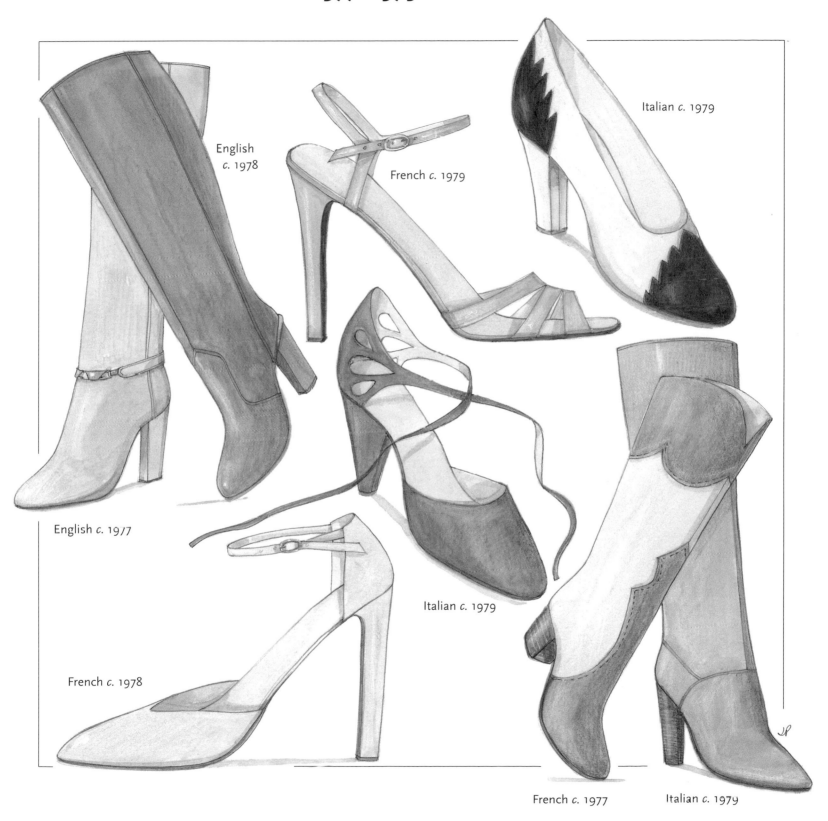

English
c. 1978

French c. 1979

Italian c. 1979

English c. 1977

Italian c. 1979

French c. 1978

French c. 1977

Italian c. 1979

Men's shoes and boots 1980–1989

Italian *c.* 1982–1983

American *c.* 1983–1985

American *c.* 1980–1982

English *c.* 1987–1989

Italian *c.* 1986–1987

Italian *c.* 1987–1988

Italian *c.* 1988–1989

Italian *c.* 1989

Italian *c.* 1988–1989

JP

Women's shoes and boots 1980–1982

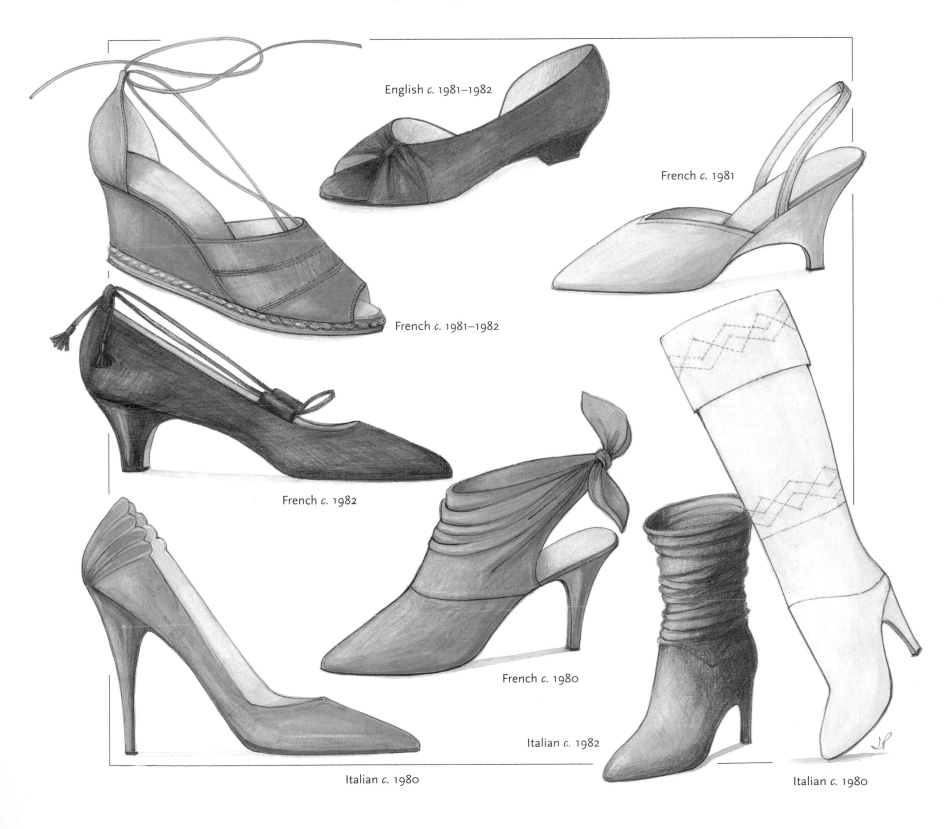

English *c.* 1981–1982

French *c.* 1981

French *c.* 1981–1982

French *c.* 1982

French *c.* 1980

Italian *c.* 1982

Italian *c.* 1980

Italian *c.* 1980

Women's shoes 1983–1984

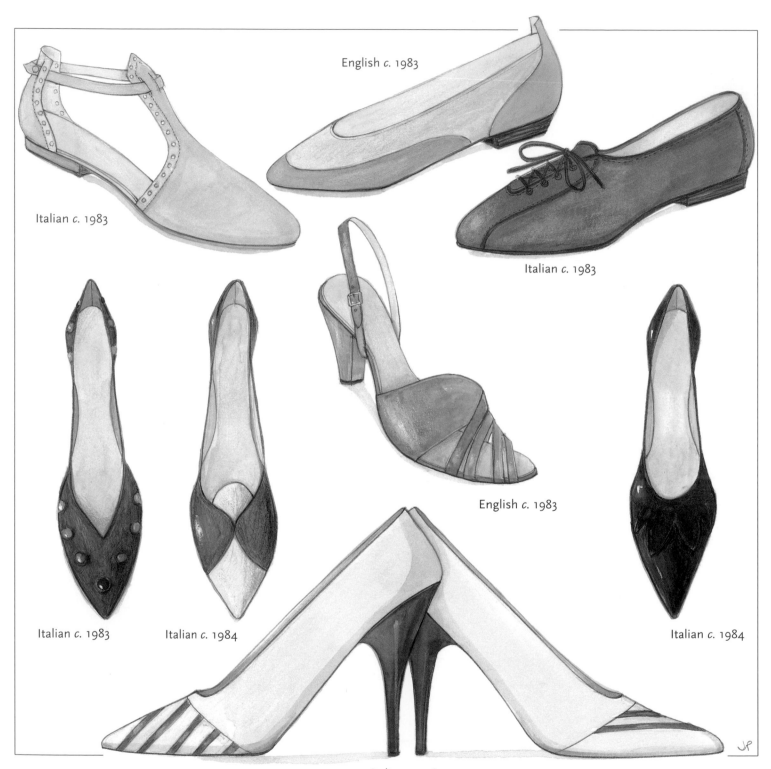

English *c.* 1983

Italian *c.* 1983

Italian *c.* 1983

English *c.* 1983

Italian *c.* 1983

Italian *c.* 1984

Italian *c.* 1984

Italian *c.* 1984

Women's shoes and boots 1985–1986

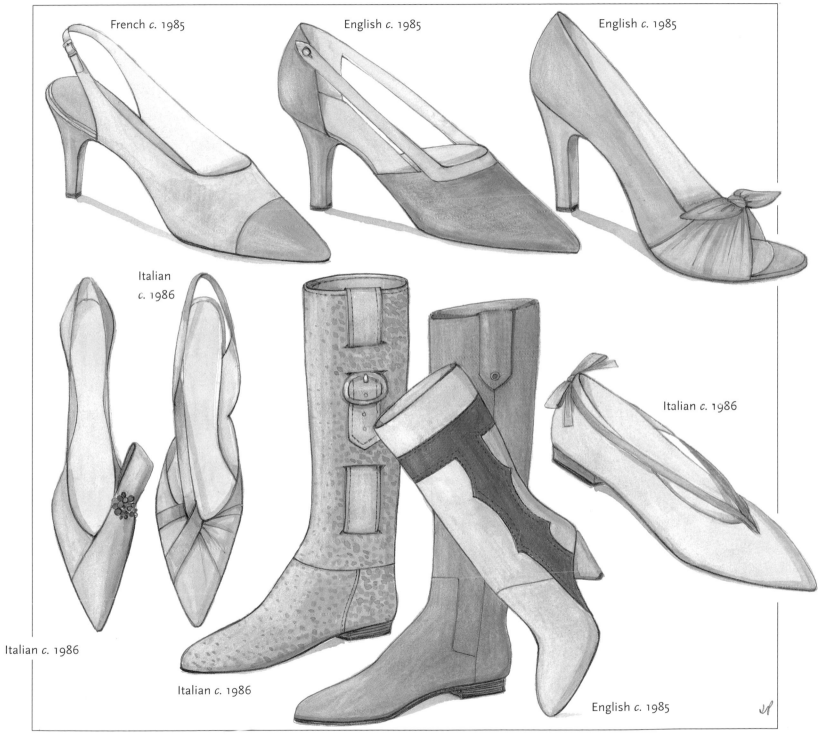

French c. 1985

English c. 1985

English c. 1985

Italian c. 1986

Italian c. 1986

Italian c. 1986

Italian c. 1986

Italian c. 1986

English c. 1985

Women's shoes 1987–1989

Italian *c.* 1988

English *c.* 1987

Italian *c.* 1988

Italian *c.* 1989

Italian *c.* 1987

Italian *c.* 1987

French *c.* 1987

Italian *c.* 1987

Men's shoes and boots 1990–present day

Italian *c.* 1995–1997

American *c.* 1999–2000

English *c.* 1996–1998

Italian *c.* 2000–2003

English
c. 1990–1993

English *c.* 1994–1996

English *c.* 1999–2003

American *c.* 1995–1999

Women's shoes and boots 1990–1992

Italian *c.* 1991

French *c.* 1990

French *c.* 1990

French *c.* 1990

English *c.* 1991

Italian *c.* 1991

Italian *c.* 1992

English *c.* 1991

Italian *c.* 1992

Italian *c.* 1991

Women's shoes and boots 1993–1994

English c. 1994

Italian c. 1994

French c. 1993

English c. 1993

American c. 1993

English c. 1994

English c. 1994

Italian c. 1994

JP

Women's shoes and boots 1995–1996

English *c.* 1995

French *c.* 1996

English *c.* 1996

English *c.* 1996

English *c.* 1995

Italian *c.* 1996

English *c.* 1995

English *c.* 1995

Women's shoes and boots 1997–1999

French c. 1997

English c. 1999

Italian c. 1998

Italian c. 1998

English c. 1999

English c. 1998

English c. 1997

English c. 1999

Women's shoes and boots 2000–present day

English c. 2001

English c. 2001

English c. 2003

English c. 2000

English c. 2002

French c. 2003

English c. 2003

Italian c. 2003

French c. 2003

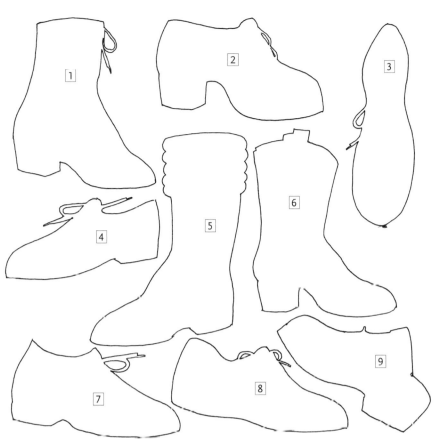

Men's shoes and boots 1970–1979

1 Italian c. 1970–1972. Leather sole, blunt toe, medium-high stacked leather heel, mid-calf-length calfskin upper with wide-spaced laced fastening through large eyelets from above low vamp over full-length tongue. 2 Italian c. 1974–1976. Composite platform sole with blunt toe and combined high heel, calfskin upper with wide toecap, heel-back and facings to laced fastening in contrast colour. 3 Italian c. 1977–1979. Leather sole, blunt toe, medium-high calfskin-covered heel, matching upper with cross-over decorative seamed panels above toes and under laced fastening, topstitched edges and detail. 4 Italian c. 1972–1973. Leather sole, blunt toe, medium-high stacked leather heel, calfskin upper with contrast-colour gussets above toes, matching piping, topstitching and laces. 5 Italian c. 1977–1979. Leather sole, blunt toe, medium-high stacked leather heel, mid-calf-length calfskin upper with straight leg, padded and stitched cuff. 6 English c. 1975. Leather sole, blunt toe, high plastic mock-stacked-leather heel, mid-calf-length calfskin upper with curved top edge to front and back, contrast-colour side pulls and panel with self-colour star in centre, contrast-colour star trim above toes. 7 English c. 1972. Thick crepe sole and combined low heel, suede upper with centre front topstitched raised seam from tip of toe to top of long tongue, self-suede thong laces. 8 Italian c. 1977. Coloured rubber sole with blunt toe and combined low wedge heel, leather and canvas upper with raised heel-back, laced fastening through eyelets and rings over high vamp, topstitched detail. 9 Italian c. 1978. Thick wood platform sole with wide blunt toe and combined heel trimmed with leather and metal studs, backless leather upper with tucked and topstitched detail above high vamp.

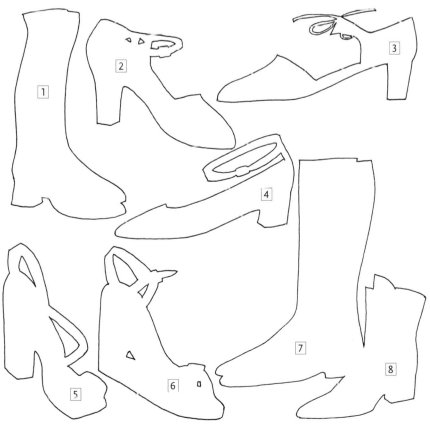

Women's shoes and boots 1970–1972

1 American c. 1970–1972. Composite soles with blunt toes and flared thick heels, above-knee-length stretch plastic leather-look fitted uppers, topstitched detail. 2 American c. 1970–1971. Leather sole, almond-shaped toe, thick high calfskin-covered heel, matching sideless upper with plain low-cut vamp, buckled ankle strap threaded through openwork detail on sides of heel-back. 3 French c. 1970. Composite sole with almond-shaped toe and thick high calfskin-covered heel, matching sideless upper with plain low-cut vamp and laced bar strap over instep combined with heel-back. 4 American c. 1971–1972. Leather sole, almond-shaped toe, thick low suede-covered heel, matching upper with plain low-cut vamp and wide buckled ankle strap attached to extension on heel-back. 5 American c. 1972. High calfskin-covered composite platform sole with square toe and high heel, matching upper comprised of a shaped strap over toes and an asymmetric strap over instep, buckle fastening on side. 6 English c. 1972. High canvas-covered composite platform sole with blunt toe and combined open wedge heel, crossed striped canvas straps over toes, matching buckled bar strap over instep and heel strap. 7 French c. 1970. Leather soles, blunt toes, low stacked leather heels, knee-length calfskin uppers with shaped and stitched cuffs, matching toecaps and heel-backs. 8 Italian c. 1970. Leather sole, almond-shaped toe, low stacked leather heel, ankle-length calfskin upper with contrast-colour ankle guard, matching facings to laced fastening.

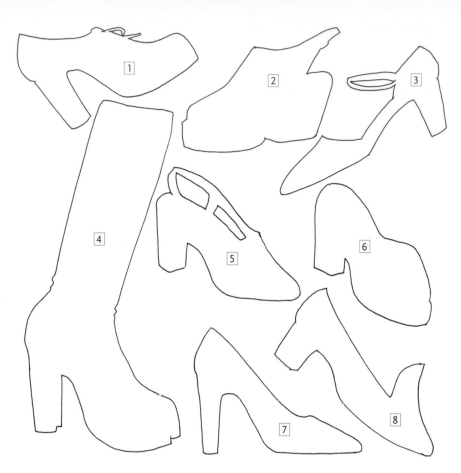

Women's shoes and boots 1973–1974

1 English *c.* 1973. Composite sole with blunt calfskin-covered cork platform and thick high heel, matching upper with multicoloured seamed facings to front laced fastening. 2 French *c.* 1973. Composite sole with blunt toe, hessian-covered wood platform sole and combined open wedge heel, multicoloured patchwork calfskin upper with open toe and high vamp, buckled heel strap. 3 German *c.* 1973. Leather sole, almond-shaped toe, calfskin-covered platform and thick high heel, matching toecap, shallow heel-back and buckled ankle strap, sideless upper with contrast-colour calfskin under plain low-cut vamp. 4 English *c.* 1973. Suede-covered exaggerated composite platform soles with deep blunt toes and thick high heels, matching fitted knee-length uppers with centre back zip fastening. 5 French *c.* 1974. Leather sole, blunt toe, thick medium-high calfskin-covered heel, multicoloured patchwork calfskin upper with wide heel strap. 6 German *c.* 1974. Composite sole with blunt toe, wooden platform and combined heel, backless leather upper with high-cut vamp and open toe. 7 Italian *c.* 1974. Leather sole, almond-shaped toe, straight medium-high heel, matching upper with plain low-cut vamp. 8 French *c.* 1974. Leather sole, almond-shaped toe, thick medium-high suede-covered heel with contrast-colour inset stripe on each side, matching stripe on centre front of upper from tip of toe to top of high tongue.

Women's shoes and boots 1975–1976

1 English *c.* 1975. Composite sole with blunt toe, calfskin-covered platform and thick high heel, matching sideless upper with low-cut vamp, asymmetric flap above narrow straps over toes, combined side carriers, heel and ankle straps. 2 English *c.* 1975–1976. Composite sole with blunt toe, calfskin-covered platform and thick high heel, matching sideless upper, low vamp with straps over toes threaded through metal ring, combined side carriers, heel and buckled ankle straps. 3 Italian *c.* 1976. Leather sole, almond-shaped toe, thick high calfskin-covered heel, metal insert trim between heel-back and top of heel, matching front of toe, plain upper with low-cut vamp. 4 English *c.* 1975. Composite sole with blunt toe, exaggerated platform covered in leather-look plastic and mock stacked leather heel, leather-look plastic upper with low-cut vamp and toecap with contrast-colour threaded detail, two matching buckled bar straps. 5 Italian *c.* 1976. Leather sole, almond-shaped toe, straight high calfskin-covered heel, matching knee-length printed calfskin upper with strap and button trim over instep. 6 English *c.* 1975. Leather sole, blunt toe, calfskin-covered platform and thick high heel, matching part of patchwork upper and buckled heel strap, insert above toes in contrast colour. 7 Italian *c.* 1976. Leather sole, square toe, calfskin-covered platform, mock stacked leather heel, calfskin upper with shallow toecap, contrast-colour front insert and tongue under wrap-over buckled fastening.

Women's shoes and boots 1977–1979

1 English c. 1977. Leather sole, almond-shaped toe, straight high calfskin-covered heel, matching knee-length fitted upper with mock ankle strap and decorative metal buckle. 2 English c. 1978. Leather sole, almond-shaped toe, straight high calfskin-covered heel, decorative metal plate inserted between base of heel-back and top of heel, knee-length fitted calfskin upper, topstitched edges and detail. 3 French c. 1979. Leather sole, almond-shaped toe, straight high calfskin-covered heel, matching sideless upper with straps over toes and combined side carriers, heel and buckled ankle straps. 4 Italian c. 1979. Leather sole, almond-shaped toe, matt calfskin-covered straight heel, matching upper, contrast-colour toecap with pointed decorative edges and matching heel-back. 5 French c. 1978. Leather sole, almond-shaped toe, straight high calfskin-covered heel, matching sideless upper with low-cut pointed vamp, shallow heel-back and buckled ankle strap. 6 Italian c. 1979. Leather sole, almond-shaped toe, matt calfskin-covered cylindrical heel, matching sideless upper with plain low-cut vamp, shallow heel-back with openwork decoration and long straps to tie around ankle. 7 French c. 1977. Leather sole, blunt toe, low mock stacked leather heel, mid-calf-length matt calfskin upper with contrast-colour front and shaped cuff, topstitched edges and detail. 8 Italian c. 1979. Leather sole, pointed toe, mock stacked leather high heel, knee-length fitted calfskin upper with seams over high instep and around heel-back.

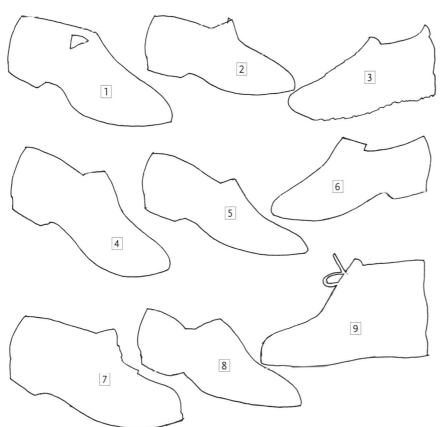

Men's shoes and boots 1980–1989

1 American c. 1980–1982. Leather sole, almond-shaped toe, low stacked leather heel, calfskin upper with open sides and apron front with topstitched edges, matching buckled bar strap fastening and decorative seam on heel-back. 2 Italian c. 1982–1983. Leather sole, almond-shaped toe, low stacked leather heel, calfskin upper with plain front, contrast-colour piping in seam over instep, matching inset leaf-shaped motif on each side of high tongue and heel-back. 3 American c. 1983–1985. Corrugated rubber sole with turned-up blunt toe and combined low heel, rubber, canvas and suede upper with contrast-colour leather trim, laced fastening over high tongue. 4 Italian c. 1986–1987. Leather sole, almond-shaped toe, low stacked leather heel, calfskin upper with apron front comprised of interwoven strips of leather, matching decoration on sides running from toe to heel-back. 5 Italian c. 1987–1988. Leather sole, almond-shaped toe, low stacked leather heel, lizard skin upper with plain front and combined short tongue, edges bound with calfskin. 6 English c. 1987–1989. Composite sole with almond-shaped toe and combined low heel, calfskin upper with plain front and combined short tongue, low-cut sides with elasticated panels, topstitched edges and detail. 7 Italian c. 1988–1989. Composite sole with blunt toe and combined low heel, suede upper with apron front and turned-down fringed tongue threaded under wide instep strap. 8 Italian c. 1989. Leather sole, almond-shaped toe, low stacked leather heel, calfskin upper with plain front and topstitched wing seam over instep, matching edges of high vamp and low-cut sides. 9 Italian c. 1988–1989. Thick crepe sole with blunt toe and combined wedge heel, ankle-length suede upper with panels of apron front running from toe to heel-back, laced fastening, topstitched edges and detail.

Women's shoes and boots 1980–1982

1 French c. 1981–1982. Composite sole with almond-shaped toe, rope edging and calfskin-covered high wedge heel, matching two of three horizontal panels on front of sideless upper with open toe, contrast colour repeated in long rouleau ties from each side centre front above vamp to fasten around ankle through loop on top of matching shallow heel-back. 2 English c. 1981–1982. Leather sole, almond-shaped toe, low calfskin-covered wedged heel, matching asymmetric upper with ruched detail on one side above open toe, low-cut vamp, single open side. 3 French c. 1981. Leather sole, pointed toe, medium-high calfskin-covered wedged heel, matching sideless upper with low-cut pointed vamp and narrow heel strap with elasticated panel in back. 4 French c. 1982. Leather sole, pointed toe, medium-high calfskin-covered heel, matching upper with plain front and low-cut vamp, rouleau lace with tasselled ends threaded through loops on top edges of sides and heel-back. 5 Italian c. 1980. Leather sole, pointed toe, very high calfskin-covered stiletto heel, matching upper, edges of low-cut vamp and shell-shaped heel-back piped with contrast-colour kidskin. 6 French c. 1980. Composite sole with pointed toe and suede-covered high stiletto heel, matching backless upper with draped ankle-length scarf effect above high vamp seam, sham knot and tie at back. 7 Italian c. 1982. Composite sole with pointed toe and straight high suede-covered heel, matching mid-calf-length upper with draped leg above plain front and shaped high vamp seam. 8 Italian c. 1980. Composite sole with pointed toe and slender high calfskin-covered heel, matching knee-length upper with shaped high vamp seam and turned-down cuff with decorative stitching, repeated at mid-calf-level.

Women's shoes 1983–1984

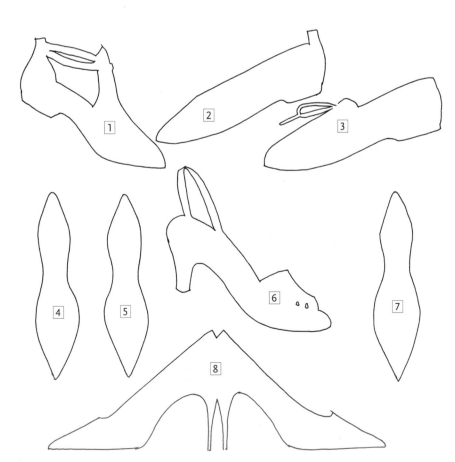

1 Italian c. 1983. Leather sole, almond-shaped toe, low stacked leather heel, sideless suede upper with plain front and T-strap fastening behind shallow heel-back, perforated and topstitched edges. 2 English c. 1983. Leather sole, almond-shaped toe, low stacked leather heel, calfskin upper with low-cut vamp, shallow wing-shaped front and heel-back with top edge extension in contrast colour. 3 Italian c. 1983. Leather sole, almond-shaped toe, low stacked leather heel, calfskin upper with laced fastening above full-length tongue, facings extend to end of toe, piped and topstitched edges and detail. 4 Italian c. 1983. Leather sole, sharp pointed toe, high calfskin-covered stiletto heel, matching upper with low-cut pointed vamp decorated with single line of multicoloured leather sequins from above toe to heel-back. 5 Italian c. 1984. Leather sole, sharp pointed toe, high calfskin-covered stiletto heel, matching upper with pointed toe and low-cut pointed vamp in-filled with contrast colour, matching front. 6 English c. 1983. Leather sole, almond-shaped toe, medium-high calfskin-covered heel, matching sideless upper with low-cut vamp and asymmetric straps above open toe, heel strap with buckled fastening. 7 Italian c. 1984. Leather sole, sharp pointed toe, high calfskin-covered stiletto heel, matching upper with pointed toe and contrast-colour leaf-shaped appliqué under low-cut vamp, matching sides and heel-back. 8 Italian c. 1984. Leather soles, pointed toes, very high calfskin-covered stiletto heels, matching asymmetric appliqué stripes under low-cut vamps on plain fronts of contrast-colour calfskin uppers.

Women's shoes and boots 1985–1986

1 French c. 1985. Leather sole, pointed toe, slender high calfskin-covered heel, matching toecap, contrast-colour upper with low-cut vamp and heel strap with buckled fastening. 2 English c. 1985. Composite sole with pointed toe and slender high calfskin-covered heel, matching sideless upper with top front edge of low-cut vamp bound in contrast colour, matching side straps connected to shallow heel-back, single button fastening. 3 English c. 1985. Composite sole with almond-shaped toe and slender high calfskin-covered heel, matching upper with draped tied scarf effect above open toe. 4 Italian c. 1986. Leather sole, sharp pointed toe, high calfskin-covered stiletto heel, matching upper with pointed toe and low-cut pointed vamp with wrap-over effect, brooch-trimmed self-calfskin loop on one side. 5 Italian c. 1986. Leather sole, sharp pointed toe, high silk-covered stiletto heel, matching upper with pointed toe and low-cut vamp ruched on one side, asymmetric silk satin heel strap from side front threaded through self-fabric ribbon, above open side to opposite heel-back connected to scalloped side edge. 6 Italian c. 1986. Leather sole, blunt toe, low stacked leather heel, knee-length textured suede upper, straight leg trimmed with vertical buckled leather strap threaded from ankle-level to top edge. 7 Italian c. 1986. Leather sole, blunt toe, low stacked leather heel, knee-length calfskin upper, straight leg trimmed on outside top edge with buttoned strap. 8 English c. 1985. Leather sole, pointed toe, low calfskin-covered cylindrical heel, matching mid-calf-length upper with inset contrast-colour horizontal stripe below top edge, repeated as scalloped vertical stripe on outside of straight leg. 9 Italian c. 1986. Leather sole, pointed toe, low stacked leather heel, silk upper with gold-coloured ribbons from centre front of low-cut vamp to behind heel-back, mock bowknot fastening.

Women's shoes 1987–1989

1 Italian c. 1988. Leather sole, almond-shaped toe, high suede-covered cylindrical heel, matching upper with plain front cut in one with short standing tongue, matching detail on top edge of heel-back. 2 Italian c. 1988. Leather sole, blunt toe, patent-leather-covered squat heel, matching upper with shaped sides, low-cut vamp trimmed with spotted velvet bow. 3 English c. 1987. Composite sole with pointed toe and very high animal-print silk-covered stiletto heel, matching upper with plain front and low-cut vamp. 4 Italian c. 1989. Leather sole, almond-shaped toe, medium-high stacked leather heel, calfskin upper with narrow-cut vamp and wide heel strap. 5 Italian c. 1987. Composite sole with almond-shaped toe and combined low heel, faux animal skin upper with open toe and asymmetric heel strap, elasticated gusset on side back. 6 Italian c. 1987. Leather sole, almond-shaped toe, medium-high velvet- and silk-covered half-cylindrical heel, sideless upper with plain velvet front and deep silk grosgrain heel strap, matching bar strap with jewelled buckle. 7 French c. 1987. Leather sole, pointed toe, high suede-covered wedge heel, matching upper with plain front and low-cut vamp, side front, sides and heel-back trimmed with contrast-colour kidskin appliqué. 8 Italian c. 1987. Leather sole, pointed toe, combined double wedge heel, calfskin upper with low-cut pointed vamp and wide elasticated heel strap, matching upper heel, silver kidskin pointed toecap, matching small lower heel.

149

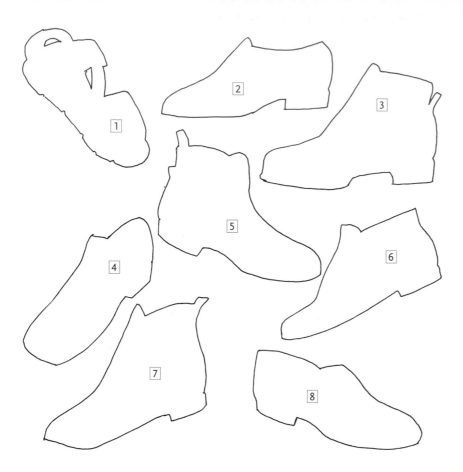

Men's shoes and boots 1990–present day

1 English c. 1996–1998. Ridged rubber sole with blunt toe and combined low heel, calfskin upper comprised of two wide adjustable straps over open toe, bar strap with Velcro fastening above padded cushion and wide heel strap. 2 Italian c. 1995–1997. Leather sole, blunt toe, low stacked leather heel, calfskin upper with plain front, contrast-colour facings to laced fastening and upper heel-back. 3 American c. 1999–2000. Ridged rubber sole with blunt toe and combined low heel, ankle-length suede upper with plain front under laced fastening from instep to padded leather ankle guard, back pull tape, topstitched edges and detail. 4 Italian c. 2000–2003. Composite sole with blunt toe and low stacked-effect heel, leather upper with two topstitched seams on front above toe to under instep strap with linked metal trim, high tongue. 5 English c. 1990–1993. Rubber sole with blunt toe and combined low heel, ankle-length calfskin upper with plain front, side flap opening with buckled strap fastening, back pull tape. 6 English c. 1994–1996. Composite sole with blunt toe and combined low heel, ankle-length calfskin upper with topstitched apron front to under high instep strap with cut-out detail, high tongue, elasticated side gussets, padded top edge. 7 English c. 1999–2003. Composite sole with square toe and low stacked-effect heel, ankle-length calfskin upper with centre front topstitched seam from tip of box-shaped toe to top of high tongue, laced fastening, back pull tape. 8 American c. 1995–1999. Composite sole with blunt toe and combined low heel, calfskin upper with contrast-colour apron front, high tongue and instep strap with cut-out detail.

Women's shoes and boots 1990–1992

1 Italian c. 1991. Composite sole with almond-shaped toe and low stacked-effect heel, satin upper with low-cut sides and vamp in-filled with self-fabric motifs forming cut-out pattern. 2 French c. 1990. Leather sole, almond-shaped toe, low stacked leather heel, patterned silk upper with plain front and narrow low-cut vamp. 3 French c. 1990. Leather sole, almond-shaped toe, low squat calfskin-covered heel, spotted silk upper with narrow low-cut vamp, cluster pearl button trim on centre front. 4 Italian c. 1991. Leather sole, pointed toe, medium-high tapered silk-covered heel, matching sideless upper with two straps on each side of centre front under self-fabric flower-trimmed low-cut vamp, attached on sides to heel strap. 5 French c. 1990. Leather sole, pointed toe, high tapered gold calfskin-covered heel, matching sideless upper with low-cut pointed vamp, heel-back and ankle-level mock-tie fastening. 6 English c. 1991. Composite sole with pointed toe and calfskin-covered Louis-style squat heel, matching ankle-length upper with plain front, wrap-over sides with concealed elasticated gussets, high pointed vamp and matching heel-back. 7 Italian c. 1992. Calfskin upper with contrast-colour facings to laced fastening extended to above pointed toe and on mid-sides. 8 Italian c. 1992. Parti-coloured calfskin upper with pointed toe, narrow low-cut vamp and stylized two-colour bow trim. 9 English c. 1991. Leather sole, pointed toe, medium-high silk-brocade-covered Louis-style heel, matching backless upper with front, high pointed tongue and narrow sides decorated with multicoloured floral embroidery. 10 Italian c. 1991. Leather sole, pointed toe, high gold calfskin-covered stiletto heel, matching upper edges and low-cut vamp of multicoloured kidskin patchwork.

Women's shoes and boots 1993–1994

1 English *c.* 1994. Composite sole with almond-shaped toe and low squat shaped calfskin-covered heel, matching upper with plain front, low-cut vamp and short tongue. 2 Italian *c.* 1994. Leather sole, pointed toe, medium-high gold calfskin-covered Louis-style heel, sideless silk velvet upper with low-cut vamp and high pointed tongue joined to pointed heel-back with gold calfskin strap on each side, matching trim and linings. 3 French *c.* 1993. Leather sole, blunt toe, shallow calfskin-covered platform, matching straight medium-high heel and upper with narrow low-cut vamp. 4 English *c.* 1993. Leather sole, pointed toe, low square calfskin-covered heel, matching ankle-length upper with centre front seam from toe to top edge, buckled strap from under side strap and button mock fastening. 5 American *c.* 1993. Composite sole with pointed toe and shallow calfskin-covered platform, matching medium-high Louis-style heel and ankle-length upper with plain front under laced fastening and high tongue, decorative pull tape. 6 English *c.* 1994. Composite sole with pointed toe and high calfskin-covered stiletto heel, matching ankle-length upper with plain front and side laced fastening above cut-away side panels. 7 English *c.* 1994. Composite sole with pointed toe and high curved silk-covered heel, matching stretch silk knee-length upper with plain front and fitted leg. 8 Italian *c.* 1994. Leather sole, elongated pointed toe, high silver calfskin-covered spike heel, matching toecap and facings of zip fastening in fitted leg of knee-length transparent plastic upper.

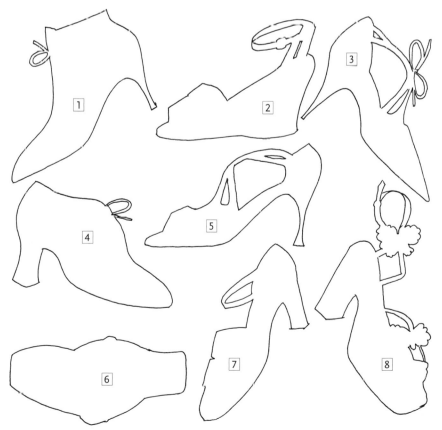

Women's shoes and boots 1995–1996

1 French *c.* 1996. Leather sole, pointed toe, shallow calfskin-covered platform, matching slender high heel, ankle-length fake-animal-skin front upper with laced fastening from instep over high tongue, transparent plastic heel-back and boot top. 2 English *c.* 1995. Composite sole with blunt toe and calfskin-covered platform combined with high wedge heel, matching shallow side panels and crossed and buckled ankle straps, two transparent plastic straps over instep and toes. 3 English *c.* 1996. Leather sole, pointed toe, high silk-covered stiletto heel, matching toecap, crossed straps and rouleau tie of sideless upper, front with low-cut vamp and heel-back in contrast colour. 4 English *c.* 1995. Composite sole with almond-shaped toe and medium-high suede-covered Louis-style heel, matching sideless upper with plain front under laced fastening above high vamp and tongue. 5 English *c.* 1996. Composite sole with blunt toe and fake pony-skin-covered thin platform, matching slender high heel and sideless upper with low-cut vamp above open toe, crossed straps over instep with buckled fastening on one side of heel-back. 6 Italian *c.* 1996. Heelless leather sole, square toe, calfskin lining, backless upper with short strap between large and second toes joined to multicoloured jewel-decorated strap over instep. 7 English *c.* 1995. Composite sole with almond-shaped toe and high card-shaped silk-covered heel, matching sideless upper with single wide strap above open toe and two straps over instep, filled-in heel-back and buckled ankle strap. 8 English *c.* 1995. Composite sole with square toe and shallow gold calfskin-covered platform, matching thick high heel and narrow criss-crossed upper straps decorated with jewelled butterflies.

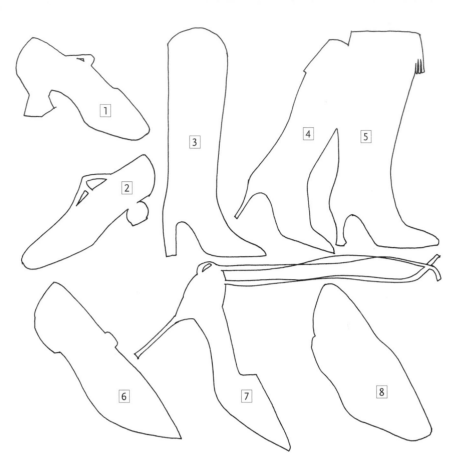

Women's shoes and boots 1997–1999

1 Italian *c.* 1998. Leather sole, narrow square toe, medium-high two-colour calfskin-covered angular heel, matching upper with low-cut vamp and buckled bar strap. 2 Italian *c.* 1998. Leather sole, almond-shaped toe, calfskin-covered spherical heel, contrast-colour calfskin upper with low-cut vamp, plain front and T-strap with side button fastening. 3 French *c.* 1997. Leather sole, elongated pointed toe, set-back straight satin-covered heel, matching knee-length stretch satin upper with plain front and straight leg embroidered with multicoloured silk dragon. 4 English *c.* 1999. Leather sole, elongated pointed toe, multicoloured jewel-encrusted slender high heel, matching turned-down cuff on embossed velvet upper with plain front and fitted leg. 5 English *c.* 1999. Leather sole, elongated pointed toe, medium-high calfskin-covered Louis-style heel, matching knee-length upper with plain front, criss-crossed leather straps over fitted leg and fringed turned-down cuff. 6 English *c.* 1998. Composite sole with pointed toe and stacked-effect low heel, calfskin upper with wide bar strap above low-cut vamp. 7 English *c.* 1997. Leather sole, pointed toe, high spiked metal heel and silk-covered heel top, matching sideless upper with low-cut vamp and bead-decorated plain front, matching heel-back with long ribbon tie from top edge. 8 English *c.* 1999. Deep crepe sole with square toe, combined wedge heel, suede upper with leather thong tie fastening on one side of wrap-over high vamp, topstitched asymmetric seam to one side of box-shaped toe, repeated on one side of heel-back.

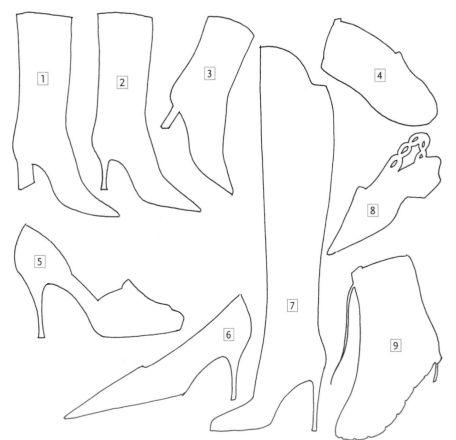

Women's shoes and boots 2000–present day

1 English *c.* 2000. Leather sole, elongated pointed toe, high card-shaped calfskin-covered heel, matching knee-length upper with fitted leg and concealed side zip fastening, tongue seam and heel-back seam piped with crenellated contrast-colour calfskin. 2 English *c.* 2002. Leather sole, elongated pointed toe, slender high calfskin-covered heel, knee-length lace-covered velvet upper with fitted leg and concealed zip fastening in back seam, Russia-braid trim on top back edge. 3 English *c.* 2003. Composite sole with elongated pointed toe and thin high metal card-shaped heel, mid-calf-length fake suede upper with straight leg, side seam and top edge whipped with contrast-colour thong. 4 English *c.* 2001. Deep rubber sole with blunt toe and combined low wedge heel, calfskin upper with low-cut vamp, wide tongue with contrast-colour stripe from top to end of toe, matching trim on heel-back seam and piped edges. 5 French *c.* 2003. Leather sole, blunt toe, calfskin-covered platform, matching slender spike heel and sideless upper with low-cut vamp and short tongue, front trimmed with two fake-lizard-skin buckled straps above open toe. 6 English *c.* 2003. Composite sole with elongated pointed toe and calfskin-covered stiletto heel, matching plain upper with low-cut vamp. 7 Italian *c.* 2003. Leather sole, pointed toe, textured-calfskin-covered platform trimmed with metal studs, matching high spike heel and above-knee-length upper with concealed side zip fastening and stud-trimmed heel-back. 8 English *c.* 2001. Leather sole, almond-shaped toe, low squat shaped calfskin-covered heel, matching backless upper with plain front, low-cut vamp and short tongue, leopard-print lining, side panels forming interweaving heel strap. 9 French *c.* 2003. Ridged rubber sole and combined wedge heel, padded man-made fabric ankle-length upper with leather facings to laced fastening, matching full-length tongue, toecap, heel-back and trim, contrast-colour side flashes.

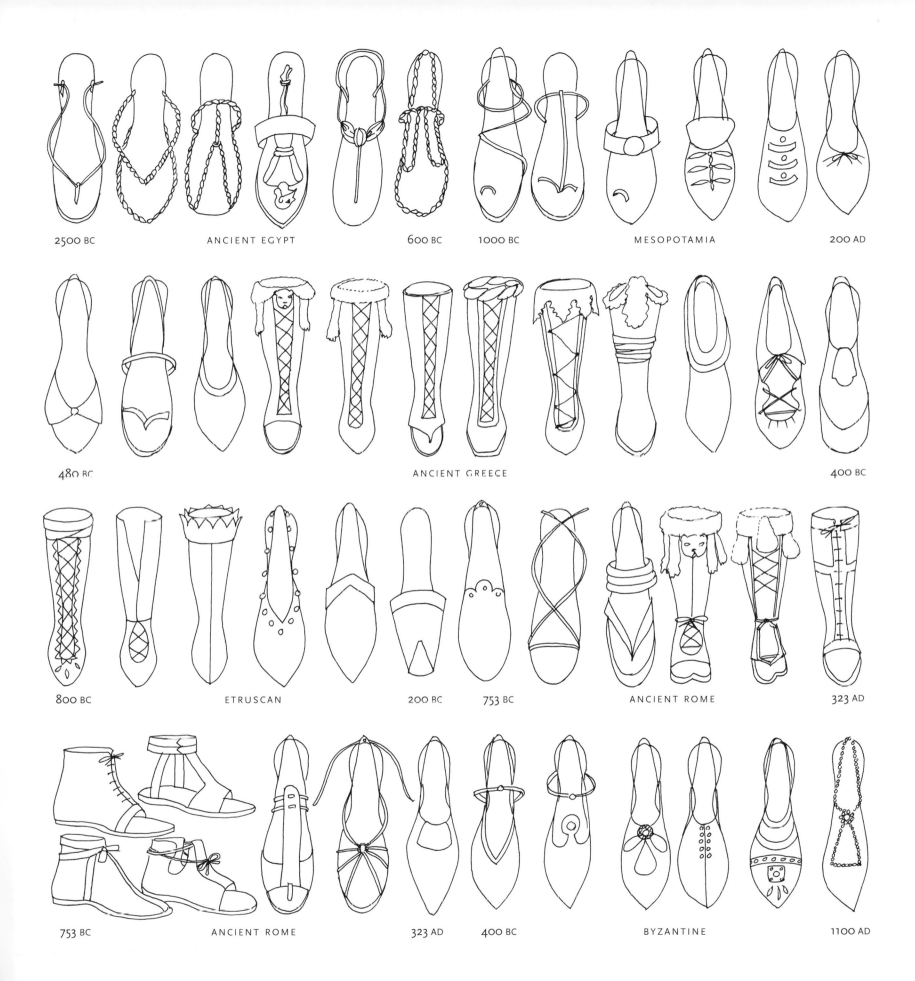

2500 BC   ANCIENT EGYPT   600 BC   1000 BC   MESOPOTAMIA   200 AD

480 BC   ANCIENT GREECE   400 BC

800 BC   ETRUSCAN   200 BC   753 BC   ANCIENT ROME   323 AD

753 BC   ANCIENT ROME   323 AD   400 BC   BYZANTINE   1100 AD

100

1099

1100

1199

1200

1299

1300

1399

1400

1499

1500

1599

1600

1699

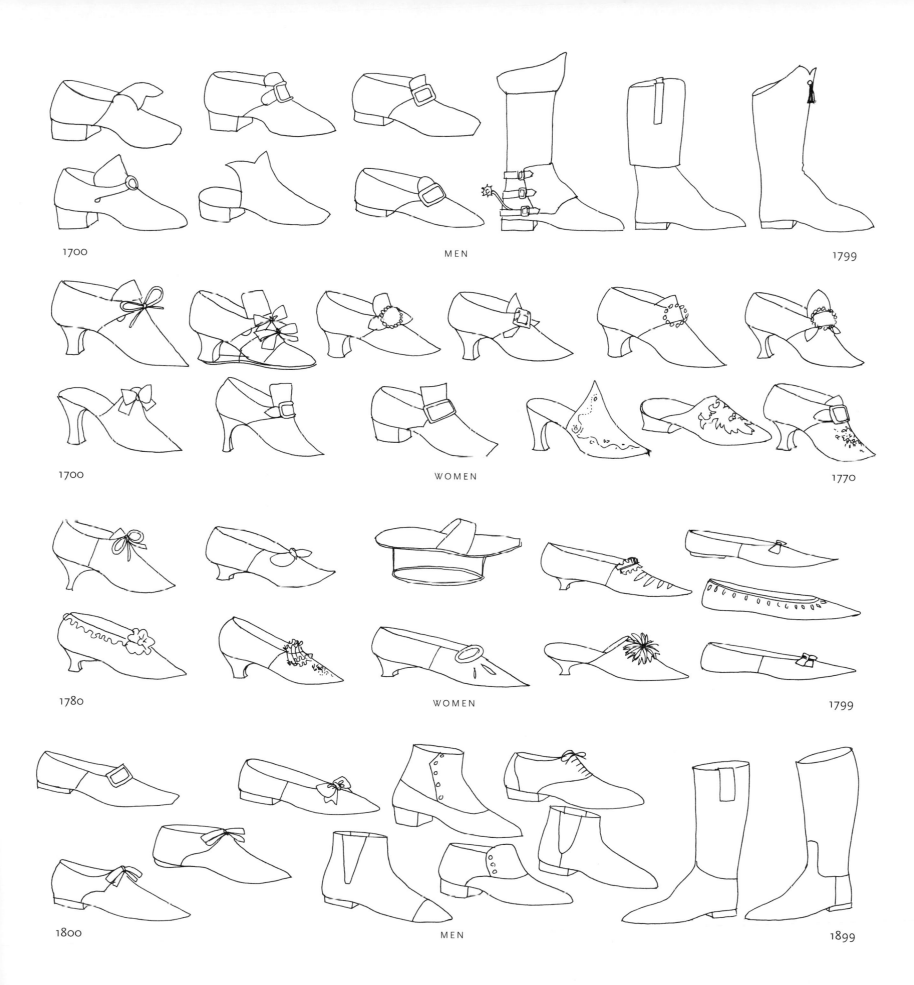

1700　　　　　　　　　　　　　　　MEN　　　　　　　　　　　　　　　1799

1700　　　　　　　　　　　　　　WOMEN　　　　　　　　　　　　　　1770

1780　　　　　　　　　　　　　　WOMEN　　　　　　　　　　　　　　1799

1800　　　　　　　　　　　　　　　MEN　　　　　　　　　　　　　　　1899

1800　　　　　　　　　　　WOMEN　　　　　　　　　　　1840

1845　　　　　　　　　　　WOMEN　　　　　　　　　　　1875

1875　　　　　　　　　　　WOMEN　　　　　　　　　　　1890

1890　　　　　　　　　　　WOMEN　　　　　　　　　　　1899

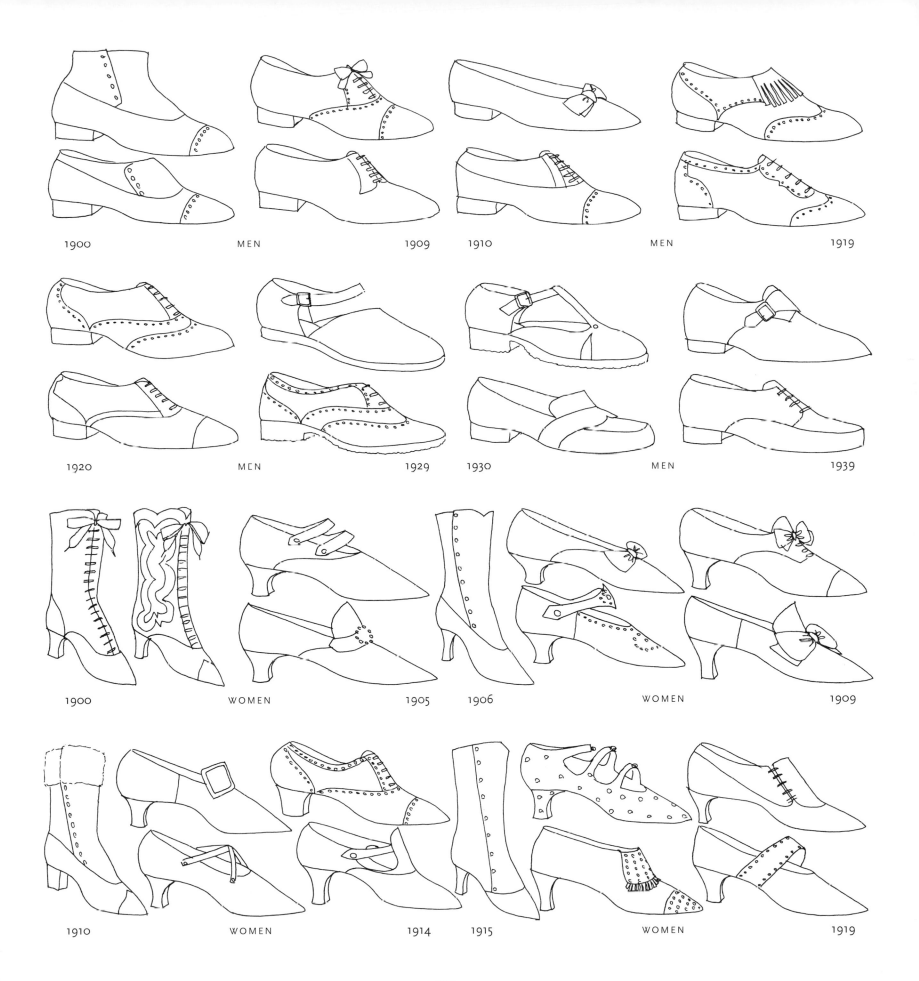

1900   MEN   1909   1910   MEN   1919

1920   MEN   1929   1930   MEN   1939

1900   WOMEN   1905   1906   WOMEN   1909

1910   WOMEN   1914   1915   WOMEN   1919

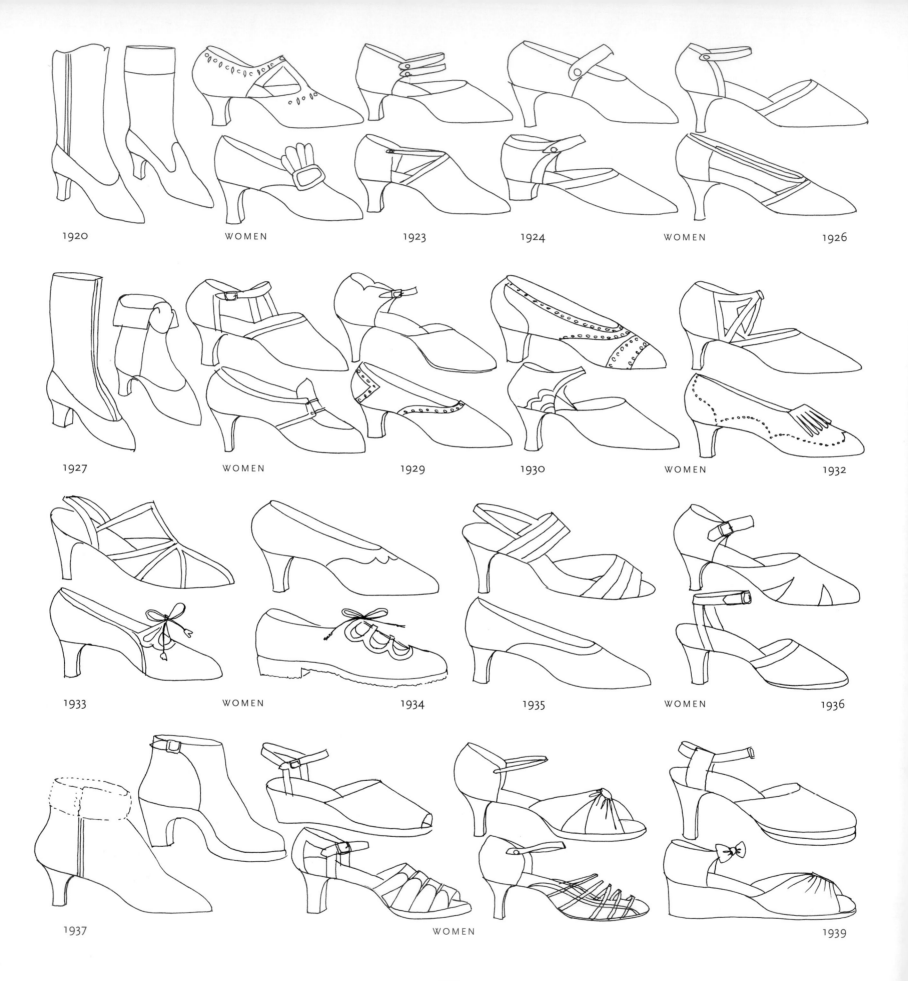

1920   WOMEN   1923   1924   WOMEN   1926

1927   WOMEN   1929   1930   WOMEN   1932

1933   WOMEN   1934   1935   WOMEN   1936

1937   WOMEN   1939

1940 MEN 1949 1950 MEN 1959

1960 MEN 1969 1970 MEN 1979

1940 WOMEN 1942 1943 WOMEN 1944

1945 WOMEN 1946 1947 WOMEN 1949

1950   WOMEN   1952   1953   WOMEN   1954

1955   WOMEN   1956   1957   WOMEN   1959

1960   WOMEN   1962   1963   WOMEN   1964

1965   WOMEN   1966   1967   WOMEN   1969

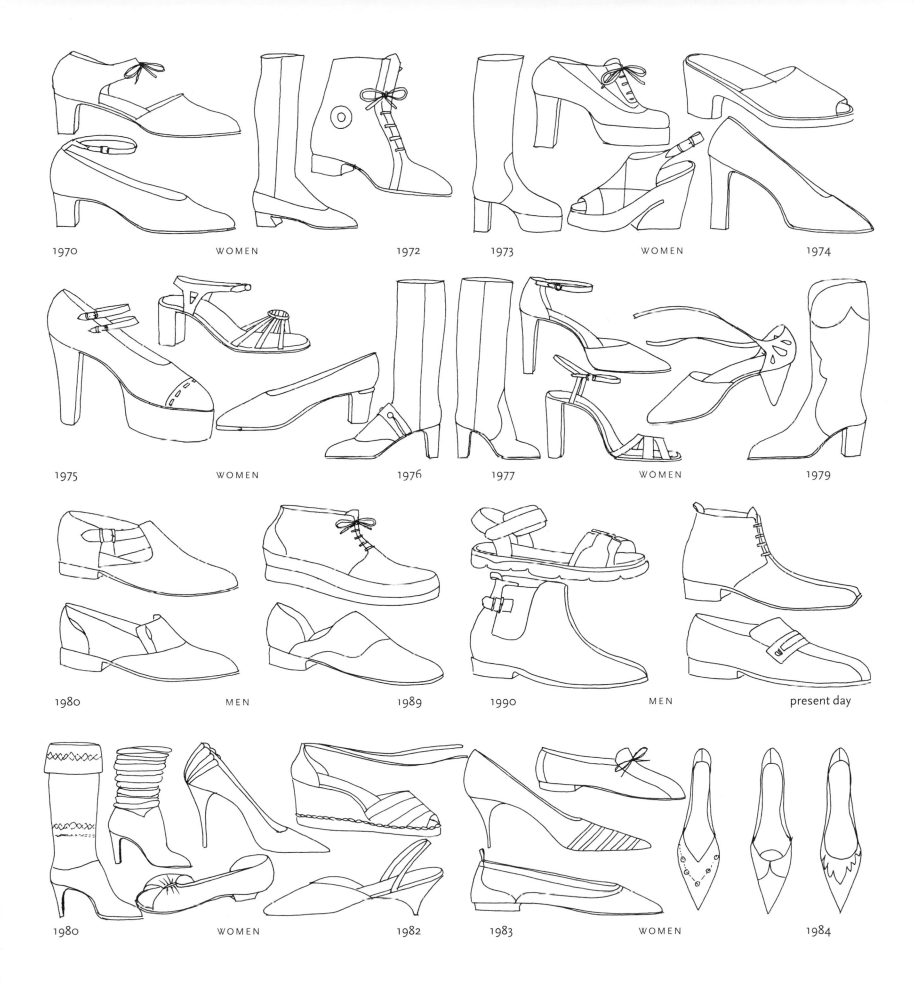

1970   WOMEN   1972   1973   WOMEN   1974

1975   WOMEN   1976   1977   WOMEN   1979

1980   MEN   1989   1990   MEN   present day

1980   WOMEN   1982   1983   WOMEN   1984

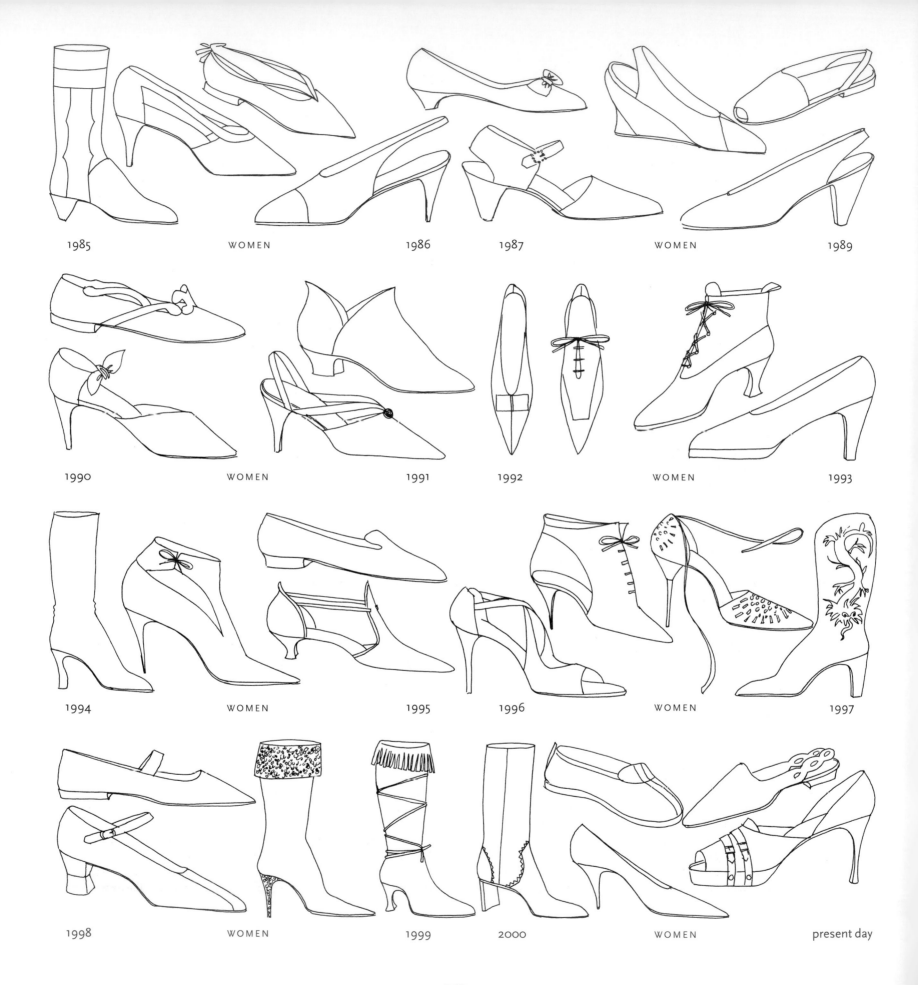

1985 WOMEN 1986 1987 WOMEN 1989

1990 WOMEN 1991 1992 WOMEN 1993

1994 WOMEN 1995 1996 WOMEN 1997

1998 WOMEN 1999 2000 WOMEN present day

Concise Biographies of Designers and Companies

adidas Founded in Germany in 1949 by Adolph Dassler, brother of Rudolf Dassler, who founded Puma*. Sponsorship of sporting heroes such as Muhammad Ali helped adidas to become the dominant force in the world sports market. While the company's trademark 'three stripes' are still used on its footwear and clothing today, adidas training shoes have transcended their sporting origins to become street fashion statements, particularly associated with hip-hop.

Bally Founded in Schönenwerd, Switzerland, in 1851 by Carl Franz Bally. The original shoe-making process was based on division of labour, with local homeworkers completing different components. By 1880 new techniques had been introduced and the company was selling across Europe, the Middle East and the Americas to become one of the world's first global luxury brands. In 1976 Bally expanded into clothing, handbags and other leather goods.

Bata Founded in Zlin, Czechoslovakia, in 1894 by Tomas Bata, together with his brother Antonin and sister Anna. Departing from the centuries-old tradition of the one-man cobbler's workshop, Bata employed a team of stitchers and shoemakers to create footwear not just for local use but also for far-off retailers. By 1938 Bata goods were being marketed in more than thirty countries. Today its products are available worldwide and are renowned for their quality and value for money.

Susan Bennis & Warren Edwards Founded in New York, USA, in 1972. Neither Bennis nor Edwards had any formal design training, but made original, exclusive shoes for both men and women. Warren Edwards now runs his own business, using over 300 different leathers and colours.

Dirk Bikkembergs Born in Bonn, Germany, in 1959, but Belgian by nationality. Bikkembergs graduated as a designer from the Royal Academy of Antwerp in 1982, and became one of the influential group of designers known as the Antwerp Six. His first shoe collection for men was launched in 1985, and was followed by menswear, womenswear and streetwear collections. His signature style is based around simple shapes, strong materials and military-style detailing.

Birkenstock In 1897 Konrad Birkenstock of Germany designed a shoe with a contoured insole. He also developed a flexible arch support, examples of which were soon being exported all over Europe. In 1964 Konrad's grandson Karl designed the first Birkenstock sandal. An American, Margot Fraser, tried a pair while holidaying in Germany and, convinced of their health benefits, started to import Birkenstocks to America, where they soon became a phenomenon. With their unique footbed, which is standard throughout the whole collection, Birkenstocks remain a by-word for comfortable, functional footwear.

Manolo Blahnik Born in Santa Cruz, Canary Islands, in 1942. Blahnik studied at the University of Geneva before moving to Paris and then London, hoping to become a set designer. While on a visit to New York in 1971 he showed his portfolio to the fashion editor Diana Vreeland, who suggested he concentrate on shoe design. Later that year he opened a shop in Chelsea, London, which is still there today. Blahnik's exquisite, often theatrical designs are made with superbly crafted, top quality materials and are a firm favourite in the worlds of fashion and entertainment.

Camper Founded in Majorca, Spain, in 1975 by Lorenzo Flux, the grandson of a craftsman shoemaker. The first Camper store was opened in Barcelona in 1981 and the company quickly made a name for its casual but sophisticated footwear in unisex designs. Today Camper (meaning 'peasant') is an international brand, drawing on its Mediterranean heritage for qualities of comfort, durability and simplicity.

Cat Manufactured since 1994 by US footwear company Wolverine World Wide under license from the construction equipment company Caterpillar. Cat shoe and clothing ranges, whether workwear or casual wear, share the same utilitarian, urban values as their industrial heritage, combining safety and comfort with rugged durability.

Jimmy Choo Born in Malaysia in 1952. Choo trained at Cordwainers College, London, and became a consultant to Bally*, before launching his own label with Gee Wee Lai. In 1996 Tamara Mellon founded the company that has rapidly become a highly successful, upmarket, fashion-forward shoe business, though Choo himself no longer designs the collections. Jimmy Choos are sold in high-end department stores and speciality stores in the UK, the US and the Far East, as well as at stand-alone boutiques in select locations including Beverly Hills and Las Vegas.

Church's Founded in Northampton, England, in 1873 by Alfred, Thomas and William Church. The hallmarks of the company's English Shoes Collection are quality and fine craftsmanship. Church's is most famous for its leather gentlemen's shoes, each pair being made over an 8-week period involving 250 operations, and hand-finished for traditional English elegance.

Clarks Founded in Street, England, in 1825 by Cyrus and James Clark, sheepskin tanners. The use of the newly invented Singer sewing machine and the introduction of William Clark's foot-friendly 'Hygienic line' established the company's reputation. In the early twentieth century Clarks expanded rapidly, offering a wide range of classic, comfortable designs. The Desert Boot, introduced in the 1950s, was to become a cult success, as was the moccasin-like Wallabee. The company has also become known for its well-fitting children's shoes.

Robert Clergerie Founded in Paris, France, in 1981, with production based in Romans. Having worked with Charles Jourdan*, Robert Clergerie went on to found his own company, which has become noted for its simple, modern designs that match clean, architectural functionality with forward-looking styling.

Kenneth Cole Founded in New York, USA, in 1982, Kenneth Cole Productions, Inc. is so-named because the only way its founder could afford to start up his business was to borrow a truck, obtain a parking permit from the mayor under the guise of being a film production company, and then sell shoes from the truck in midtown Manhattan while 'filming'. A global presence today, Kenneth Cole is a leader in fashion footwear with a wide variety of high-style ladies' and men's shoe designs.

Cole Haan Founded in Chicago, USA, in 1928 by Trafton Cole and Eddie Haan. One craftsperson is responsible for each pair of shoes from the beginning of the process right through to boxing up the finished shoes at the end. The company, having started with men's shoes, now produces women's footwear as well as hosiery, belts, handbags and other small leather goods. Classic Cole Haan hallmarks include artisan quality, from hand-crafted leather to hand-stitched seams, and a spirit of casual luxury.

Converse Founded in the US in 1908 by Marquis M. Converse. This industry-standard athletic shoe brand produces sports performance, sports lifestyle and sports classic footwear, the latter including the iconic Chuck Taylor All Star basketball shoe. Converse use functional design, progressive technology and innovative styling to create athletic shoes that have also become fashionable streetwear.

André Courrèges Fashion house founded in Paris, France, in 1961 by André Courrèges, who had previously been a designer for Balenciaga. Courrèges was responsible for introducing the Mod look to high fashion and is also credited with inventing the mini-skirt. His Spring '65 catwalk show presented geometrical white dresses accompanied by shiny, white, space-age, mid-calf-length go-go boots, which were later made famous by Nancy 'These Boots are Made for Walking' Sinatra.

Patrick Cox Born in Edmonton, Canada, in 1963. Cox trained at Cordwainers College, London, and created shoes for fashion

designers such as Vivienne Westwood*, Body Map and John Galliano before making his own private label collection available in 1987. In 1991 he opened his first shop in London. The company has now expanded into the US, France and the Far East, and is perhaps best known for its Wannabe loafers. In 2003 Cox was made designer at Charles Jourdan*.

Charles David Founded in California, USA, in 1987 as a wholesale importing and distribution company bringing European shoes to the US market. This family business, with factories in Spain and Italy, has quickly established itself as a leader in women's footwear. Its trendsetting designs and fashionable styling are achieved by a team of in-house designers. Other Charles David shoe lines include Charles David Collection and Guess Footwear.

Delman Founded in California, USA, in 1895 by Herman B. Delman. After World War I he opened stores in Hollywood and New York, and from the late 1930s worked in partnership with Bergdorf Goodman. Delman made shoes for a number of renowned designers, including Roger Vivier*, and specialized in upmarket, expensive lines. His signature glamour, whether attained by using movie stars in his advertisements or through the theatricality of his stores, made him one of the foremost shoemakers of his day.

Dr Martens Founded in Germany in 1945 by Dr Klaus Maertens and Dr Herbert Funck. When Maertens injured his foot whilst skiing, he hit upon the idea of developing a shoe with an air-cushioned sole to provide extra comfort and support. With Funck's help, the world's first heat-sealed, air-cushioned sole was created. R. Griggs & Co. in the UK acquired the global rights to the sole and developed a range of complementary footwear. The first pair of boots was produced on 1 April 1960 (hence the name by which the boots are often known, '1460s'). Since then the Dr Marten boot, with its trademark yellow stitching, sole pattern and attitude, has been adopted by countless youth sub-cultures, from skinheads to punks, and has become a modern design icon.

Dr Scholl's Founded in the US in 1906 by Dr William Matthias Scholl. The grandson of a shoemaker, Scholl worked as an apprentice shoe repairer and later as a shoe sales clerk. Realizing the need for shoes that not only fit well but also corrected or alleviated foot pain, he enrolled in Illinois Medical College and, after graduating, began to manufacture orthopaedic foot products, including the now-famous Dr Scholl exercise sandal. The company's products, with their contoured beechwood footbeds and distinctive blue and yellow livery, sell all over the world.

Ecco Founded in Bredebro, Denmark, in 1963 by Karl Toosbuy. This family-owned business, which operates using hi-tech production methods and its own state-of-the art tanneries, is today one of the largest shoe brands in the world and renowned for its comfortable walking and leisure shoes.

David Evins Born in England but emigrated to the US at the age of 13. Having studied illustration at the Pratt Institute in New York, Evins secured a contract with I. Miller* in 1941 to produce his own label. His refined, glamorous designs made him a favourite of Hollywood and high society, and his clients included Ava Gardner, Grace Kelly, Elizabeth Taylor and the Duchess of Windsor. He also designed the pumps that Nancy Reagan wore to her husband's presidential inaugurations.

Salvatore Ferragamo Born in Naples, Italy, in 1898. A shoemaker's apprentice at 11, Ferragamo was put in charge of his own shop at 13 but emigrated to Boston a year later. After a move to California he opened a shoe-repair and made-to-measure shoe shop, and soon began to produce footwear for the growing cinema industry. His elegant, witty shoes, often in unorthodox materials, were bought by customers such as Mary Pickford, Rudolph Valentino and Douglas Fairbanks, and Ferragamo became known as 'Shoemaker to the Stars'. To perfect his craft he studied human anatomy at the University of Los Angeles. In 1927 he returned to Italy, where he found workers skilled enough to make the high-quality shoes he desired, and he invented classics such as the cork wedge. Today the company is based in Florence, where lasts of celebrated customers can be seen. After Ferragamo's death in 1960 his wife and eldest daughter continued to run the company.

Maud Frizon Born in Paris, France, in 1941. For many years Frizon worked as a model, and was a particular favourite of Courrèges*. She launched her first shoe collection in 1970. Each pair was hand-cut and finished, and the collection was an immediate success. The cone-shaped high heel of the 1980s became a signature style, and Frizon made a name for her sophisticated and witty designs, often in unusual combinations of materials.

Kurt Geiger Founded in 1963 in London, England, by Kurt and Irmgard Geiger of Austria. The brand has gone through several changes of ownership, but has retained its positioning as a purveyor of confident, modern, sleek, men and women's footwear designs pitched at a grown-up and glamorous market.

Gucci Fashion house founded in Florence, Italy, in 1921, as a small luggage and saddlery company. In 1932 Guccio Gucci designed the loafer that was to become a worldwide phenomenon. This slip-on dress shoe, with its distinctive snaffle, is now a by-word for modern-day style and sophistication.

Terry de Havilland Began working for the family firm in 1960. De Havilland first drew attention for his wedge-heeled sandals, and his customers included Bianca Jagger, Anita Pallenberg and David Bowie. In the 1970s he became head of the family business and opened his first shop. Current fashion trends have revived interest in his brand of glamour and, with the signature high stiletto or platform heels and bespoke fabrics designed by his partner and muse Liz Cotton, de Havilland designs are prominent once again.

Emma Hope Established in London, England, in 1985. Hope trained at Cordwainers College, London, and attracted attention with her first own-label collection of brocade mules. The inspiration for her 'regalia for feet' often comes from historical sources. A line of handbags has now been introduced to compliment the clean, simple and softly sculpted footwear.

Hush Puppies Founded in the US in 1958 and manufactured by Wolverine World Wide. Named after a Southern US speciality – deep-fried cornmeal balls used to quieten barking dogs ('barking dogs' was 1950s slang for sore feet) – these soft suede shoes were the first to epitomize the American casual look. Today Hush Puppies, with their distinctive basset hound logo, are available in eighty countries worldwide.

Jan Jansen Born in the Netherlands in 1941, the son of a sales manager in a shoe factory. Having served his apprenticeship in Rome, Jansen went on to work under the Jeannot label. His creations, including the clog-like Woody, the High-Heeled Sneaker and the heelless high heel, are notable for their technical innovation and for the exuberant flamboyancy of their materials, including metallic goat leather, rattan and crepe.

Joan & David Founded in Massachusetts, USA, in 1968 by Joan and David Halpern. David was chairman of Suburban Shoe Stores when he met Joan, and she decided to learn the rudiments of the business at a small shoe company in Boston. Joan & David is today well-known for its smart, classic shoes, designed for the active, modern woman. Now based in Italy, the company has branched out into purses, accessories and clothing.

Johnston & Murphy Founded in New Jersey, USA, in 1850 by William J. Dudley. In 1880 Dudley teamed up with James Johnston, and on Dudley's death in 1882 Johnston went into partnership with William H. Murphy. Now based in Nashville, Tennessee, the company is famous for its elegant, understated, hand-crafted shoes in styles including the oxford, the tie shoe and the captoe, which have been worn by every US president since the 1850s.

Charles Jourdan Born in Romans, France, in 1883. In 1919 Jourdan set up his first shoe shop and the business prospered, particularly in the sale of women's shoes. In the 1930s, Jourdan was the first shoe designer to advertise in fashion magazines, and the company's reputation for stylish, avant-garde promotion has continued to this day. After World War II, Jourdan's three sons joined the company and in 1957 they opened, in Paris, the first of several boutiques. Now one of the biggest names in French luxury, ready-to-wear footwear, Charles Jourdan is associated with a chic, conservative look.

Stéphane Kélian Founded in Romans, France, like Robert Clergerie* and Charles Jourdan*. Stéphane Kélian is known for original, high-fashion, wearable shoes, and has a particular reputation for hand-woven designs. The company also distributes Maud Frizon*.

Beth and Herbert Levine Founded in the US in 1950. Like David Evins*, Beth Levine worked at I. Miller* in the 1940s. When in 1950 she married Herbert, a salesman and shoe designer, they set up a joint company. This became known for its use of unexpected materials, including bamboo and clear acrylic, and for its innovative styling, such as heels and soles attached to pantyhose. Their designs are still influential today.

John Lobb Founded in England in the mid-1880s. Noted particularly for its handmade men's brogues, oxfords and loafers in over 50 different types of leather, John Lobb has a vast collection of customers' lasts arranged in alphabetical order, including some of the most famous names of the twentieth century, such as Winston Churchill, Alfred Hitchcock, Gregory Peck and Katharine Hepburn. Today the company enjoys three Royal Warrants and a reputation for quality bespoke craftsmanship.

Christian Louboutin Born in Paris, France, in 1963. Louboutin trained with Charles Jourdan* and freelanced for Chanel and Yves Saint Laurent. His designs are renowned for their inventiveness and wit. With their trademark red-painted soles, his 'follow me' shoes have heels that leave behind a rosette imprint.

Bruno Magli Founded in Bologna, Italy, in 1936. In the 1970s and '80s the company's franchises achieved international success, partly through the efforts of its North American agents, Buddy and Harriet Palter. Bruno Magli maintains a reputation for upscale craftsmanship and, in addition to women's and men's shoes, produces leather clothing, handbags, luggage items, small leather goods and other accessories.

I. Miller Founded in New York, USA, in 1880. Under Israel Miller the firm was a renowned supplier of theatrical footwear, mainly for Broadway productions. After Miller's death in 1929 the company expanded into making and retailing fashion footwear for the upper end of the market, employing the best designers to create collections. The shoes became famous during the 1930s and '40s for the superior quality of their design and manufacture.

Nike Founded in Oregon, USA, in 1962 by Phil Knight and Bill Bowerman, under the name of Blue Ribbon Sports. The Nike brand shoe was launched in 1972, and in 1978 the company was re-named Nike, after the Greek goddess of victory. With its unmistakeable 'swoosh', Nike footwear, including the famous Air Jordan basketball shoe, is noted for its technical advances and for the company's innovative marketing and branding practices.

André Perugia Born in Nice, France, in 1893 of Italian parentage. Perugia trained in his father's workshop and at the age of 16 opened a shop in Paris, where he sold handmade shoes. He later moved to the famed Rue Faubourg St Honoré, where all the fashion designers had their salons. After World War I, he made shoes for fashion designer Paul Poiret, and it was through this connection that his clients came to include celebrated dancers and movie actresses such as Josephine Baker and Gloria Swanson. By experimenting with new materials, shapes and textures, Perugia created glamorous footwear of startling originality.

Andrea Pfister Born in Pesaro, Italy, in 1942. After designing for Lanvin and Jean Patou, Pfister showed his first collection in 1965, and in 1967 opened his first shop in Paris. Famous for his colourful, highly decorated and amusing footwear, such as the feather-covered Papageno shoe or the cocktail-glass-heeled Martini Dry pump, Pfister is at the vanguard of stylish fantasy footwear.

François Pinet Born in France in 1817, the son of a shoemaker. Generally credited with being the first important 'bottier', Pinet established his company in 1855 and quickly began supplying made-to-order boots and shoes to Parisian high society. The company's reputation was based on the Pinet heel, a more refined version of the popular Louis heel. Pinet's son took over on his father's retirement and the company's shoes remained fashionable well into the 1930s.

Puma Founded in Herzogenaurach, Germany, in 1948, by Rudolf Dassler, brother of Adolph Dassler, who founded adidas*. One of the best-known sports shoe brands in the world, Puma products come with a trademark 'formstrip'. Though its classics are enduringly popular, the company is also at the vanguard of technological innovation.

H & M Rayne Founded in London, England, in 1889 by Henry and Mary Rayne. Having started as theatrical costumiers, providing clothing, cosmetics and footwear for the stage, H & M Rayne decided to concentrate on shoes. The company became well-known for supplying the Royal Family – the future Queen Elizabeth II wore a pair at her wedding. Rayne shoes are distinguished for their unostentatious, classic designs.

Reebok Started in Bolton, England, in 1895 by Joseph William Foster, who made himself a pair of spiked running shoes. Soon he was manufacturing the shoes for other athletes and his company J. W. Foster & Sons prospered. In 1958 the company became Reebok, named after an African gazelle. With its trademark 'vector' logo, the company was the first to introduce an athletic shoe, the Freestyle, especially for women. Following the boom period of the 1980s exercise movement, the company was also at the forefront in promoting athletic footwear as street and casual wear.

Fratelli Rossetti Founded in Parabiago, Italy, in 1953 by Renzo Rossetti and his brother Renato. One of the foremost Italian shoe producers, Fratelli Rossetti became well-known for its brown loafer for men. Today the company's elegant and fashionable men and women's shoes are available worldwide.

Sergio Rossi Established in San Mauro Pascoli, Italy, in the 1960s. The son of a shoemaker, Rossi began by producing women's shoes for an urban, sophisticated market. By the 1980s bags and menswear had been introduced, and the company had established a reputation for high quality, superior fit and a uniquely sexy sensibility. In 1999 the company entered into a strategic partnership with the Gucci Group. Sergio Rossi luxury goods are now available in Europe, the US and Asia.

Russell & Bromley Established as a boot and shoe manufacturing business in East Sussex, England, c. 1820, by John Clifford Russell. In 1874 Russell's granddaughter Elizabeth married George Frederick Bromley, and when the couple took over the running of one of the family store branches, Russell & Bromley was born. Still family-owned today, the company are highly successful retailers of a wide array of fashionable women's, men's and children's footwear and handbags.

Walter Steiger Born in Geneva, Switzerland, in 1942. Steiger followed family tradition by undertaking an apprenticeship in shoemaking at the age of 16, after which he went to work for Bally* in Paris. After a stint in London, he opened his own Paris store in 1973. Renowned for his luxurious materials, including crocodile, Persian lamb and mink trim, Steiger makes shoes for an upmarket clientele and has also designed shoes for a number of couturiers, including Chanel, Oscar de la Renta and Nina Ricci.

Timberland Founded in New Hampshire, USA, in 1952 by Herman and Sidney Swartz, sons of Nathan Swartz who owned the Abingdon Shoe Company. In the 1970s the Swartz brothers tapped into a resurgence in interest in the great American outdoors and the environment. The durable, sturdy boot they created, with its heavily cleated sole and striped laces, was a pioneer in the trend for hiking-style boots.

Tod's Established in Italy in 1979 by Diego Della Valle, who turned his family's century-old shoe business into one of the world's leading luxury leather goods brands. Tod's chic moccasins, made popular as driving shoes by the Fiat magnate Gianni Agnelli, are available in a range of materials, including mock-croc and lizard, and have as their trademark distinctive nubbly soles.

Ugg Founded in Australia by Brian Smith, who in 1978 introduced his sheepskin boots to the United States. From its early beginnings as a small-time surf brand, Ugg has grown to be a hippy-chic phenomenon and the global leader in luxury sheepskin footwear.

Roger Vivier Born in Paris, France, in 1913. Vivier abandoned his studies in sculpture at the Ecole des Beaux-Arts in Paris in order to take up an apprenticeship in shoemaking. After World War II he worked with Christian Dior. Experimenting with distinctive heel shapes, including the stiletto, the platform and the comma, Vivier is often cited as one of the most innovative shoe designers of the twentieth century.

Stuart Weitzman Weitzman learned the art of shoemaking from his father, Seymour Weitzman, whose family ran a small shoe factory in Massachusetts, USA. His trademark is the use of exotic materials, including cork, vinyl, wallpaper and gold, and he designs over 300 new styles of high-fashion women's shoes and handbags a year.

Vivienne Westwood Born in Derbyshire, England, in 1941. Westwood's avant-garde footwear, made to complement her often outrageous clothing designs, includes the vertiginous-heeled mock-croc platform lace-ups infamously worn by Naomi Campbell on the autumn/winter 1994 catwalk.

Pietro Yanturni Born in Calabria, Italy, in 1890. An authority on shoes, Yanturni worked as the curator of the shoe collection at the Musée Cluny in Paris. Styling himself 'the most expensive shoemaker in the world', he made extraordinarily well-crafted shoes for a highly exclusive clientele.

Sources for Shoes

Anderson Black, J., and Madge Garland, *A History of Fashion*, London 1975

Barton, Lucy, *Historic Costume for the Stage*, London 1935

The Bata Shoe Organization, *All About Shoes: Footwear Through the Ages*, Toronto 1994

Baynes, Ken, and Kate Baynes (eds), *The Shoe Show: British Shoes Since 1790*, Rugby 1979

Blum, Stella, *Everyday Fashions of the Twenties As Pictured in Sears and other Catalogs*, New York 1981

— (ed.), *Victorian Fashions and Costumes from "Harper's Bazaar', 1867–1898*, London 1974

Boucher, François, *A History of Costume in the West*, London 1965

Bradfield, Nancy, *Historical Costumes of England, from the Eleventh to the Twentieth Century*, London 1958

Broby-Johansen, Rudolf, *Body and Clothes: An Illustrated History of Costume*, London 1968

Brooke, Iris, *English Costume in the Age of Elizabeth: The Sixteenth Century*, London 1948

—, *English Costume of the Early Middle Ages: The Tenth to the Thirteenth Centuries*, London 1949

—, *English Costume of the Later Middle Ages: The Fourteenth and Fifteenth Centuries*, London 1948

—, *English Costume of the Seventeenth Century*, London 1948

—, *A History of English Costume*, London 1937

—, and James Laver, *English Costume of the Eighteenth Century*, London 1949

Buck, Anne M., *Women's Costume: 1800–1835*, The Gallery of English Costume, Manchester 1952

—, *Women's Costume: 1870–1900*, The Gallery of English Costume, Manchester 1953

—, *Women's Costume: The 18th Century*, The Gallery of English Costume, Manchester 1954

Byrde, Penelope, *The Male Image: Men's Fashion in England 1300–1970*, London 1979

Contini, Mila, *Fashion*, London 1965

Cunnington, Cecil Willett, *English Women's Clothing in the Present Century*, London 1957

—, and Phillis Cunnington, *Handbook of English Mediaeval Costume*, London 1952

—, Phillis Cunnington and Charles Beard, *A Dictionary of English Costume*, London 1974

Dorner, Jane, *Fashion in the Forties and Fifties*, London 1975

—, *Fashion in the Twenties and Thirties*, London 1973

Drake, Nicholas, *The Fifties in Vogue*, New York 1987

Ewing, Elizabeth, *History of Twentieth Century Fashion*, London 1974

Fowler, Kenneth, *The Age of Plantagenet and Valois*, London 1967

Gaunt, William, *Court Painting in England from Tudor to Victorian Times*, London 1980

Girotti, Eugenia, *Footwear: Fifty Years History: 1945–1995*, Milan 1995

—, *Footwear: History and Customs*, Milan 1986

Gorsline, Douglas, *What People Wore: A Visual History of Dress from Ancient Times to the Twentieth Century*, London 1978

Halls, Zillah, *Men's Costume 1580–1750*, Her Majesty's Stationary Office, London 1970

—, *Women's Costume 1600–1750*, Her Majesty's Stationary Office, London 1970

—, *Women's Costume 1750–1800*, Her Majesty's Stationary Office, London 1972

Hartley, Dorothy, *Mediaeval Costume and Life*, London 1931

Houston, Mary G., *Ancient Greek, Roman and Byzantine Costume*, London 1931

—, and Florence S. Hornblower, *Ancient Egyptian, Assyrian and Persian Costume*, London 1920

Howell, Georgina, *In Vogue: Six Decades of Fashion*, London 1975

Kohler, Carl, *A History of Costume*, London 1928

Laver, James, *A Concise History of Costume*, London 1969

—, *Costume in Antiquity*, London 1964

—, *Costume Through the Ages*, London 1963

Lee-Potter, Charlie, *Sportswear in Vogue Since 1910*, London 1984

Lynam, Ruth (ed.), *Paris Fashions: The Great Designers and Their Creations*, London 1972

Mazza, Samuele, *Scarperentola*, Milan 1993

McDowell, Colin, *Shoes: Fashion and Fantasy*, London 1989

Mulvagh, Jane, *Vogue: History of Twentieth Century Fashion*, London 1988

O'Hara, Georgina, *The Encyclopaedia of Fashion from 1840 to the 1980s*, London 1986

O'Keeffe, Linda, *Shoes: A Celebration of Pumps, Sandals, Slippers and More*, New York 1996

Pattison, Angela, and Nigel Cawthorne, *Shoes: A Century of Style*, London 1998

Pratt, Lucy, and Linda Woolley, *Shoes*, Victoria and Albert Museum, London 1999

Scott, Margaret, *Late Gothic Europe: 1400–1500*, London 1980

Smith, Desire, *Fashion Footwear 1800–1970*, Atglen 2000

Stevenson, Pauline, *Edwardian Fashion*, London 1980

Swann, June, *Shoes: The Costume Accessories Series*, London 1982

Trasko, Mary, *Heavenly Soles: Extraordinary Twentieth-Century Shoes*, New York 1989

Wilcox, R. Turner, *The Dictionary of Costume*, London 1969

—, *Five Centuries of American Costume*, New York 1963

—, *The Mode in Footwear*, New York 1948

Yarwood, Doreen, *English Costume: From the Second Century BC to 1967*, London 1967